ATLANTIS <u>AND</u> 2012

"I have reviewed dozens of books on the year 2012 and its meaning and consequences, but Frank Joseph's *Atlantis and 2012* presents us with many facts and research ignored by most of the other guides. I have especially high regard for Frank Joseph's courage to question what the majority of academia, government, and media around the world have concluded about global warming. They have ignored the research showing global warming is actually the precursor to a new ice age. In addition to all the other fascinating bits to be found in *Atlantis and 2012*, I find the most important is Joseph's emphasis on the reminder that global warming may just be the trigger for an oncoming ice age, which we now know can manifest in as little as 20 years!

"The Mayan civilization gave a gift to future humanity in the form of their Mayan calendar. Having witnessed periodic extinctions, they documented these cycles in the hopes of preparing and maybe even preventing what they could not: a dark end for our age. Their message is one of balancing the material and spiritual dimensions, because an imbalance brings on social decay and physical annihilation. Vested interests and the domination of the corporate world, which enforces its status quo, have brought us to the edge of extinction. Although humankind may be vastly diminished, the planet will survive.

"The Atlanteans were much like us—in fact, they *are* us if you consider reincarnation. Their insatiable appetite for material prosperity and military might mirror the world governments of today. Frank Joseph has used the works of two great seers, Plato and Edgar Cayce, to guide us through our past and future. Thanks to the Atlantis code (which we know as the Mayan calendar), he shows that we still have hope that we might be able to avoid what the Atlanteans failed to avoid. You must read this book—today!"

ROBERT R. HIERONIMUS, PH.D., AUTHOR OF
UNITED SYMBOLISM OF AMERICA
AND HOST OF *21ST CENTURY RADIO*

ATLANTIS
AND 2012

**The Science
of the
Lost Civilization
and the
Prophecies
of the
Maya**

FRANK JOSEPH

Bear & Company
Rochester, Vermont • Toronto, Canada

Bear & Company
One Park Street
Rochester, Vermont 05767
www.BearandCompanyBooks.com

Bear & Company is a division of Inner Traditions International

Library of Congress Cataloging-in-Publication Data

Joseph, Frank.
 Atlantis and 2012 : the science of the lost civilization and the prophecies of the Maya / Frank Joseph.
   p. cm.
 Summary: "Traces Maya astronomy back to Atlantis"—Provided by publisher.
 Includes bibliographical references and index.
 ISBN 978-1-59143-112-1 (pbk.)
 1. Maya astronomy. 2. Atlantis (Legendary place) 3. Two thousand twelve, A.D. I. Title. II. Title: Atlantis and two thousand twelve.
 F1435.3.C14J67 2010
 529'.32978427—dc22

                                                                    2009048113

Printed and bound in the United States by Lake Book Manufacturing

10   9   8   7   6   5   4   3   2   1

Text design by Jon Desautels
Text layout by Virginia Scott Bowman

This book was typeset in Garamond Premier Pro and Eurostile with Footlight, Greco, and Gill Sans as display typefaces

Chapter 9 first appeared as "The Remarkable Inca Calendar," by Frank Joseph, in *Atlantis Rising* magazine 12, no. 72 (November/December 2008). It is republished here with permission.

Chapter 10 first appeared as "The Significance of the Number 11 in the 2012 Prophecy," by Frank Joseph, in *Mysteries* magazine, no. 23 (2009). It is republished here with permission.

To send correspondence to the author of this book, mail a first-class letter to the author c/o Inner Traditions • Bear & Company, One Park Street, Rochester, VT 05767, and we will forward the communication.

CONTENTS

PART ONE
2012

PART TWO

THE SEER

Countdown to 2012

9400 BC	The Atlantean flood occurs, according to a literal reading of Plato's Dialogues, the *Timaeus* and *Kritias*.
3814 BC	The Age of Atlantis begins with the zodiacal Age of Taurus.
3114 BC	The Mayan calendar's Long Count opens on 4 Ahau 3 Kankin (August 11), coinciding with the first of four global catastrophes. It is referred to by the Mexihcah as Jaguar, 4-Ocelotl.
2193 BC	Earth's brush with Comet Encke results in a worldwide catastrophe—the Mexihcah 4-Ehecátl, or Windstorm.
1628 BC	The Mexihcah Fire from Heaven, 4-Quihuitl, was aptly named for Comet Encke's return barrage of meteoric material that generated a series of gigantic tsunamis to obliterate Lemuria.
1198 BC	The final destruction of Atlantis is associated with the Mexihcah, 4-Atl, or Water.
561 BC	Solon returns to Athens from Egypt with the story of Atlantis.
399 BC	Plato composes his account of Atlantis based on Solon's copy.
AD 391	The memorial column from which Solon had transcribed the history of Atlantis is lost when Christians demolish Egypt's temple of Neith, where it was preserved.
1514	Pope Leo X declares that the world will end five hundred years hence.
1479	The Aztec Calendar Stone is erected atop Tenochtitlán's Great Pyramid.
1521	Tenochittlan falls to Spanish invaders on August 13.
1790	Sewer workers in Mexico City accidentally excavate the Aztec Calendar Stone on December 17.
1930	Serbian scientific genius Milutin Milanković discovers the relationship between recurring ice ages and variations in Earth's rotation.
1945	Edgar Cayce dies.
1968	The Bimini Wall is discovered.
1972	The U.S. government launches Project Stargate.
1973	Unaware of the Mayan calendar's end date, Nahui-Ollin, Dennis and Terrence McKenna calculate the "end of time" from the Chinese I Ching: December 22, 2012.
2012	The Mayan calendar ends on the morning of the winter solstice, December 21, 2012.

Map of the ancient world showing the location of Atlantis and the Lemurian Islands, drawn by artist Kenneth Caroli.

END TIMES
OR GOLDEN AGE?

Scientific thinking often benefits from the throwing of
"bombs"—the publication of ideas so revolutionary that
one half of the profession is scandalized, while the other
half is captivated by the prospect of daring, new solutions
to old problems.

ROBERT BAKKER, *THE DINOSAUR HERESIES*[1]

A groundswell of interest in the winter solstice of 2012 gathers world-wide momentum as time hurtles inexorably toward that anticipated date. No other December 21 throughout recorded human history has attracted such far-flung attention, even concern. Foreshadowed by a burgeoning number of books, magazine articles, and television specials, public fascination duplicates itself the nearer that fateful date approaches. A catastrophic scenario popularly associated with this soon-to-be-experienced incident is underscored by the collapse on a grand scale of long-established economic institutions in concert with Earth's ecological instability.

The free fall of such formerly unassailable corporate titans as General

Motors and Freddie Mac seems ominously paralleled by unprecedented firestorms scourging the American West or the Arctic ice cap's shockingly rapid disappearance. Some commentators believe these forces are escalating toward a climax in late 2012.

Intrigued by these speculations, computer experts have wondered if high-tech software is capable of making a valid projection for that year. They have resorted to a system known as the Web Bot Project, which is already developed for predicting financial trends. With the expansion of the Internet, it has evolved exponentially since its inception in the early 1990s.

As reporter Krzys Wasilewski explains for the *Student Operated Press,* programmers compose "a set of words or phrases such as 'crisis' or 'stocks,' which are searched for on the Internet. Whenever one is traced, the system copies it and sends [it] to the server" and presents it "in the right context." The system is not a game, but "hard core computer science and radical linguistics."[2] It was originally conceived to follow Wall Street cycles and define stock patterns that could provide advance notice of market fluctuations. By the end of the decade, however, Web Bot's success tempted some programmers, curious to learn what the next century might hold, to widen its focus from exclusively financial concerns to a broader perspective, and everything passing through the Internet was fed into the prognosticating software.

In early summer 2001, the computer program promised that a "world changing event" would take place that autumn. Web Bot had correctly, if imprecisely predicted the attacks of September 11. Throughout January 2003, the Project repeatedly warned of a vessel soon to be involved in a tragic accident. Some analysts misinterpreted this as a maritime disaster. On February 1, the space shuttle *Columbia* was lost with all hands aboard when it exploded while reentering the atmosphere.

Based on the accuracy of hits such as these, the program was directed to the controversial year ahead. "The records provided by the Web Bot have confirmed the ancient Mayan and Chinese prophesies that the year 2012 will bring an unspecified disaster," Wasilewski reports. "The Bot program also predicts a worldwide calamity taking place in the year 2012."[3]

Doomsday predictions range from a planet-wide purge to Armageddon—from a natural upheaval that will precipitate some new order of international peace to the end of the world. The coming event horizon is far less frequently dismissed as absolutely insignificant. Even scientific observers bored by prophesies of global upheaval openly express awe at the unique set of celestial circumstances they know will take place on the appointed day and hour.

Astronomers know that in the late morning of December 21, 2012, the ecliptic (the Sun's apparent path across the sky) will intersect with the galactic ecliptic (the projection of the Milky Way's disc on the sky) to place the Sun at the very center, in the crosshairs between the solar path and that of our galaxy, when the sun is one degree above the horizon at the equator (73 degrees West).

Though the ability of Maya astronomers more than two millennia ago to anticipate this cosmic happening with such pinpoint accuracy seems remarkable, it is nothing when compared to the real significance of their prediction. From our Earth-bound perspective, the sun moves into the ecliptic crosshairs only once every 26,000 years. Astronomers refer to this moment as the Precession of the Great Year of the Equinox.

Late advances in astrophysics, however, tend to confirm that this great precession is entirely subjective and theoretical—meaningless—because of the disintegration of observations extending into space beyond 18,000 light-years. In that case, the winter solstice sunrise of 2012 takes place only once in the whole history of the universe! More amazing still, modern scientists did not even discover the whereabouts of the galactic center until 1963. How could the ancient Maya have known its exact location? And why did they choose this cosmically unique event as the date to terminate their calendar?

The source for this accelerating anticipation lies, as almost everyone knows, in the Mayan calendar. Few, however, understand that it was neither a calendar in the usual sense nor originally Maya. It was, instead, an astrological almanac with roots in the Olmec. They built America's first civilization, which appeared along the northeast coast of Mexico in the vicinity of Veracruz, around 1500 BC. Yet this official foundation date has been called into question by some important scholars, especially Zechariah Sitchin.

He presented evidence in the April 2001 issue of *Ancient American* magazine on behalf of much earlier beginnings. He cites a critical discovery made by *Mercury 7* astronaut Gordon Cooper, who, accompanied by a *National Geographic* photographer, retrieved some Olmec artifacts from a small island in the Gulf of Mexico. Repeated radiocarbon dating of the objects at a Texas forensic lab confirmed their 5,000-year-old provenance.

Unconvinced by these findings, Mexican archaeologists headed by Pablo Bush-Romero joined Cooper when he returned to the site. Additional materials were removed for independent testing at Mexico City's National Archaeology Department, where the related items compared identically with Cooper's finds: all shared the same, late-fourth-millennium BC time frame. Accordingly, at Mexico's Jalapa Archaeological Museum, the world's foremost institution dedicated to Olmec culture, America's first civilization was publicly backdated to 3000 BC. Conservative scholars later pressured the Jalapa Museum curator to replace his heretical revision with their previous 1500 BC estimate.[4]

But 1500 BC itself was not much earlier than the 1200 BC date hotly contested among mainstream authorities convinced that no advanced society could have flourished in Mexico before 1200 BC. In fact, 1500 BC too, was vigorously opposed until the mid-twentieth century by a majority of scholars who insisted that the Olmec preceded the Maya by no more than a few hundred years. Apparently, despite entrenched academic opinions, continuing discoveries, such as those made by Gordon Cooper, have progressively pushed Olmec origins much deeper into the past. Such backdating is cogent, even crucial to our understanding of the Mayan calendar and its so-called "prophecy."

The first day of the calendar's Long Count began in 3114 BC—some 29 centuries before the officially recognized advent of the Maya—but the same time frame assigned by the latest, carbon-dated evidence for the sudden birth of Olmec culture. It is clear, then, that the Maya did not invent their calendrical system but were instead the inheritors of a sophisticated technology introduced millennia before their ascendancy. "This calendar's development is without doubt very old," concluded Mexico's leading archaeologist, Alfonso Caso, "and it must have been the creation of a people who attained a high degree of culture prior to that of all the peoples with whose culture we are now familiar."[5]

The same calendar originated by the Olmec and handed down to the Maya was passed on to subsequent Central American cultures, culminating in the Aztecs, who encoded its high principles in their famous Calendar Stone. As such, this deeply pre-Columbian calendar was less Maya than Mesoamerican in that it served Mexican civilizers before and after the Maya. Its true identity as an astrological almanac or zodiacal computer means that its chief function was to forecast fortuitous or unfavorable days. The prehistoric inhabitants of Central America did not merely dabble in astrology, however. They were controlled by it, individually and as a society. We may gain some inkling of their condition if, by analogy, we discovered that federal law in the United States was entirely replaced by the rules governing astrology. In Mesoamerica, all aspects of a person's entire life were regulated by his or her horoscope. When we understand that ancient Americans were so absolutely dominated by their place in the cosmic scheme of things, the significance of such astrological regimentation becomes clear. Regulation of personal and civil behavior was deemed inseparable from a universal order upon which all creation was predicated and operated.

In this, Mesoamerican cosmology was remarkably similar to the dynastic Egyptian principle of Maat, or Balance. Symbolized by a perfectly poised feather standing upright, it was nothing less than a national ethic that permeated and determined Egyptian character and culture from the first day of Nile Valley civilization in the late fourth millennium BC to its last gasp more than 3,000 years later. Maat was personified by a goddess representing pervasive harmony, a fundamental goodness inherent in the phenomenal world. Its core mechanism was universal equipoise, whose opposite—imbalance—defined evil. Hence, the orderly proportion of monumental architecture and art remained unchanged throughout pharaonic history, because to depart from the spiritual-aesthetic canon would have been—and in fact *was*—regarded as a blasphemy against the divine order, which culture was supposed to embody and project.

King Amenhotep IV—better remembered as the self-styled Akhenaton—tried to replace all cultural expression with portraits of himself and his family continuously worshipping the One and Only God, thereby supplanting traditional spirituality with his egomaniacal monotheism. The resultant chaos shook dynastic civilization to the brink of collapse. Fortunately, the heretical king's religious experiment was as short-lived as his reign, and Egypt rebounded immediately after his death, when Maat was once more allowed to flourish throughout the Nile Valley.

Life in both pharaonic and Mesoamerican societies was absolutely dependent on a national feeling of cosmic order that put individual men and women in accord with a greater harmony regulating both heaven and Earth. From this metaphysical interdependence stemmed the hermetical concept "as above, so below." This fundamental parallel between early civilizers in the Valley of Mexico and the Nile Valley is by no means circumstantial. Neither people on either side of the world claimed to have originated this guiding principle. Instead, they allegedly received it as a foreign legacy from overseas flood survivors at the very start of high culture in both parts of the world.

According to Manetho, a third-century BC Egyptian historian, Thaut, god of wisdom, arrived on the shores of the Nile Delta in predynastic times with Emerald Tablets containing all the know-how necessary to build civilization. He retrieved them from Sekhet Aaru, his island home in the far west, where this "Field of Reeds," as it was known, had been condemned to a watery grave for the arrogance of its otherwise great people.

The Aztecs repeated their version of Mesoamerican origins in the story of Quetzalcoatl, the Plumed Serpent who evacuated Aztlán, his homeland across the ocean to the *east,* before it sank into the sea under the weight of its sinful inhabitants. Egyptian Sekhet Aaru and Aztec Aztlán share an identical significance—Field of Reeds—in both languages. Reeds were used by both the ancient Mexicans and Egyptians as writing utensils, regarded by both peoples as symbols of literacy. Hence, an entire field of reed pens was metaphorical for a place of profuse learning.

Parallels grow closer still when we learn that the first Egyptian dynasty was inaugurated around 3100 BC—just when Mesoamerican civilization began with the Olmec. So too, the Mayan calendar began in 3114 BC. That events of such high cultural and prehistorical magnitude must be entirely coincidental does not appear credible. Even so, First Dynasty or even predynastic Egyptians completing a transatlantic voyage on a simultaneous mission to found a civilization in Mexico seems no less improbable than Olmecs making an expedition to the Nile Delta for the same purpose.

Moreover, for all their pyramids and hieroglyphs, Mesoamerica and ancient Egypt were not identical. One was not the colonial extension or transplant of the other. Rather, their similarities suggest an outside source that independently affected both, allowing some fundamental cultural features to develop under local influences. Such a foreign impact naturally would have been inflected by uniquely indigenous forces, resulting in a combination or synthesis of domestic and alien influences responsible for resemblances and differences between Mesoamerica and ancient Egypt.

A clue to the identity of that external stimulus lies in Quetzalcoatl's overseas home, Aztlán. Its name and description immediately evoke another island kingdom—Atlantis, as it is known in German and English-speaking lands—characterized by the fourth-century BC philosopher Plato as a high culture in the Atlantic Ocean that flourished before the rise of other civilizations, but which succumbed to a natural catastrophe. Among Spaniards and Slovenes, this island kingdom is called Atlantida. Plato's Greeks knew it as Atlanikos. The original name is unknown, though it may have resembled the Old Frisian version as it appears in the mid-twelfth-century *Oera Linda Bok* (Book of What Happened in the Old Time): Atland, with *at-* referencing a foremost mountain.[6]

The Frisians are at least dialectically set apart from the Germans and

Dutch with whom they share living space along the coast of the North Sea. According to the *Oera Linda Bok,* it is there that their ancestors settled as refugees after the loss of Atland. The name Atland bears a striking resemblance to Aztlán, which the Aztecs believed suffered an identical fate. Proof for the existence of Atlantis rests on the testimony of world folk traditions and conclusions of modern science.

Yet these entirely historic and scientific considerations penetrate only halfway to an enigma so profoundly strange that they cannot exceed their rational limits to reach the bottom of this ancient mystery with its end hooked to the immediate future. Only the transrational at once goes beyond hard facts without leaving them behind, but rather incorporates them into a final disclosure. These different but complementary methods of investigation into the Mayan calendar require two parts: the scientific Normal must work with the psychic Paranormal to break the Atlantis code and reveal its predictions for 2012.

If part 1 of this book arises from the ancient past, as personified by Plato among its greatest minds, then it seems fitting that the preoccupation of part 2 with the near future should be dominated by one of modern time's greatest seers: Edgar Cayce. Here you will find a selection of Cayce's so-called life readings, because they uniquely illuminate Atlantis as the Mayan calendar's original mainspring and the origin of its 2012 prophesy. He spoke too of a sister civilization—Lemuria—on the other side of the world, a fellow player in a cataclysmic drama that consumed both Atlantis and this fellow civilization, but not before she set certain influences in motion long after her prehistoric demise.

Some material concerning Cayce, the Sleeping Prophet has been drawn from the out-of-print *Edgar Cayce's Atlantis and Lemuria,* but all of it is revised here, corrected and updated in an entirely new context. As he showed, both civilizations were different though blood-related players in an ancient drama, because the former was founded during remote antiquity by the latter at the outset of its existence. The Atlanteans were neo-Lemurians, from whom they inherited a truly primeval if perennial wisdom.

Their combined genius invented the Mesoamerican calendrical system that subsequent generations of Olmecs, Mayas, and Aztecs used to synchronize human society with the eternal cycles of creation, destruction, and renewal. As such, answers to questions posed today by the rapid approach of 2012 may lie in the calendar's profoundly ancient origins among memories of Atlantis. There only, at its true source, a code to unlocking the enigma may yet be found.

PART ONE

2012

WHAT WAS ATLANTIS?

Though neither the first nor only one of its kind, Plato's account is the best-preserved description of Atlantis to have survived antiquity. It is, therefore, the most important document available to students of this sunken realm, made all the more invaluable by the Greek philosopher's prestige among Western civilization's most influential thinkers.

He cites Atlantis in two Dialogues—the *Timaeus* and *Kritias*—as an example illustrating the point he was attempting to make: human societies begin to self-destruct when their citizens no longer regard organic relationships between the spiritual and the material spheres of existence. Imbalance in one, he states, sets up a similarly deteriorating resonance in the other. Such a bond is unseen until the consequences of cosmic disharmony reveal themselves in physical destruction. This fact alone— that Plato used Atlantis to exemplify his argument—is sufficient internal evidence to verify the drowned kingdom's historical authenticity.

The account did not originate with him; he inherited it from his grandfather, Solon, the famous lawgiver, who learned of the sunken civilization while visiting Egypt around 565 BC. During his tour of a Nile Delta's temple of the goddess Neith, a high priest translated the story of Atlantis as it had been recorded in hieroglyphic text on a monumental pillar.

Atlantis was a Greek interpolation of the Egyptian Etelenty. The name also appears in the Book of the Coming Forth by Day (better

Fig. 1.1. Solon learned about Atlantis from a temple priest who translated from a memorial column an account of the lost city. In 561 BC, the famous legislator returned to Athens, and the story was cited 63 years later in Plato's Dialogues the *Timaeus* and *Kritias.*

known as the Book of the Dead), a compilation of liturgical texts buried with the deceased to help the soul along its underworld journey through death to new life. Etelenty, according to Dr. Ramses Seleem's 2001 translation, means "the land that has been divided and submerged by water."

Variations of Atlantis occur often in ancient Egyptian literature. Thaut, the god of wisdom, referred to by Classical Greeks as "Thoth," was enraged by the decadence of an antediluvian humanity. "I am going to blot out everything which I have made," he declared in the Theban Recension of the Book of the Dead. "The Earth shall enter into the waters of the abyss of Nun (the sea-god) by means of a raging flood, and will become even as it was in the primeval time!"[1] Thaut appears again in the Edfu Texts, which locate the "Homeland of the Primeval Ones" on a great island overwhelmed by the sea with most of its inhabitants during the Zep Tepi, or First Time. Thaut escaped the deluge in the company of seven sages, who brought their preflood technology to the Nile Delta, thereby sparking pharaonic civilization.[2]

After returning from Egypt with the story of Etelenty, Solon was preparing a Greek rendition when he passed away in 559 BC. Plato's version presents most of the facts, but in a more straightforward form than the unfinished epic. Ignoring this documented pedigree, skeptics claim that Atlantis was unknown before Plato supposedly invented it. They fail to recognize, however, that Atlantis had already been memorialized in a public event conducted throughout ancient Greece. During the Lesser Panathenaea, female participants in the all-Athenian festival wore a garment caught at the shoulders and draped in folds to the waist. Known as a *peplum,* it was adorned with images, "which showed how the Athenians, supported by Minerva (Latin version of the Greek goddess Athena), had the advantage in the war with the Atlantes," according to the renowned nineteenth-century classical scholar Philip August Boeckh.[3] Because the Panathenaea was celebrated annually for centuries before Plato's birth, he could not have fabricated Atlantis, which was already well known to generations of his fellow countrymen. Furthermore, their long familiarity with the story underscores his purpose in using it as a veritable historical example for the philosophic argument he made in the *Timaeus* and *Kritias*.

Some skeptics claim he merely conflated a similar natural disaster that occurred during his own lifetime into a fictional Atlantis. They refer to Helike, located little more than a mile from the Gulf of Corinth. During major seismic activity, the large, important city and its immediate vicinity, with all its inhabitants, suddenly collapsed 1.25 miles beneath the surface of the Earth. The sea rushed in, dragging down ten Spartan ships riding at anchor. There were no survivors. Over time, the sunken ruins of Helike were gradually silted over and lost until excavations brought them to light near the village of Rizomylos in the summer of 2001. Their archaeological discovery has since been added to the World Monument Fund's list of One Hundred Most-Endangered Sites.

Yet Plato's account could not have been based on Helike's fate, because the Greek city was destroyed during the winter of 373 BC, some 25 years *after* he wrote the Atlantis narrative immediately following Socrates' suicide in 399 BC. Moreover, Plato would never have succeeded at trying to pass off Helike as Atlantis, because the Achaean city's demise was an infamous affair that occurred during the lifetime of his fellow Greeks.

Other skeptics insist that the Aegean island of Thera was really Atlantis, but their arguments are no less flawed, and they unravel under scrutiny. (See Frank Joseph, *The Destruction of Atlantis,* Rochester, Vt.: Bear & Company, 2002, chapter 2, "Where Is Atlantis?") Suffice it to say here that Thera lies in the Mediterranean Sea, not the Atlantic Ocean, and additionally bears little in common with Plato's description of Atlantis. None of the names cited in his account are found on Thera, which was too tiny for wars with Egypt, Italy, and Greece, as specified in the *Kritias*. Nor was Thera surrounded by a ring of mountains, populated by elephants, home to a mining or mineralogical center, in possession of three harbors, the site of an imperial city, or the capital of religious worship for the sea god Poseidon.

Attempts by conventional scholars to minimize or debunk Plato's account invariably fall on the facts he presents so clearly. He begins by telling us that Atlantis was a large island "greater than Libya and Asia combined."[4] His characterization has led some investigators to conclude that he was describing a massive continent. Yet the Libya and Asia of his time—2,400 years ago—comprised only a fraction of the territories encompassed by those places as they are understood today. During the fourth century BC, Libya was no more than a thin strip of North African coastline running from the western Egyptian border to perhaps Morocco, at most, while Asia meant Asia Minor, roughly the western third of what is now Turkey. Combined, these areas might result in an island as large as Portugal, but never anything approaching a true continent.

Atlantis lay in the Atlantic Ocean, outside the Straits of Gibraltar, where it was almost entirely surrounded by a ring of high mountains, which opened on the south. A temperate climate allowed for two growing seasons, typical of other Atlantic islands, such as Madeira or the islands of the Canaries. The island was thickly forested, facilitating the construction of a large navy the Atlanteans used to pursue their imperialist agendas, and it was inhabited by scores of wild animals—most remarkably, the elephant. The appearance of this creature on an island in the middle of the Atlantic Ocean was a point used by skeptics until 1967 to discredit Plato's account. In 1967, however, *Science* magazine reported the discovery of thousands of elephant teeth from forty different underwater locations along the Azores-Gibraltar Ridge. Recovering elephant remains validated Plato's account as few other finds have done in recent times.

The pachyderms evidently crossed from the shores of northwest Africa over a former land bridge that extended into the eastern Atlantic. When the land bridge collapsed sometime within the last 25,000 years, the elephants were stranded on the island of Atlantis. Standard translations of Plato's account perpetuate an error that, once corrected, suggests this former land bridge was used by the migrating elephants:

"For in those days, the Atlantic was navigable" (*Timaeus,* 24).[5] Florida Atlantologist Kenneth Caroli states that "the original Greek word does not mean navigable. It means passable 'on foot'. It is their assumption of a maritime context that convinced scholars to twist the translation."[6]

From an aerial perspective, the city itself on the island resembled a target, laid out as it was in concentric circles of alternating moats and land rings. At the hub of the central, artificial islet stood the holy of holies: a small, golden shrine dedicated to the sacred marriage between a native woman, Kleito, and the sea god Poseidon. From their union sprang five sets of male children, the progenitors of a dynasty that ruled the Atlantean empire. The island derived its name from the firstborn, Atlas—Atlantis means Daughter of Atlas.

Fig. 1.2. Fifth-century BC relief statue of Atlas from the Athenian Parthenon (Elgin Marbles, British Museum)

The city was surrounded by an extensive, cultivated plain irrigated via an immense canal system fed by numerous rivers and freshwater springs of both cold and hot water, thermal sources typical of volcanically active islands.

Approaching from the south, visitors would have seen three harbors, testimony to Atlantean sea power. Just beyond the broad marketplace, busy day and night with international commerce, reared a colossal wall of red tufa, white pumice, and black lava rock arranged in tricolor bands and sheeted with broad panels of polished bronze. Abutted by watchtowers, the great rampart entirely surrounded the city.

A single canal 300 feet wide and 100 feet deep ran from the outer wall to the coast, 5.5 miles away. A fully armed battleship was thus able to sail directly from the sea to the outer wall and through it to the first and largest moat on the other side. The other two moats were connected by four bridged canals 500 feet across, guarded by towers and gates wherever the bulwarks touched solid ground and cut into an unequal pair of land rings, which allowed vessels to pass through them from one to the next.

At the perimeter of the nearest land ring stood another wall of red, white, and black volcanic rock plated with gleaming tin. Behind it was a racetrack that ran round the entire, 1,800-foot-wide islet otherwise given over to temples; priestly residences; gymnasia; separate public baths for men, women, and horses; stadiums; and public gardens.

The second, smaller land ring, at 1,200 feet wide, was the seat of naval headquarters, with training facilities and marine barracks. The central and smallest islet was surrounded by a red, white, and black wall adorned with *orichalcum,* high-grade copper. It enclosed the imperial palace, which was set in a large garden with an adjoining winery. Nearby was the monumental Temple of Poseidon, 600 feet long, half as wide, and 150 feet high.

The exterior of the structure, which resembled archaic Greek or early Etruscan sacred architecture, was covered in silver, save for, in the pediment over the entrance, golden figures signifying various deities. Inside, a colossus of the sea god held his emblematic trident in his right hand while seizing with his left the reins to six winged horses that pulled the chariot in which he stood. The statue was so huge that its head almost brushed the ivory ceiling flecked with gold. Around the base of Poseidon were one hundred Nereids, representations of boys riding dolphins, symbolizing initiates into the sea god's mystery cult.

The temple was a veritable hall for statuary, with figures of the original ten kings and their queens, "and many others dedicated by monarchs and private persons belonging to the city and its dominions,"[7] according to Plato. They were grouped around a magnificent altar and holy pillar inscribed with the laws of the empire.

Adjacent to the temple was a bullpen from which a sacrifice was selected by the ten regents when they convened in the temple alternately every fifth or sixth year. They subdued the animal with nooses and clubs, then slit its throat with stone daggers to spill its blood over the sacred column. Thereafter, the attendees made pledges to uphold the laws with royal golden cups filled with toasts of wine mixed with bull's blood.

Not far from the Temple of Poseidon, at the midpoint of Atlantis itself, stood the small shrine dedicated to his primeval union with Kleito. This innermost islet was just 3,000 feet across, although large enough to accommodate the imperial palace, great temple, and golden-walled holy of holies. Atlantis was a citadel and ceremonial center, not an urban setting. Its only permanent residents were imperial family members, their bodyguards, naval and army personnel, and priests and attendants. Instead of a city where people lived, Atlantis was a public gathering place visited for military, political, ceremonial, and religious activities. The population resided in cities and towns or on farmsteads throughout the island. Its volcanic soil was highly fertile, allowing for a flourishing agriculture.

Atlantis was surrounded by a rectangular, uniformly flat plain nearly 350 miles long and 230 miles wide. This vast, cultivated space was serviced by streams and rivers from adjacent mountains. The descending waters were conveyed into a gigantic irrigation canal 100 feet deep and 600 feet wide and circling the entire plain—1,118 miles long.

While this public works project may seem to some skeptics beyond the capabilities of any premodern civilization, archaeologists know that the Hohokam culture of the American Southwest, as long ago as the eleventh century, built a canal system that, if placed end to end, would have stretched more than 1,000 miles from Phoenix, Arizona, to well beyond the Canadian border. Plato describes the Atlanteans as extraordinary irrigationists. They created a network of river ways to float timber and produce by boat—again reminiscent of the Hohokam, who identically employed their canal system—to various parts of the island. Such prodigious feats of agriculture were necessary to feed the 1,034,800 inhabitants of the island.

At the zenith of its power, Atlantis was the capital of an imperial enterprise that extended from "the opposite continent," as Plato referenced America, to Western Europe as far as Italy and North Africa on the Egyptian border. Names of the original ten kings listed by Plato suggest something of the empire's extent, because they correspond with certain geographical realms, mythical figures, and foreign peoples far removed from Plato's Greece. For example, Elasippos, Euaemon, Autochthon, and Azaes were the names of Atlantean kings cited by Plato. Similarly, Lisbon was originally known as Elasippos, as the Portuguese capital was called even in late Roman times, while Spanish Cadiz was referred as Gades, from the Atlantean Gadeiros. Euaemon echoes Eremon, a royal flood hero who led his fellow deluge survivors to the shores of pre-Keltic Ireland after the catastrophic inundation of his island kingdom. The Autochthones were described by Herodotus, Plato's fifth-century BC predecessor, as Atlanteans dwelling along the western shores of Morocco, just as King Autochthon is cited in the *Kritias*. King Azaes appears to reference Plato's "opposite continent," where the Itzás were a Maya people occupying coastal Yucatán.

While Ampheres (Joined or Fitted Together on Both Sides), Diaprepres (Bright Shining One), Mestor (Counselor), and Musaeus (Of the Muses) are less certainly associated with any particular people or place, flood stories featuring identifiable Atlantean themes were prevalent in Portugal, Spain, Ireland, North Africa, and Mexico, where most of Plato's Atlantean monarchs seem philologically connected. These holdings granted the Atlanteans fabulous wealth, particularly in the form of copper mining.

The emperor of Atlantis commanded the ancient world's most powerful armed forces, comprising 76,600 warriors. These included 14,400 archers, slingers, and heavily armed infantry, together with 10,000 chariots carrying 20,000 drivers and soldiers. There were also elite units, troops of royal bodyguards, officers, and an army of supply personnel.

Yet Atlantis was primarily a thallasocracy—a naval power—and its fleet of 1,200 warships was manned by 14,400 sailors, marines, shipwrights, and dockhands. These impressive forces were augmented by the nine other affiliated kingdoms that made up the Atlantean empire. Though Plato does not provide their disposition of arms, together they formed a potent military phenomenon unequaled until the advent of Imperial Rome. Nor does Plato explain why Atlantis gathered its military might to launch an attempted conquest of the Mediterranean world. In any case, the Atlantean juggernaut seemed irrepressible, subjugating Western Europe as far as Italy and steamrolling across North Africa to penetrate the Egyptian frontier. The armies of pharaonic Egypt were crushed, and the entire kingdom tottered on the verge of surrender, when their Athenian allies scored a stunning victory against the invaders. Henceforward, the bloodied Atlanteans were progressively forced to relinquish their conquests in a series of defeats that eventually expelled them from the Mediterranean.

Sometime thereafter, widespread seismic upheavals swallowed up the Greek armies, and the island of Atlantis disappeared "during a single day and night" of catastrophic flooding.

The *Kritias* inexplicably breaks off just when Zeus, the supreme Olympian god, is about to condemn the Atlanteans for their degeneracy. The same kind of detailed description that brought their civilization to life would have doubtless re-created its destruction. While some scholars speculate the Dialogue was left incomplete for various, unknown causes, it is more likely that the missing section was finished but lost, like most classical literature.

Fig. I.3. British artist Peter Bellingham's 1871 oil painting *Island Volcano* is a facsimile of the final destruction of Atlantis.

More troubling is the only incredible anomaly in the entire account: Plato's repeated insistence that the Atlanto-Athenian War took place 11,400 years ago. The discrepancy between this remote period and the details portrayed by both the *Timaeus* and *Kritias* have compelled many investigators to dismiss the whole narrative as a work of fiction.

Plato's elaborate description of Atlantis unequivocally identifies it as a Late-Bronze-Age kingdom dated roughly from the sixteenth to thirteenth centuries BC. Yet some 7,000 years earlier—when its forces supposedly invaded the Mediterranean Sea—neither Greek nor Egyptian civilization existed. Far from any temple containing detailed records of Atlantis, Egyptians had invented nothing more technologically sophisticated than grindstones for making flour from wild grass seeds. The Athens portrayed by Plato as a victorious military power did not exist 114 centuries ago. In fact, the Greek peninsula was not even inhabited at the time.

Literalists who insist that Plato's ice age time frame must be upheld despite everything science understands about the period are obliged to explain how Atlantis could have flourished when the wheel had not yet been invented. There were no metal tools or weapons in 9400 BC, no chariots, no irrigation projects, no urban centers, no large-scale agriculture, no monumental art, no ships, no written language, no armies—in short, nothing described by the Dialogues. The temperate, mid-ocean climate Atlantis was said to have enjoyed did not exist during the Late Pleistocene Epoch, as that postglacial period is known. It is an entirely impossible setting for Bronze-Age Atlantis, no less outrageously erroneous than assigning U.S. history to the Middle Ages.

Literalists assume that their concept of time is identical to Plato's. As Caroli rightly observes, "The Greek system of numbers used throughout Roman times and after did not exist in Plato's day, let alone Solon's. The potential to confuse the earlier and later Greek systems is rarely considered. The older system was more decimal."[8] Moreover, the Nile Delta priests who supplied the original account were known to use a *lunar* calendar. Transposing his 9400 BC–date from solar to lunar years brings Atlantis squarely into its proper temporal surroundings during the Late Bronze Age, circa 1200 BC. It seems likely, then that the ancient translator of the Egyptian text did not trouble himself with recalculating its lunar years into solar time, but transcribed them, as he did all other information, verbatim from the inscription.

While his fidelity is an assumption, Plato's troublesome chronology might be more simply explained by what the British scholar Desmond Lee describes as the Greeks' "bad sense of time. . . . And though the Greeks, both philosophers and others, were interested in origins, they seem to have been curiously lacking in their sense of the time-dimension. . . ."[9] Perhaps nothing more than notorious Greek sloppiness concerning proper dating may have been responsible for Bronze-Age Atlantis's incongruous placement at the end of the Pleistocene Epoch. It is nonetheless curious that this period defined a major cultural surge known as the Mesolithic, or Middle Stone Age, when northwestern Europe was resettled after the Last Glacial Maximum by extraordinarily creative invaders. The Upper Paleolithic people were named after La Madeleine, a Vézère valley rock shelter in the French Dordogne.

The Magdalenians first appeared on the shores of Normandy, as though arriving from the sea, then spread in all directions, from Portugal to Poland. Unlike their far less sophisticated predecessors, they dwelled in tents; manufactured superior flint tools; worked both utilitarian and aesthetic forms in bone, antler, and ivory; and sculpted stone figurines of passing skill. Their greatest, surviving achievement is stupendous cave art, as preserved at such subterranean galleries as Lascaux in France or Spain's Altamira.

If the Magdalenians were not exactly Plato's Atlanteans, they may have been their Upper Paleolithic ancestors. Their appearance on the shores of Western Europe—when major coastal flooding occurred due to glaciers melting into rising sea levels—coincided with his Pleistocene time frame. Though less probable than the direct transcription of a lunar date, it is nonetheless conceivable that the time cited by Plato for the existence of Atlantis—"11,400 years before present"—might refer after all to its Mesolithic roots. Atlantean beginnings around 9400 BC may have been enough to satisfy him for the whole narration, given Greek indifference toward accurate chronologies of any kind.

Caroli brings out a more troubling possibility: the original Greek account was deliberately tampered with for religious reasons. He points out that not one of the earliest known versions

> . . . predates the 9th Century, and most are no earlier than the 12th or 13th. To equate the destruction of Atlantis with Noah's flood required reducing Plato's dates. But the oldest manuscripts assigned the Atlantean catastrophe to one thousand years before Solon's time. Later translators "corrected" it to match the then accepted figures from Plato. In many of the early texts of the *Timaeus,* it read 1,009, not 9,000 years. It was mainly monkish scribes doing the many copies of copies. But they expanded Plato's original chronology from 1,009 years in the *Timaeus* to 9,000 years, though the former is suspiciously precise, and so the more likely.[10]

While we may never satisfactorily reconcile a tenth-millennium BC time frame for the events surrounding Atlantis, that curious period seems nevertheless to reflect on the sunken capital from the radically different perspectives of Magdalenian Europe and the Bronze Age. Perhaps both—separately or simultaneously—were meant, for whatever causes, to illuminate various aspects of the multifarious lost fatherland of civilization.

THE OTHER SIDE OF
THE MIRROR

Chapter 1 defined the exoteric or former physical reality of Atlantis. Yet its historical (prehistoric) existence was the material expression of esoteric energies that underpinned the lost civilization, drove its destiny, and today most concerns us as clues to the forthcoming enigma of 2012.

Plato tells us that the Atlanteans were more interested in spiritual than material power:

> For many generations, as long as the divine nature lasted in them, they were obedient to the laws, and well-affectioned toward the gods, who were their kinsmen. They retained a certain greatness of mind, for they possessed true and in every way great spirits, practicing gentleness and wisdom in the various chances of life, and in their relationships with one another. They despised everything but virtue, not caring for their present state of life, and thinking lightly on the possession of gold and other property, which seemed only a burden to them. Neither were they intoxicated by luxury, nor did wealth deprive them of their self-control. By such reflection, and in the continuance in them of a divine nature, all that which we have described waxed and increased in them.[1]

His characterization of the Atlanteans as "kinsmen" of the gods was not merely a national myth, like Japan's pre–World War II belief in Emperor Hirohito's divinity. It was generated instead by a small shrine at the absolute midpoint of Atlantis, where a golden enclosure surrounded the holy of holies. It was here that Kleito, the mortal woman, entered into a *hieros gamos,* Greek for "temple marriage" or "holy union" with a god, Poseidon. The name Kleito, in fact, exemplifies the hieros gamos. It is is a normative for the Greek verb *kleito,* "to touch or titillate lasciviously, to be inclined to pleasure," according to sexologist Ian Kerner.[2]

Another writer, Joseph Wells, adds that Kleito is a diminutive of Kleitoris, from which the English word *clitoris* derived. He goes on to point out that Poseidon is partly formed from Greek words for "penis" (*peos, posthe,* and so forth), and *eidon,* or "idol."[3] The erect male and female sex organs are therefore represented in both names, embodying as they do the Atlantean temple marriage between a mortal woman and an immortal deity cited in the *Kritias.* Its description of Poseidon's laws inscribed on a pillar ritually libated with bull's blood signified the *hieros gamos* implicit in Kleito and Poseidon.

These observations contribute to Plato's fundamental veracity, for he could hardly have been expected to bother about such minute, internal subtleties on behalf of mere fiction. They are, instead, part of the numerous, otherwise superfluous details he included to affirm the historical reality of Atlantis.

As the sacred patron of all things pertaining to the sea, Poseidon esoterically personified the subconscious. Water—particularly the ocean—is a metaphor for mind: its surface (consciousness) reflects the phenomenal world, but just below the surface lies a darker, entirely contrary dimension of dynamic energy forms incessantly engaged in devouring each other. Kleito's holy union with such a mythic conception signifies an altered—or, more accurately stated, an *exalted*—state of consciousness.

The purpose of such a transformation lay in accessing human psychic potential for its application in the life of an already high, progressive civilization. Plato does not specify how this form of empowerment was achieved, because it was probably lost with the mystery cult that prevented

Fig. 2.1. Fifth-century BC bronze colossus of Poseidon retrieved from the bottom of the Aegean Sea and currently at the National Museum of Archaeology, Athens, Greece. A monumental temple to the sea god stood near the center of Atlantis.

such knowledge from being publicly disclosed. Plato himself was believed to have been an initiate in the Pythagorean Brotherhood. Followers who violated their oaths of secrecy forfeited their lives—including, it would appear, Pythagoras himself, who was stoned to death in a bean field for sharing his own principles with uninitiated outsiders. It may not have been coincidental that Psonchis, the Nile Delta priest who translated the story of Atlantis from its hieroglyphic text on a temple column, bore the same name as one of Solon's Pythagorean teachers in Egypt.

Archaeobiologists believe adherents of the far-famed Eleusinian Mysteries were administered ergoline alkaloids from the fungus ergot, an early form of LSD, to expand their consciousness. During the mid-twentieth century, an important contributor to ethnobotany, R. Gordon Wasson, demonstrated that such hallucinogens were integral to virtually every spiritual discipline throughout the ancient world. These mystery cults comprised the mainspring of Near Eastern and European mysticism, with its emphasis on direct, personal experience of the divine, as mythically dramatized by Kleito's hieros gamos. It was believed that through such experiences were released psychic insights and powers endemic to, but otherwise dormant, in every human being. Psychoactive-ingesting practioners of the Atlantean mystery cult were thus able to plumb the depths of subconscious potentiality—mythically personified by Poseidon fishing up choice catches on his trident—that granted them an otherworldly awareness.

This emblematic device—the trident—was symbolic of supreme spiritual power, topped as it was by three prongs. It is not unlike the three-pointed wand held by the Hindu master of Creation, Shiva. The three-pronged weapon wielded by the Roman *retiarius* (gladiator), with his net of interdependent relationships ensnaring all things, made him a sacred impersonator of Uranus, the creator sky god. The Kelts worshiped their deities in groups of three, and identified them with three heads or faces. The Hindu trinity of Brahma, Vishnu, and Shiva personify, respectively, *sat,* or being; *cit,* consciousness; and *ananda,* love—the components of godhood cyclically creating, maintaining, and destroying the universe. Height, breadth, and length comprise the three dimensions of space or the stages of matter proceeding from solid and liquid to gaseous states—all elements of creation or creativity. Stylistically representing male genitalia, Poseidon's trident, grasped commandingly in his right hand, yet again underscores his role as divine bridegroom in the temple marriage, suggesting the tantric concept of sexual energy as a power to attain enlightenment.

One hundred Nereids surrounding the base of his statue are yet other symbols of the transconsciousness associated with this deity. He was also honored by the Greeks for his creation of the horse, which they associated with virility and—when endowed with wings—spiritual illumination. Both of these hieros gamos qualities were exemplified by the winged horses pulling his chariot in Atlantis's Temple of Poseidon. The number of these horses, however, are keys to the Atlantean mysteries, and may yet unlock that enigma in 2012, which we are rapidly approaching.

SACRED NUMERALS

Plato reports in the *Kritias* (4, 119) that monarchs from across the empire assembled in Atlantis at the Temple of Poseidon "alternately every fifth and sixth year, thereby showing equal respect to both the odd and even numbers."[1] These regular meetings were not part of some formal religious convention, but instead represented a pair of sacred numerals that incorporated the Atlanteans' entire civilization and determined the disposition of their daily lives.

Plato's Atlantis account is literally constructed with the numbers 5 and 6 and their multiples. Poseidon's colossus stood in a chariot drawn by six winged horses. The citadel itself embodied 5 in its three moats and two land rings—or, simultaneously, 6, including the central islet, which itself was 5 stades across. Atlantis's great canal ran 50 stades from the seacoast to the ceremonial city, as did its outer wall at a uniform distance from the largest land ring.

An irrigation ditch surrounding the cultivated plain was 10,000 stades in length, and the Atlantean empire itself comprised ten kingdoms. Allotments of land were parceled out in plots of 10 square stades, with the total number of allotments at 60,000. Kleito bore five sets of twin boys who formed the royal houses of Atlantis. Military leaders were obligated to provide a sixth part of the equipment for a war chariot. The Atlantean armed forces fielded ten thousand chariots, together with twelve hundred warships.

Why were 5 and 6 chosen as sacred numerals, with preference for 5? What did they mean to the Atlanteans? Five represents humankind as signified by the five senses and five fingers to a hand: manual dexterity; solar, male energy; light and enlightenment. It stands for conscious action, acquisition, material achievement, technology, scientific inquiry, organization, civilization, militarism, conquest, justice, honor, duty, hard facts, self-control, and discernment. Five is the sacred center—symbolized by a circle enclosing a cross or a single point at the center—where the imperceptible is perceived (or where it manifests).

The number 6 connotes woman. It is concerned with lunar or female energy, intuition, nature, emotion, fecundity, liberty (always represented by a woman), instinct, premonition, creativity, peace, fairness, and forgiveness. The Romanian mythologist Mircea Eliade stated that 6 "is the number of mother-love. . . . It is an even number, which means it is female and passive . . . the number of marriage from the female point of view. . . . Six is essentially the number of the wife and mother."[2] Eliade cites an anonymous numerologist, who observed that marriage license bureaus in the United States are forced to either work overtime or multiply their staffs to accommodate increased numbers of applicants during 6-year periods.

Six exemplifies the hieros gamos, the "holy union" between Father Sky and Mother Earth—the sacred bond between fertilizing force from above and innate potentiality below operating in the well-known principle of "as above, so below." The sixth tarot trump is known as The Lovers.

The significance of Plato's sacred numbers remarkably characterizes the lost culture, particularly the mysticism he described. In 5 resonate the Atlantean dynamics of technology, organization, militarism, conquest, and imperialism. This aggressive consciousness is contrasted with but complemented by 6, the numeral of intuition, instinctiveness, nurturing consolidation, fertility, and creativity. These active and passive principles—solar-male and lunar-female energies—appear where they were wedded in the Temple of Poseidon, its exterior sheeted with gold and silver, the light of the sun and moon, each conveying its own set of mystical implications. Their holy union of the conscious and subconscious mind signified a simultaneous florescence but deliberate control of psychic potential—the next step in human evolution.

The first son Kleito bore to Poseidon was Atlas. His pre-Greek name in Sanskrit means the Upholder, or He Who Supports or Holds Up, because he was envisioned in non-Platonic myth as a nude, bearded titan who crouched on one knee, bearing on his shoulders the sphere of the heavens or zodiac (not the world, as commonly mistaken in modern times). This figure anthropomorphized a tall peak far out at sea: when it was overcast, cloud cover concealed the summit, making the mountain appear to hold up the sky. Such imagery appropriately personified the disciplines of astronomy and astrology, both created by Atlas—in other words, their origins went back to Atlantis, the "daughter of Atlas." The island derived its name from the titan—transformed by myth into a foremost mountain—as did the sea it dominated, the Atlantic Ocean.

Again, in non-Platonic tradition, the island of Atlas was home for him and his four daughters, the Hesperides, known by this name after their mother, Hespera, the Evening Star. She was associated with the distant West across the sea, where Atlas island was located. Also referred to as the Western Maidens, the Daughters of Evening, Erythrai, and the Sunset Goddesses, Aegle, Arethusa, Erytheia, and Hesperia tended a garden at the center of which stood the Tree of Life, another version of Poseidon's phallic pillar in his temple at the Atlantis acropolis.

Representing the Four Cardinal Directions, the Hesperides surrounded their father, thereby rendering him the sacred fifth numeral as a midpoint. Clearly, 5 was the Atlanteans' supreme holy number, because they identified it with their eponymous first king, Atlas. They also revered him as the creator of astrology, which played a pivotal role in their society. The kingly sacrifice of a bull in the Temple of Poseidon was an entirely astrological ritual. Its victim was the astral bull whose slaughter meant the end of the Age of Taurus, something other Bronze-Age peoples—such as the contemporary Trojans, Minoans of Crete, or Mycenaean Greeks—would have understood as a prelude to renewal. Taurus was similarly synonymous with rejuvenation and revival, which he engendered by having his own throat cut, thereby enabling plants and animals to spring from his blood. His myth was reenacted in a rite called the *taurobolium* to commemorate the death and resurrection of the hero Mithras, who personified the next age and baptized initiates into his cult.

Atlas was said to have invented astronomy and astrology simultaneously, because what later came to be known as two, distinct disciplines was originally a single concept. Throughout the ancient world, astronomy was the precise observation of the heavens and documentation of their movement for the accurate interpretation by earthly astrologers of cosmic influences. They believed that all physical phenomena were intrinsically connected to metaphysical actions and causes; that both were reciprocal and interactive. Therefore, one could be used to explain the other. After centuries of separation, scientists are gravitating back toward this ancient principle in their discovery that merely the physical presence of an experimenter influences the outcome of his experiment on a subtle yet critical level.

So, too, physicists understand that there are no fundamental differences between energy and matter; that the latter is but a subatomic variant, rearrangement, or recomposition of the former. Interchange of energy forms is again worthy of consideration, thereby allowing for infinite possibilities in which astrology or prophesies are no longer so easily dismissed, condemned, or ridiculed.

THE ATLANTO-MAYAN
CALENDAR

The form that Atlantean astrology or its predictive procedures took may, in fact, have best survived in the Mayan calendar or, more properly, Mesoamerican calendrics, of which the Maya were a part.

As mentioned in chapter 1, Azaes was listed by Plato as one of Kleito's sons who ruled a province of the Atlantean empire. His name bears a striking resemblance to the Itzás, a Maya people who occupied coastal Yucatán, where they are most famously remembered for their impressive ceremonial city, Chichén Itzá. Its centerpiece is the pyramidal Temple of Kukulcan, the Feathered Serpent.

While the term *serpent* was often used as a title signifying "power," the Mayas were unable to grow facial hair, and therefore possessed no word to describe Kukulcan's bearded appearance. They had to rely on their next closest adjective—*feathered*—to characterize the bearded founding father of Mesoamerican civilization. Had they not seen this foreigner from the ancient Old World with their own eyes, they would never have been able to dream up such a figure.

His conception as a bearded white man is by no means confined to pre-Columbian oral traditions. The walls inside a small, masonry structure at the north end of Chichén Itzá's Great Ball Court are covered with bas-relief carvings clustered around the representation of Kukulcan

Fig. 4.1. This relief carving inside the Temple of the Bearded Man at Chichén Itzá's Great Ball Court represents the non-Indian profile of Kukulcan, the Maya founding father. We can compare this image to the ancient Greek conception of Atlas, the eponymous emperor of Atlantis, portrayed in a fifth-century BC stone relief in chapter 1.

as a male figure with a Semitic nose and long, full beard. This structure itself is known as the Temple of the Bearded Man.

He reappears nearby, atop the 90-foot-high Kukulcan pyramid, inside the walls of its shrine at the summit, among an identical quartet of bearded men holding up the Mayan glyph for "sky."

The Maya referred to these self-evident depictions of Atlas as Bacabs, twins representing the Cardinal Directions. So, too, Plato informs us

Fig. 4.2. Relief carving of a Bacab, or Atlantean figure, inside Chichén Itzá's shrine room at the Pyramid of the Feathered Serpent.

that Kleito's sons from whom the royal houses of Atlantis descended were twins. As Atlas was the creator of astrology, so each brother Bacab presided over one year in a 4-year cycle, because they were deities of astrological time. They were believed to have come to Chichén Itzá just after a world-class deluge destroyed their capital across the sea. This lost homeland was described as "the Red and Black Land," recalling Plato's description of the red (tufa) and black (lava) natural formations on the island of Atlantis.

The Itzás were a Maya people named after a variant of the Feathered Serpent, Itzamna. In a Maya cosmology known as the Chilam Balam and Juan Darreygosa's sixteenth-century *Historia de Zodzil*, Itzamna bears the title Serpent from the East and is described as "the first after the flood" that engulfed his island kingdom in the Atlantic Ocean.[1]

He arrived on the island of Cozumel, off the Yucatán coast, where some temples dedicated to him still stand. Proceeding to the Mexican mainland, he built Chichén Itzá, or Mouth of the Well of Itzá, and one

Fig. 4.3. Line-drawing impressions of Bacabs, or Atlantean figures, on the interior walls of the shrine atop Chichén Itzá's Pyramid of the Feathered Serpent.

hundred forty-nine other cities. In temple art such as friezes at the Maya ceremonial center of Tikal, in Guatemala, he is portrayed as a long-nosed, bearded man rowing his boat across the sea from which he came. In the background of this sculpted frieze running around the top exterior of the acropolis is a volcanic island in the process of a major eruption while a stone city topples into the sea and a blond-haired man drowns in the foreground.

The identity of this scene could hardly be more self-evident. When Teobert Maler, the Austrian archaeological photographer who found the frieze, saw it for the first time in 1915, he exclaimed, "until that moment, I dismissed Atlantis as a baseless myth. I knew at once that I had been mistaken."[2]

Itzamna's followers from the Red and Black Land of Tutulxiu, the Land of Abundance or the Bountiful, far across the sea, "where the sun rises," were the Ah-Auab: "foreigners to the land," "white men," or the True Men.[3] On the twenty-seventh stele at Yaxchilan, the eleventh stele at Piedras Negras, and on the Temple of Warriors at Chichén Itzá, they are portrayed as bearded, with long, thin noses, and European facial features.

The Chilam Balam tells of life in the Red and Black Land as ideal for many centuries. One day, however, "a fiery rain fell, ashes fell, rocks and trees crashed to the ground. Then the waters rose in a terrible flood.

The sky fell in, and the dry land sank into the sea"—doubtless the same event depicted on the acropolis at Tikal.[4]

The Red and Black Land was also known as Tayasal, and described in the *Popol Vuh* as "the lost homeland of the Ah-Auab, who came from the other part of ocean, from where the sun rises, a place called Patulan-Pa-Civan."[5] These oceanic origins were naturally embedded in the very name of the people that built Chichén Itzá. It stems from the Mayan *itz*, for "magic," and *(h)á*, meaning "water," to form "magicians of (or from) the water (i.e., sea)."

Given their city's abundant Atlantean pedigree, evidence for the sacred numerals in its ceremonial architecture might be expected, such as the Temple of Kukulcan's ten levels. Buried in the heart of the step pyramid, directly beneath the summit's Bacabs positioned at the Cardinal Directions on the four walls of its shrine, reposes a blue-eyed statue, known as a *chac-mool,* to create the sacred center and fifth numeral.

A few paces to the northwest, a sculpted panel in the Great Ball

Fig. 4.4. Buried deep inside Chichén Itzá's Pyramid of the Feathered Serpent, in its own chamber, is the blue-eyed statue of a reclining male figure known as a chac-mool.

Court depicts a decapitated victim from whom six streams of blood transform into serpents. Feathered serpents from Atlantis carried the technology and spirituality of their overseas homeland to establish a colony in Middle America at Yucatán—Plato's Azaes—from which their descendants, the Itzás, derived their name and identity. As such, they were culture bearers who sparked Mesoamerican civilization, a synthesis of introduced Atlantean know-how and indigenous influences.

Among the most important gifts carried away from the island kingdom of Atlas was a scientific reckoning of time. Its original configuration was gradually eroded and eventually lost through the influence of successive, native inflections from the late fourth-millennium BC Olmec and third-century BC Maya, over the millennia to its last custodians, the Aztecs, in the early-sixteenth century AD. Yet its core mechanism remained intact as developing cultural variations succeeded one another. The better known of these are the Mayan calendar and the so-called Aztec Calendar Stone.

The latter was accidentally dug up by sewer workers on December 17, 1790, before the large cathedral of Mexico City's El Zócalo Plaza Mayor, almost parallel to the front of the viceroy's palace. They pried the 24-ton disk from 2 feet below street level, then set it upright against the cathedral's eastern wall. Spectators were awestruck by the 13.5-foot-tall monolith sculpted from a single, 4-foot-thick piece of gray-black basalt still bearing traces of its original, polychrome artwork.

Centuries earlier, the 50,000-pound slab had been hewn from quarries in the mountains south of today's Mexico City, near the floating gardens of Xochimilco. It was then transported somehow about 30 miles to the main square of Tenochtitlán and lifted more than half way up the steep steps of the Great Pyramid. Laying flat on a broad landing, sculptors and artists undertook the complex task of carving and painting the bas-relief masterpiece during the reign of Emperor Axayacatl. Their labors were finished by the late-fifteenth century, when the great disk was installed upright on its rim in a thronelike cradle. There the monumental symbol of eternity stood, above the Aztec imperial capital, for just 40 years. It presided over the fall of Tenochtitlán on August 13,

1521, and the attendant collapse of Mesoamerican civilization.

The city had not even been envisioned by the Aztecs, who seized it from its original occupants after the Calendar Stone's completion in the late-fifteenth century AD. Long before, Mexihcah founding fathers built Tenochtitlán on an island and patterned the capital, with its canals and causeways, after their ancestral homeland, Aztlán, a mountainous White Island in the Atlantic Ocean.

Any doubt concerning Aztlán's identification with Plato's sunken kingdom is dispelled by the Temple of Ehecátl, a circular pyramid of red, white, and black stone (the same described in the *Kritias*), rising in five steps (the Atlantean sacred numeral), located at Tenochtitlán's precise center, where it enshrined a statue of the god supporting the sky on his shoulders. His resemblance to the Atlantean titan even extended to an obvious philological comparison: Ehecátl, Atlas.

Little is known of the historic Mexihcah save their obvious civil engineering skills, conquest by the Aztecs, and extermination during the Spanish Conquest. They or their ancestors may have been responsible for building that earlier, even larger ceremonial center 30 miles north of Mexico City, Teotihuacan, famous for its colossal Pyramid of the Sun and Avenue of the Dead. In any case, Mesoamerica's foremost cultural area was known as the Valley of Mexihcah—as it still is today—long before the Aztec usurpers arrived.

In the process of converting the natives to Christianity by demonizing their culture, Catholic friars learned and recorded something of Mexihcah origins in Aztlán, but not much else from the few, dwindling survivors of the disease epidemics unintentionally yet effectively introduced by the Spaniards. Previous to the catastrophic epidemics, Tenochtitlán was a sprawling urban center with some 212,500 residents occupying a metropolitan landscape more than 8 square miles in extent. The first Europeans to visit declared that its civil organization, sophistication, and beauty rivaled those of Paris, Seville, or Venice. "When we saw so many cities and villages built in the water and other great towns on dry land," remembered the veteran conquistador Bernal Diaz del Castillo, "we were amazed, and said that it was like an enchantment, on account of the great towers and boulevards and buildings rising from the water, and all built of masonry. And some of our soldiers even asked whether the things that we saw were not a dream. I do not know how to describe it, seeing things as we did that had never been heard of or seen before, not even dreamed about."[6]

Favorable first impressions did not prevent the conquistadors from systematically destroying the city and leveling it to the ground for mostly religious reasons. The Calendar Stone was dislodged from its cradle and sent careening down the front of the pyramid. It came to rest face downward in the dirt. Spanish Catholic friars cursed what they imagined was a "demonic altar," then ordered it ritually buried. Something of their fanaticism survived into the late-eighteenth century, when priests at the Cathedral Metropolitana informed parishioners they could gain heavenly grace by spitting on the freshly excavated disk and chipping off pieces with hand tools. To prevent its slow disintegration through vandalism, Mexico City authorities removed the Calendar Stone to an improvised shelter in Chapultepec Park that eventually grew into the National Museum of Anthropology, where the artifact is now preserved.

At the bottom of the monolith are the ornately head-dressed profiles of two male figures facing each other. The man on the left is Quetzalcoatl, an Aztec version of the Feathered Serpent, confronting his evil twin, Tezcatlipoca, or Smoking Mirror. The name referred to his talisman, a flint mirror he used to glimpse the future—appropriate enough, in view of the Calendar Stone's prognosticating features. Despite his divine patronage of divination, he was also the god of enmity, discord, war, and strife, in opposition to the civilizing Feathered Serpent. Tezcatlipoca's appearance on the Calendar Stone demonstrates its pre-Aztec—probably even pre-Mexihcah—origins. The Maya knew Smoking Mirror as K'awil, but a far older version was worshipped by the Olmec from the beginning of pre-Columbian civilization, thereby demonstrating the very ancient roots of Mesoamerican calendrics.

The serpentine bodies of both Quetzalcoatl and Tezcatlipoca are divided into sections adorned with images of flames and jaguar limbs amounting to the 52 years in the Mexihcah-Aztec century. As such, they appear as *xiuhcoatls,* or "fire serpents," and therefore part of the overall catastrophic theme pervading the Aztec Calendar Stone. At the top of its rim, between the xiuhcoatl snake tails, is a square containing the date—13-Acatl; 13-Cane, or AD 1479—in which the Calendar Stone was completed. The outer circle, interrupted at the top by this box and at the bottom by the Sacred Twins, is otherwise given over entirely to mathematical notation, as are the next four concentric rings. Even the smallest details—to the lone dot and a single diagonal line—signify arithmetical values.

For example, the squares at the outer perimeter contain representations of the manguey plant, whose leaves and stem each add up to one Xiuhmolpili, a unit of 365 days, to complete one solar year. Square sections contain five dots, each representing weeks of as many days. Four larger indicators above four lesser pointers are, respectively, the Major and Minor Cardinal Directions. They simultaneously signify the eight divisions of the Mexihcah-Aztec day from sunrise to sunset in eight intervals of 3 hours' duration each. All this data rises from the Calendar Stone to compute accurately the solstices, equinoxes, and days of the zenith, which began or divided the Mexihcah-Aztec year.

An innermost arrow atop a ring encircling the anthropomorphic image of the sun indicates the day when the sun rises to its highest point directly over Tenochtitlán. At celestial moments such as this one, small obelisks, known as *gnomon,* around the edge of the Stone cast shadows over different details of its sculpted face, pointing to the occurrence of solstices, equinoxes, and zeniths. The gnomon also marked the annual rotation of the circumpolar star groups and the apparent course of the sun each year.

The next ring features the twenty day signs of the Mexihcah-Aztec month. Their original names and significance begin at the top right and go around to complete the circle: Xochitl (flower, life); Tecpatl (flint, violence); Olin (movement, potential); Cozcaquauhtli (vulture, disease); Cuauhtli (eagle, time); Ocelotl (jaguar, transformation); Acatl (cane, emptiness); Quihuitl (heavenly fire, judgment); Ozornatli (monkey, baser instincts); Itzcuintli (dog, loyalty); Malinalli (grass, peace); Atl (water, life); Tochtli (rabbit, alertness); Mazatl (deer, harmony); Miquiztli (skull, death); Coatl (serpent, wisdom); Cuetzpallin (lizard, dreams); Calli (house, preservation); Ehecatl (windstorm, travel); and Cipactli (alligator, earth).

The Calendar Stone aided in the observation of important religious ceremonies observed each month. These included petitions to the rain god Tlaloc, Altcualcaco, or Wants Water, and the Birth of Flowers during Tlaxochimaco, the Aztec "month" (from July 12 to the 31), when fertility celebrations took place. Military reviews paraded during Ochpaniz, the Month of Brooms, but the Atemoztli, Fall of Waters music festival, climaxed in the Izcalli mass sacrifice of tens of thousands of human victims taken from across the Aztec empire.

At the center of the Calendar Stone is the ghastly face of Tonatiuh. A flaming fire pot hangs over the sun god's forehead, or Third Eye, while his tongue lolls for bloody sacrifice. Flames sprout from his ears and nostrils, and the solar eagle's talons (in circles on either side of his face) grip human hearts.

The Aztecs and, presumably, their Mexihcah predecessors revered Tonatiuh, because he made mortal redemption possible when, at the beginning of the world, he threw himself into a fire. Rising from his own immolation, he took with him into heaven the souls of those who died heroically. All others descended into nine levels of hell before vanishing forever, like mist. Acceptably honorable deaths included falling in battle for men and expiring during childbirth for women. Voluntarily sacrificing their hearts to the flint knife, represented by Tonatiuh's greedy tongue, guaranteed paradise for both sexes.

He is surrounded at the center of the monolith by four circles repeating his calendrical title, 4-Olin, or 4-Movement. It is also the name of the present epoch he personifies and the manner in which it will end. Like their Maya and Olmec precursors, the Mexihcah believed that several, defining cataclysms shook our planet in the ancient past. Each natural catastrophe was an event horizon delineating the end of a particular time period, or sun, in human history and the beginning of another. Those

Fig. 4.5. Tonatiuh, the solar god of destruction, who will terminate our age on December 21, 2012, is portrayed at the center of the Aztec Calendar Stone.

preceding 4-Olin—our time—are symbolically represented in a quartet of boxes with Tonatiuh in the middle.

The most recent in order of its occurrence appears in the bottom-right square, referred to as 4-Atl, or 4-Water, when the world was destroyed by a great flood.

The previous sun, at the bottom-left of Tonatiuh, is 4-Quihuitl, or 4-Fire from Heaven. It too depicts an overturned bucket, but this one dumps flames on a burning pyramid.

Fig. 4.6. This square at the central section of the Aztec Calendar Stone (restoration) symbolically represents the end of a former age—4-Atl—with the figure of a pyramid inundated by water.

At the upper-left, 4-Ehecatl, or 4-Windstorm, is an eagle blowing on a pyramid as a dragonfly—synonymous with "change"—scoots away. The first and earliest sun is at the upper-right, 4-Ocelotl, or 4-Jaguar, in which early humans and a race of giants were destroyed by wild animals.

The numeral 4—signifying the Four Cardinal Directions—precedes each one of these cataclysms to indicate their worldwide impact. The 4-Ocelotl box is unique, because it is the only one that does not feature a pyramid, implying that this earliest sun took place before man attained civilization. The 4-Atl square frames the image of a pyramid sinking under a flood streaming from an overturned bucket signifying the wrath of Chalchiuhtlicue. Our Lady of the Turquoise Skirt, a name graphically identifying her with swirling or stormy water, was often represented in Aztec temple art as a goddess seated upon a throne surrounded by whirlpools of drowning men and women. It was her disaster that ended a former age of civilized greatness and ushered in a new one in Middle America with the arrival of survivors.

On her feast day, Chalchiuhtlicue was honored by priests, who collected reeds and ceremoniously placed them around her temple to signify her identification with the island home of Mexihcah forefathers. Literally, Place in the Water, Aztlán was also known by several other titles, including the Field of Reeds, synonymous with a place of great learning, because reeds were used as writing instruments. As pointed out in the introduction to this text, ancient Egyptians half a world away identically referred to their ancestral homeland Sekhet Aaru as an island of high culture before it was engulfed by the Atlantic Ocean.

These numerous connections to Atlantis are graphically multiplied by the quartet of squares surrounding the Calendar Stone's central hub. They match the four global catastrophes that punctuated Atlantean history and ended it. A consensus of scientific opinion at Britain's Fitzwilliam College, in Cambridge, during the summer of 1997, found that our planet had been subjected to a set of celestial bombardments beginning somewhat more than 5,000 years ago.

In 1984, archaeo-astronomer Marc Davis, paleo-geologist Piet Hut, and climatologist Richard A. Muller suggested "extinction of species by periodic comet showers." Their controversial article in *Nature* magazine eventually led to an international symposium of scientists convening under the banner "Natural Catastrophes During Bronze-Age Civilizations: Archaeological, Geological, Astronomical and Cultural Perspectives." Pooling their multidisciplinary expertise in 1997, they concluded that a recurring comet or comets narrowly missed Earth on four separate occasions—circa 3100 BC, 2200 BC, 1600 BC, and 1200 BC. Each close pass showered Earth's northern hemisphere with meteoric material, resulting in cataclysms on a worldwide scale.[7]

Further, the four catastrophes correspond to global event horizons in the early history of civilization: the rise of high cultures in Mesopotamia, the Nile Valley, and the Valley of Mexico at the turn of the fourth millennium BC; collapse of Egypt's Old Kingdom and Mesopotamia's Akkadian empire and the rise of China's first dynasty (the Xia) around 2200 BC; the end of Europe's Old Bronze Age, the implosion of the Hittite Old Kingdom, and the sudden termination of China's Xia

Dynasty about 1600 BC; the close of the Late Bronze Age, abandonment of Britain's Stonehenge after 18 centuries of continuous occupation, and the the beginning of the decline of pharaonic Egypt (from which it never recovered) circa 1200 BC.

All these and numerous other related circumstances were preceded or accompanied by natural disasters of historically unprecedented magnitude and destructiveness. The late-fourth millennium BC witnessed violent volcanic outbursts from Iceland to Mount Saint Helens and planet-wide flooding from the Amazon River, which swelled into a gigantic lake, to the Dead Sea, where water levels rose 300 feet.

In 2200 BC, an extensive land bridge connecting Malta to a nearby island fell into the Mediterranean Sea, causing tsunamis that flooded the entire archipelago, while virtually all of Europe's peat bogs burst into flames. The volcanic island of Thera detonated in the Aegean Sea during 1628 BC with the equivalent force of ten thousand 50-megaton atomic bombs, just as an eruption of comparable magnitude took place in New Zealand. Earth suffered a severe climate regression when several thousand cubic miles of ash were ejected into the atmosphere by global volcanism combined with meteor strikes from the eastern Atlantic Ocean and North America to Australia in 1198 BC.

Each of these four natural catastrophes coincided with the close passage of Comet Encke, named after the German astronomer who first calculated its orbit, Johann Franz Encke, in 1822. Their parallel to the quartet of worldwide cataclysms cited on the Aztec Calendar Stone is not unique. Ancient India's own calendrical system was separated into major divisions of prehistoric periods known as *yugas*—the Maha yuga is dated to 3100 BC, the Krita yuga came to an end by 2214 BC, the Treta yuga ended in 1621 BC, and the Davpara yuga terminated in 1213 BC. These yugas compare closely to the geologic catastrophes of the late-fourth millennium BC, 2193 BC, 1628 BC, and 1198 BC. Moreover, their identifiably Atlantean character is especially apparent in the Davpara yuga, during which Krishna's palace, Dwarka, was supposed to have sunk to the bottom of the sea after a great war.

On the other side of the world, Inca priests told of successive waves of overseas mass migration to coastal Peru undertaken by the pioneering Ayar-manco-topa, wandering Ayar-chaki, civilizing Wiracocha, and warlike Ayar-aucca—all separated by several centuries and set in motion by their own natural upheavals.

The Hopi Indians of the American Southwest believe that the world has been destroyed four times over. Followers of Zoroastrianism's Zurvanite predecessor, Plato's contemporaries in the fourth century BC, contended that four previous world ages had each been brought to a violent end through the recurring visitation in Earth skies of Tistrya. Although identified as a star, it generally signified an unspecified, bright light in the heavens. Tistrya's Zoroastrian version, Ahriman, is more specifically described as a comet or meteor shower "attacking the axis and deranging the heavens, thereby causing the catastrophes," in the words of Florida Atlantologist, Kenneth Caroli.[8]

The ancient Greeks recalled the great floods of Ogygea, Phoroneus, Deucalian and, of course, Atlantis. Foreshadowing its cometary and/ or meteoric annihilation, which he does not describe, Plato states in *Timaeus*:

There have been and will be many different calamities to destroy mankind, the greatest of them by fire and water, lesser ones by countless other means. Your own story of how Phaethon, child of the Sun, harnessed his father's chariot, but was unable to guide it along his father's course, and so burnt up things on the Earth, and was himself destroyed by a thunderbolt, is a mythical version of the truth that there is at long intervals a variation in the course of the heavenly bodies, and a consequent widespread destruction by fire of things on the Earth.[9]

Plato does, however, provide some remarkable, internal evidence demonstrating that the Atlanteans were not only aware of these cataclysms, but also structured their most important religious ritual around them. His detailed description of a bull sacrifice undertaken by the ten kings in the Temple of Poseidon every fifth or sixth year (*Kritias, 4f,* 119, 120) was, as mentioned above, an astrological ceremony commemorating the Age of Taurus. According to Max Heindel (1865–1919), the renowned Danish authority on the zodiac, it ended in 1658 BC.[10]

His calculation coincides with the third, worldwide catastrophe occasioned by the close passage of Comet Encke that triggered the nuclearlike eruption of Thera's volcanic mountain in the Aegean Sea, and the penultimate destruction of Atlantis. Neither Heindel nor Plato could have known that the end of the Age of Taurus was an almost perfect template for the global cataclysms of 1628 BC. The kings of Atlantis ritually sacrificed a bull to commemorate the close of this zodiacal age while they prayed to Poseidon to protect them from another such disaster. A 30-year discrepancy between the geophysical date for Thera's detonation, with its attendant upheavals around the world, and the end of the Age of Taurus suggests that the calculations of either the geologists or Max Heindel, or both, are off the mark by an insignificant trifle. Yet the kings' celebration of their bull sacrifice throws an extraordinarily revealing light on their time parameters, because it at once removes Plato's Atlantis from some impossibly incongruent setting during postglacial times to a time squarely in the Bronze Age, at the close of the Age of Taurus, after 1628 BC.

If, as it would appear, the Age of Taurus corresponded with the age of Atlantis—at least until the end of the Middle Bronze Age—then Taurus and Atlantis must have shared a common beginning. According to Heindel, the Age of Taurus began in 3814 BC. This date, too, is a remarkable fit, suggesting the likely birth of Atlantean civilization. Its founders would have required several centuries of development before their society reached cultural levels high enough to begin impacting the outside world by the end of the fourth millennium BC.

Additional internal evidence for Atlantis is found in the second day sign of the Aztec Calendar Stone: Mazatl. It represented the Mexihcah deer god and goddess, who "raised a great mountain" called Place Where the Heaven Stood in the middle of the Atlantic Ocean. Their offspring were pairs of twin sons, the builders of glittering palaces and shrines, until they were mostly killed by a massive flood that sank to the bottom of the sea the mountain Place Where the Heaven Stood. One pair of royal deer twins survived the calamity, however, by sailing to the shores of Middle America, where they built the first postdeluge kingdom.

Comparisons are too obvious between Place Where the Heaven Stood, a "great mountain," and Mount Atlas; the inundation that overwhelmed either location; and Mazatl's and Kleito's pairs of twin princes, both of which built glittering palaces and shrines.

The famous Argentine author Jorge Luis Borges, director of Buenas Aires' Biblioteca Nacional (National Public Library), cited a North African correspondence to the Mexihcah myth of Mazatl. He wrote that Jakob Ben Chaim, a sixteenth-century rabbi in Fez, quoted a fragment from the Sibyl of Erythraea on an obscure Moroccan tribe who "had their original dwelling in Atlantis, and are half-deer."[11] The Erythraean Sibyl was Herophile, a Chaldean prophetess from Babylonia, who presided over Apollo's oracle at the Ionian town of Erythrae during the Late Bronze Age, just when Atlantis was destroyed.

The Aztec Calendar Stone obviously belongs to a worldwide memory of global cataclysms so traumatic they became defining moments in ancient man's prehistory and his reckoning of time. They appear in the squares clustering around the hub of the Stone, beginning particularly with the most recent catastrophe, the great deluge, a clear reference to the destruction of Atlantis in every respect.

The Maya legend of the Four Suns recounted how death came to their overseas' ancestors from out of the sky: "It rained fire upon them. They were swallowed by the waters."[12] This was the Unuycit, when an ancestral homeland, Patulan-Pa-Civan, perished with all but a handful of survivors, who sailed to the shores of Yucatán during the remote past. Mentioned in the Dresden Codex, the Haiyococab was the Water over the Earth, from which the "Earth-upholding gods fled when the world was destroyed by the Deluge."[13] The Mayas' Popol Vuh, or Book of Counsel, a cosmological collection of their fundamental historical and spiritual beliefs, describes the Hun yecil—the Drowning of the Trees—when the U Mamae, or Old Men, survivors of an Atlantic cataclysm, built their first postdeluge temple near the banks of the Huehuhuetan

River in thanks to the gods for their escape.[14] Plato's description of Atlantis inundated "during a single day and night" is seconded by the Mayas' Chimalpopca Codex, which reports that their ancestral island came to a bad end "in one day of deluge. Even the mountains sank into the water."[15] Tulan, yet another name for the Feathered Serpent's homeland, was smothered by

> . . . a resinous thickness descended from heaven. The face of the Earth was obscured, and a heavy, darkening rain commenced; rain by day, and rain by night. There was heard a great noise above their heads, as if produced by fire. Then were seen men running, pushing each other, filled with despair. They wished to climb upon their houses. And the houses, tumbling down, fell to the ground. They wished to climb upon the trees, and the trees shook them off. They wished to enter into the grottoes, and the grottoes closed before them. Water and fire contributed to the universal ruin at that time of the last great cataclysm which preceded the Fourth Creation.[16]

Out of these violent upheavals, the last migrations arrived in what is now Guatemala: "Those who gazed at the rising of the sun had but one language. This occurred after they had arrived at New Tulan, before going west. Here the language of the tribes had changed. Then speech became different. All that they had heard or understood when departing from (Old) Tulan had become incomprehensible to them."[17] Reflecting the quartet of natural disasters that struck during Atlantean times, four different Tulans appear in the Cakchiquel Manuscript: "It is where the sun set that we came to (New) Tulan from the other side of the sea, and it is there that we were conceived and begotten by our mothers and fathers."[18]

These accounts preserved by the Maya in their most sacred documents unquestionably reflect the destruction of Atlantis. Even 4-Atl's translation as 4-Water shares its meaning with the Sanskrit *atl,* because both "support."

The previous event horizon 4-Quihuitl, 4-Fire from Heaven, graphically describes the effect of Comet Encke's disastrous brush with Earth in 1628 BC. Its earlier near-miss during 2193 BC is likewise characterized by 4-Ehecátl, or 4-Windstorm, by Swedish geologists Lars Franzen and Thomas B. Larrson, whose material evidence for the late-third-millennium BC catastrophe revealed "indications of strongly increased atmospheric circulation in rhythmically appearing periods" caused by numerous, mid-air bursts of meteors and asteroids, resulting in, literally, worldwide windstorms.[19]

Although 4-Jaguar, or 4-Ocelotl—the first cataclysm and the near-annihilation of humanity by wild beasts—seems less clearly associated with the upheavals of 3100 BC, its celestial character survived in the Aztec version, which told that the evil Tezcatlipoca turned himself into another sun a very long time ago. To save Earth from being burned by twice as much heat, Quetzalcoatl knocked Smoking Mirror out of the sky, but as he fell, Tezcatlipoca transformed himself into a monstrous jaguar and took out his frustration on men and women by attacking them everywhere. He was prevented from utterly devouring the human race when Quetzalcoatl again intervened to drive him off, thereby inaugurating a new age or "sun" for the world. Tezcatlipoca eventually returned to blow the Feathered Serpent high into the sky with a powerful wind that devastated the whole Earth (4-Ehecátl). While wandering among the stars, Quetzalcoatl collected a sufficient number of heavenly flames to hurl them down at his enemy, forcing him yet again from power, but setting the entire planet on fire in the process (4-Quihuitl). The water goddess Chalchihuitlicue, Our Lady of the Turquoise Skirt, finally doused the conflagration with a global flood, from which a few humans survived to begin life over again (4-Atl).

While this myth self-evidently describes a series of celestially induced natural disasters, the Calendar Stone's original identity is more brightly illuminated by its incorporation of the sacred numerals of Atlantis. The disk design itself is made up of five alternating elements—six, if the central sun face of Tonatiuh is included—the same fundamental arrangement Plato described for the layout of "that sacred isle," Atlantis. On the Calendar Stone, the concentric ring just inside the outer circle carries square sections, each one containing five dots representing weeks of five days. Five more dots inside the circle signify intercalary days, making the system correspond to a solar year by bringing the total number to 365.

Groupings of the fifth numeral were so frequent in and integral to the workings of the Calendar Stone that they were assigned their own designation as *nemontemi*. Two nemontemi of five dots surround each manguey plant on the monolith to represent one decade. It bears twenty such squares, plus two more squares on three sides with sixteen dots, for an additional 6 years.

Dots standing alone were referred to as *chalchihuitls,* after Our Lady of the Turquoise Skirt, the sea goddess who presided over the Atlantis-like destruction of 4-Water. Five chalchihuitls are positioned prominently in the central hub around Tonatiuh's glaring sun face.

The third ring from the outermost rim is composed of fifty-two *quincunxes* (squares containing four dots in each corner with one at their center). Although only forty are visible, the remaining twelve are obscured by the eight directional indicators. Fifty-two quincunxes total the 260-day count harkening back to the earlier Maya Tzol'kin: a sacred calendar used for divination purposes and to determine the time of religious or ceremonial events.

The Maya also operated a solar calendar, the Haab, comprising 18 months of 20 days each, together with a 5-day month at year's end known as the Wayeb, or Nameless Days.

The fifth numeral plays a pivotal role in the Mayan calendar, when five *tun* cycles—groupings of 5,125-year periods—made up the Precessional Year, also known as the Great Zodiacal Year, comprising some 25,630 solar years and upon which the whole time-counting system was based.

Mesoamerican civilizations before and after the Maya used a vigesimal, or base twenty, in conjunction with a base five numbering system.

Tezcatlipoca, who plays such a vital role in the Stone's symbolism, celebrated his main feast day during Toxcatl, the fifth month in the Mexihcah calendar. After the last of the four cataclysms, they claimed the era in which they lived and we live was the Fifth Sun, the last re-creation of the world, oscillating between the Great Flood and the next global catastrophe to come in 2012.

Arizona's Hopi Indians preserve very much the same belief, even to use of the same terminology, stating that our time is the Fifth Sun, which is set to end violently on the winter solstice of 2012—if the world is still in a condition of Koyaanisqatsi, "life of moral corruption and turmoil," or "life out of balance."

It is clear, then, that the sacred numerals of Atlantis, particularly 5—synonymous with "civilization"—are the Mayan calendar's fundamental denominators and its later expression in the Aztec Calendar Stone.

The name Calendar Stone, however, is a misnomer in every respect. As already mentioned, the Aztecs appropriated astronomy and astrology from a previous people they conquered, the Mexihcah. Nor was the Stone a calendar, but a highly complex, sophisticated almanac—an astrological computer—for divination. It was known as the Aztec Calendar Stone only from the beginning of the twentieth century. The monolith's original name was Cuauhtlixicalli: House of the Eagle, Eagle Bowl—but the Vessel of Time was closest to its real meaning. The eagle symbolized the sun, which in turn embodied the passage of time.

To the Mexihcah and Aztecs, time was the supreme deity, because it brings everything into existence, destroys everything, and brings new forms into being through a cycle of creation, destruction, and re-creation that nothing in the universe escapes. As we have discovered, they believed that Earth had been successively blasted by four cataclysms that wiped out society and each time pushed humanity to the brink of extinction. After generations of misery and hardship, the survivors and their descendants gradually repopulated the world and built new cultures. When humankind again forgot the past and grew corrupt, moral imbalance eventually upset cosmic law to call down another holocaust. As before, a few were spared to start the long, painful ascent back to civilization. The god of time is accordingly depicted in his most horribly ruinous aspect as Tonatiuh at the center of the Calendar Stone, because he signifies the world disasters arrayed around him.

Fig. 4.7. In this Aztec representation of their capital city, an eagle signifying the destructive aspect of time devours a snake (synonymous with Earth and physical existence) at the center of Tenochtitlán, where the Eagle Bowl, better known as the Aztec Calendar Stone, was located.

This cyclical pattern of human nature alternating with global calamities convinced the Mesoamericans that they were required to behave within the observable laws of nature as expressed in the timetables of the heavens and the regular movements of celestial bodies. Each day, by the great disk gleaming from the steps of the Great Pyramid the inhabitants of Tenochtitlán were reminded of the delicate balance between their behavior and cosmic judgment.

Zelia Nuttall, a renowned pioneer in Middle American archaeology for Massachusetts' Peabody Museum, realized as long ago as the late-nineteenth century that Mexico City's ancient sun stone had been "designed to control the actions of all the human beings of the state, bringing their communal life into accord with the periodic movements of the heavenly bodies."[20] She recognized how Mesoamerican awe of temporal cycles absolutely dominated the lives of the Aztecs and their forerunners for the previous 45 centuries, going all the way back to the first Olmec.

At the moment of birth, the rest of the child's life was determined by its horoscope, and the day sign under which the infant was born prearranged everything from the cradle to the grave. Each day had its own deity whose glyph was a stylized portrait of its functions and character, which the mortal born on that day was obliged to assume in some way. Marriages were contracted, travels were undertaken, rituals were enacted, wars were declared, treaties were proclaimed, buildings were erected, business deals were concluded, sexual activity was allowed or forbidden—in fact, virtually all human activity was regulated—by an astrological regimen monumentalized in the multicolored Cuauhtlixicalli glowering from atop its pyramid over the people of Tenochtitlán.

Each day was overseen by a different deity that impacted the fate of anyone born under its influence. Men and women were, therefore, obliged to identify with the calendric divinity in some way. Priests known as day keepers cast the horoscopes of all new babies, and assigned them names from the days on which they were born. A case in point was a native mistress of the conquistador leader Hernán Cortés. He referred to her as La Malinche (doña Marina), a corruption of her real name, Ce Malinalli, One Grass, from the Aztec Calendar. Tezcatlipoca, its mythic figure whose dynamic actions kept the Vessel of Time filled with life-giving energies, was appropriately known as Ipalnemoani, He by Whom We Live, and Titlacauan, We Who Are His Slaves.

Far from being the first of its kind, the Aztec Calendar Stone may actually be a monument to a kind of sacred device, some portable instrument used to compute significant astronomical data. The sculpture is perhaps a faithful reproduction of a much smaller original device probably no larger than 2 or 3 feet in diameter. The sculpted monolith plainly shows five or six disks within its shallow bowl and superimposed on one another like stacked plates, as though they were meant to turn either clockwise or counterclockwise, independently of each other, aligning with certain figures to obtain desired coordinates.

Each of the Cuauhtlixicalli's eight pointers, or indicators, may have been affixed to different rings of the smaller instrument after which the sun stone was modeled on a larger, monumental scale. Turning the rings to a different position would move its arrow to the desired numerical value, thereby arriving at a particular computation.

The Eagle Bowl's real identity as an apparatus is additionally suggested by the notches and gears that make up its outer circles. When they and their various, meshing parts are highlighted separately, they resemble the internal mechanism of a working instrument. If so, there was probably more than one—so many, in fact, that every high priest may have possessed an astrological calculator, and the so-called Aztec Calendar Stone memorialized a standardized type.

That it was, in fact, reproduced on a smaller scale was reported firsthand by Bernal Diaz del Castillo in 1521, when he and his fellow conquistadors were approached by *caciques,* or imperial representatives of Moctezuma II, the Aztec emperor, bearing goodwill gifts. These included

> a wheel like a sun, as big as a cart-wheel, with many sorts of pictures on it, the whole of fine gold, and a wonderful thing to behold, which those who afterward weighed it said was worth more than ten thousand *reales.* Then another wheel of greater size made of silver of great brilliancy in imitation of the moon with other figures shown on it, and this was of great value, and very heavy.[21]

Because such important though nonetheless perishable devices were commonly associated with the priesthood, its members had a permanent testimonial to their craft erected in a prominent position of authority atop the capital's Great Pyramid, where it overlooked central Tenochtitlán.

While the Eagle Bowl's function as a monument to some kind of sacred computer operated by influential holy men is unproved, its identity as an astrological almanac is more certain. So, too, the Cuauhtlixicalli's Atlantean character is steeped in the related myths of the Feathered Serpent, Smoking Mirror, and Our Lady of the Turquoise Skirt. It becomes especially apparent, however, in the Eagle Bowl's profuse incorporation of the sacred numerals 5 and 6—especially 5—which Plato tells us were the mystical common denominators of Atlantis.

A REBELLION OF
THE EARTH

Because time repeats itself, the Maya believed, they should be able to predict the future. This was the fundamental tenet upon which their calendar was based: coming events were foreshadowed in the past. From this supposition, Maya astronomers developed a complex system of timekeeping based on the scientific inheritance of their U Mamae ancestors—the Old Men who carried the principles of celestial mechanics from doomed Aztlán-Atlantis to the shores of Yucatán. There, they evolved the Tzol'kin's 260-day calendar, a 365-day calendar for the Haab, plus the calendar round—a 52-Haab that synchronized the cycles of both Tzol'kin and Haab.

These intricate organizations of time were not intuited by shamans during altered states of consciousness, nor were they the religious hallucinations of controlling priests presuming to speak for the gods. On the contrary, they were the exclusive results of close and accurate observations of natural phenomena faithfully documented over the course of numerous generations. For example, the Tzol'kin's 260 days derived from the 260-day period covering the length of human pregnancy, leading some archaeologists to conclude that the calendar was developed by midwives to predict the arrival of newborn infants.

Because the solar circumambulation of Venus is 1.6 times faster than that undertaken by our planet, its thirteen revolutions around the sun require 8 Earth years to complete. Proof that the Maya were aware of this 13:8 ratio is expressed by the numbers they used to identify Venus and calculate its movements—13 and 8. In fact, their calculations of the Venus cycle were accurate within a 2-hour margin of error.

Most amazing of all was their knowledge of an event at the heart of our investigation. On the morning of December 21, 2012, the winter solstice sun will be aligned with the galactic equator, the central line of our galaxy as it appears from Earth. The alignment will include an apparent rift at the galactic core, a lightless region formed by dark clouds of interstellar dust extending along the Milky Way's hub beyond the constellation Aquila, the Eagle (the Aztec Calendar Stone's Eagle Bowl). Remarkably, neither this dark rift nor the 2012 alignment were known to modern science until the mid-twentieth century. How the Maya or their Atlantean predecessors could have learned about either astronomical phenomena without the use of deep-space telescopes and super computers is a mystery. Yet the fact that the Maya were in fact aware of these alignments powerfully underscores the credibility of their statements regarding the controversial winter solstice to come.

Predictions for this date appeared in their so-called Long Count of 1,872,000 days beginning on August 11, 3114 BC and set to terminate 5,125 solar years later on December 21, 2012. The present Long Count began with the destruction of the Fourth World. At present, we are living in the Fifth World that is due to end shortly. As Mexihcah calendrics were usurped by the Aztecs, so the Maya obtained much of theirs from the Izapa. Inhabiting a ceremonial capital likewise known as Izapa, near Mexico's Pacific coastal plains of Chiapas, close to the modern border with Guatemala, they were a transitional people connected with Mesoamerica's first civilization. More likely, they were the Olmec themselves or, at least, their last remnants, known to possess the Long Count, which they passed on to the Maya.

"There are no specific markings or statements about the year 2012 on the archaeological artifacts at Izapa," observes John Van Auken of Virginia's Association for Research and Enlightenment. "But there are numerous images at Izapa that portray a rare celestial alignment that appears in the skies in the years around 2012. This galactic alignment marks the rebirth of the December solstice and the rebirth of the Sun Lord over Seven Macaw's attempts to replace him. The Sun Lord rises through the Dark Rift in the Milky Way, located between Sagittarius and Scorpio."[1]

The celestial alignment Van Auken refers to is depicted on a late-pre-Classic (circa 600 BC) stela at Izapa. In the Mayas' Popol Vuh and, presumably, Izapa myth, Vucub Caquix, or 7-Macaw, was a demonic bird that tried to take over the sun and moon in a twilight zone between the Fourth and Fifth Worlds. Although his complex story is not entirely comprehensible, he was doubtless intended to signify an evil influence, given the nature of his sons, Cabracan and Zipacna. They were the instigators of earthquakes, implying 4-Ollin's Earth movement set to end our present world.

The earliest and so far only known written Mayan reference to 4-Ollin was found in the former Izapa-Olmec realm of Chiapas at Tortuguero, site of a Classic Maya city (AD 200 to 700) north of the better known ceremonial center at Palenque. The incomplete, partially legible inscription on Tortuguero's Monument 6 has been translated by Mayan epigrapher David Stuart: "At the end of 13 Baktuns, on 4 Ahau 3 Kankin, 13.0.0.0.0; [something] occurs when Bolon Yokte descends."[2] Our present era of the Fifth Sun comprises 13 Baktuns, each one containing 144,000 days. 4-Ahau 3-Kankin, 13.0.0.0.0 is December 21, 2012.

Archaeologists Nikolai Grube, Simon Martin, and Mark Zender (University of Texas) offer a complimentary translation: "'[I]t will happen' (*utom*), [effaced section] 'and he will descend' (*yem*). They involve the 'coming down' of B'olon 'Ok, or Bolon yokte K'uh. The Thirteenth Bak'tun will be finished [on] Four Ahaw, the Third of K'ank'in.' [Effaced] will occur. '[It will be] the descent [?] of the Nine Support [?] God(s) to the' [effaced]."[3]

Bolon Yokte, who is depicted, as well as mentioned on the Izapa stela, was the terrible lord of the underworld, leader of all the forces of destruction, the personification of triumphant chaos and conflict. His spotted jaguar pelt signifying the starry night sky identifies him with his place of origin in the heavens, while "the mouth of the jaguar represents

Fig. 5.1. At the ceremonial center of Copán, in Honduras, stone representations portraying the god of the underworld threaten to destroy humankind at the end of the Mayan calendar, "when Bolon Yokte descends" on the world, December 21, 2012.

the Underworld Portal, which is seen in the sky as the Dark Rift in the Milky Way," according to researcher John Major Jenkins.[4]

The descent of the Nine Support Gods indicates that as many levels of hell will descend upon Earth on the winter solstice of 2012. Interestingly, the words describing exactly what will take place "when Bolon Yokte descends" have been lost, probably due to weathering over the course of time—or they may have been intentionally effaced by someone who could understand them long before modern archaeologists were able to translate the inscription on Monument 6. Perhaps a literate Maya reading it was so horrified by the prediction that he deliberately blotted out all words identifying the precise nature of the coming event in a magical effort to prevent its occurrence. In any case, there can be no doubt that the Maya—from their Olmec predecessors at Izapa to their Aztec inheritors in Tenochtitlán—consistently regarded 4-Ahau 3-Kankin, the close of the Fifth World in which we live, as an all-encompassing catastrophe unrivaled for its destructiveness.

The coming of a Sixth World is neither mentioned nor implied anywhere, because humanity is not supposed to survive "when Bolon Yokte descends" at the close of 13-Baktun. Twenty-first-century scholars endeavor to put a positive spin on the Maya prophecy, arguing that it merely refers to a transition from one age to another. The passage may be accompanied by a natural upheaval here or there, and social disruption may shake up a few cities, but humankind is supposed to survive. More than that, some modern interpreters claim the winter solstice of 2012 will signal a new golden age of renewal for all the peoples of our planet. The world will be purged of its mistakes so that humanity may at last dispense with all the inequalities that have so far hampered indefinite progress.

These Pollyanna prophecies are largely baseless. Researchers who instead confine their investigations to the Mesoamerican source materials come away with entirely opposite conclusions. Bolon Yokte may appear once in temple art beside the Tree of Life, but such a single, uncertain reference cannot make the God of Creation out of the Lord of Hell. Nor do edifying versions of 4-Ahau 3-Kankin square with the Mexihcah's own term for the nature of the Fifth Sun's closure: Macuilli-Tonatiuh; literally, the Clenched Fist of Tonatiuh.

Readers will recall Tonatiuh's bug-eyed portrayal at the center of the Aztec Calendar Stone, where his blood-spattered tongue drips with human hearts, while others are held in the grasp of his pitiless talons. His forehead is adorned with a pot spilling flames. Fire blazes from his nose and ears. As such, Tonatiuh is disappointing as the messenger of a new era characterized by international peace and human renewal. In fact, he embodies the end of our 13 Baktuns in the Nahui-Ollin, or 4-Ollin. This period is, moreover, ruled by Xolotl, the dark and malevolent aspect of the Evening Star, the Planet Venus, which plays such a vital role in Mesoamerican calendrics. For example, the winter solstice of 2012 is transited by Venus, just as, according to the Maya, the Long Count was set in motion 5,125 years before by Kukulcan, the Feathered Serpent and beneficent incarnation of Venus.

Fig. 5.2. A relief sculpture from the Aztec capital, Tenochtitlán, depicting Macuilli-Tonatiuh, Clenched Fist, a vengeful god who will bring chaos to the world at the end of the Fifth Sun, the present age, on the winter solstice of 2012.

As this planet's evil incarnation, Xolotl was the Mexihcah death god, who conveyed souls to Mictlán. It was into this underworld that the sun disappeared each night under Xolotl's control. Depicted in sacred art as a skeleton, he was additionally the god of misfortune and fire. All these dire characterizations tell us far more about the real nature of Nahui-Ollin than all the good-natured spin put on it by today's upbeat interpretations.

Yet for everything the Maya and those who came after them had to say about the calamitous end of the Fifth World, the precise nature of its closure was never spelled out. The Mexihcah originally told their Spanish inquisitors in the early-sixteenth century that the Nahui-Ollin meant simply "movement." Other native informants elaborated slightly, indicating more specifically that Nahui-Ollin signified "Earth movement," which Catholic friars presumed must have signified an earthquake.

Of the more than six million mixed descendants of the Maya living today across Guatemala, Mexico, and Belize, the Lacandones are the Mayas' most direct linear descendants. They still preserve the authentic meaning of 4-Ollin: the Rebellion of Earth. They refer to themselves as the Hach Winik, or True People, for their devotion to the Mayas' original principles, a claim emphasized by their residency near the ancient ruins of Bonampak, with its vibrantly polychrome frescoes painted during AD 790.

Hach Winik pilgrims still conduct religious activities at this famous ceremonial center in Chiapas, where Olmec ruins of Izapa and its nearby surviving inscription of the 2012 prophesy may be found. Perhaps five hundred of these True People still survive in a single village, Lacanja Chansayab, close to the border with Guatemala. Their ancient calendar appears to have chronicled the four natural catastrophes that struck our planet during the Bronze Age, and rightly predicts 2012 winter solstice alignment with the galactic center.

Yet how accurate were ancient Mesoamerican projections for Nahui-Ollin? At least some degree of their accuracy may be gleaned from the Aztec Calendar Stone's success rate in anticipating historically verifiable events. For example, it warned of the Feathered Serpent's disastrous return on Reed-1, or AD 1519. The prophecy came true when Hernán Cortés first set foot on the shores of Mexico that very year at Veracruz, just where Quetzalcoatl made his Mesoamerican debut long before. His fair-complected physical resemblance to their ancient culture hero and the superior technology both figures possessed combined with the Spaniard's fortuitous appearance at the prehistoric flood survivor's landing site just when the Calendar Stone specified it would happen. This convinced the Aztecs that Cortés was himself the returned Feathered Serpent. It was because of this tragically mistaken identity that an empire of millions was caught off balance and subdued by five hundred conquistadors with thirteen horses and a small number of cannons.

Atop the Calendar Stone appears Reed-13, a box enclosing the image of a manguey plant and surrounded on three sides by thirteen dots, each representing thirteen heavens, which comprise a single sun. The glyph signifies the end of a World, or major epoch, corresponding to the year AD 1479. Precisely thirteen years later, Christopher

Fig. 5.3. A sculpted monolith at the Honduras National Museum from the Mayas' ceremonial city of Copán depicts the underworld god, Bolon Yokte, who they believed would unleash destructive forces on the world at the end of their calendar.

Columbus dropped anchor off the island of San Salvador in the Bahamas, opening the New World to European colonization and the subsequent eradication of Mesoamerican civilization.

Appropriately, Reed-13 occupies the top position of the Calendar Stone, where arrowheads touch it on either side and the uppermost indicator points at its underside, as though all the elements of the Eagle Bowl were culminating in this particular sign. As such, Reed-13 represents the supreme date of the entire object, and suggests that the Cuauhtlixicalli was made just then, because the astrologer-priests determined that 1479 to 1492 would simultaneously encapsulate in units of thirteen the year of its creation and that of their society's downfall.

Apparently, the Vessel of Time was created when it was and erected over the residents of Tenochtitlán primarily to announce this impending doom. To them, it was a monstrous timepiece winding down the last years of the Aztec empire, reminding its subjects to brace themselves for the inevitable end of their world.

Only this dire prediction, and that yet broader prognostication for 2012, can account for the numerous, graphic references circling in concentric rings around the horrid face of Tonatiuh, the personification of time in its thoroughly destructive aspect.

6

THE GREAT WINTER

Whether the rebellion of Earth predicted by ancient Mesoamerican ancestors and calculated for the near future heralds a global renewal, as some twenty-first-century investigators predict, or the worldwide catastrophe suggested by the Maya themselves remains to be seen. Its very name—the rebellion of Earth—does, however, suggest an ecological catastrophe of the kind conservationists have been warning against and Hollywood producers have been making movies about since the late-twentieth century. To be sure, a rebellion of Earth seems to anticipate the disastrous consequences of environmental abuse some observers believe have been accumulating in Earth's biosphere since the onset of the Industrial Revolution. If—or especially when—such a calamity takes place is cogent to the impending 4-Ollin.

More certain, however, than debatable scenarios for some abrupt adversity sparked by a polluting global economy are prospects for a coming ice age. The last one ended around 9500 BC, which means that another is due just now, according to paleoclimatologists. Their study of the geologic record shows that ice ages begin and end about every 100,000 years, punctuated by less cold, geologically briefer intervals every 12,000 years. Some researchers conclude that the past dozen millennia more likely represent a warm interlude in the last ice age still in progress. If so, the resumption of far colder conditions worldwide is not only unavoidable, but is also due to snap back with a suddenness that can paralyze most life on Earth.

Pravda's online Web site caused an international stir in early 2009 when it headlined "Earth on the Brink of an Ice Age." The article by science writer Gregory F. Fegel tells of a growing consensus among climatologists concerning "the very real threat of the approaching and inevitable Ice Age, which will render large parts of the Northern Hemisphere uninhabitable. . . . The data from paleoclimatology, including ice cores, sea sediments, geology, paleobotany and zoology, indicate that we are on the verge of entering another Ice Age, and the data also shows that severe and lasting climate change can occur within only a few years."[1]

Fegel refers to recent studies by Dr. Oleg Sorokhtin, a staff researcher with the Oceanology Institute (Moscow) at the Russian Academy of Natural Sciences. Sorokhtin and his colleagues found that their research of Earth climate change over the past 100,000 years "strongly indicates the imminent climax of the Holocene (our present geological epoch) and its sudden replacement by a new glacial age during the first half of the present century."[2]

Other Russian climate experts concur. "By the mid-21st century the planet will face another little ice age similar to the Maunder Minimum (the previous little ice age)," according to Khabibullo Abdusamatov, head of the Russian space research laboratory. It must come, he stated, "because the amount of solar radiation hitting the earth has been constantly decreasing since the 1990s and will reach its minimum approximately in 2041."[3]

Most of Abdusamatov's colleagues disagree only with his relatively moderate assessment of the coming glaciation. They anticipate something far colder and enduring than the Maunder Minimum. "The Earth is now on the brink of entering another Ice Age, according to a large and compelling body of evidence from within the field of climate science," reports Fegel. "Many sources of data which provide our knowledge base of long-term climate change indicate that the warm, twelve thousand year-long Holocene period will rather soon be coming to an end, and then the earth will return to Ice Age conditions for the next 100,000 years."[4]

Russian scientists are not alone in their prognostications for a new ice age in our immediate future. Climatologists of the Western Institute for Study of the Environment Colloquium (a non-profit collaboration of environmental scientists, practitioners, and the interested public in Lebanon, Oregon) agree that the Northern Hemisphere is in immediate danger of "an imminent transition to ice." In their Institute article, "An Urgent Signal for the Coming Ice Age," Peter Harris and John Faraday point out how "the geological record shows that the transitions are sudden, long term and extreme."[5]

Scientific awareness of ice age causation and its cyclical return is not new. As long ago as 1842, the French mathematician Joseph Alphonse Adhemar first proposed that our planet's glacial episodes resulted from regular alterations in its angular relationship to the sun.[6] Although contemporary scholars rejected Adhemar's theory, it was taken up and elaborated 33 years later in Scotland by James Croll, an elected fellow of the Royal Society and correspondent of Charles Darwin. In *Climate and Time in Their Geological Relations,* Croll cites variations of Earth's orbit on climate cycles. He was the first scientist to identify positive ice-albeo's reflecting power to magnify solar feedback. During periods of high orbital eccentricity, he argued, ice ages take place in regular cycles.[7]

Building on the ideas of Adhemar and Croll during 1930, a geophysicist genius in the Balkans, Milutin Milanković, demonstrated a correlation between glacial activity and Earth's gradually alternating angles toward the sun. Earlier, he revised the Julian Calendar for the Serbian Orthodox church. *Wikipedia* states, "His calendar is, in fact, the most accurate calendar in the world today."[8]

Milanković found that ices ages responded to the tilt of our planet over a 41,000-year time-span; the shape of its orbit, which alters during a 100,000-year period; and the Precession of the Equinoxes, or "wobble" gradually rotating in the direction of Earth's axis every 26,000 years. These cycles effect the amount of solar radiation reaching our planet and combine to produce the alternating ice age maximums and warm interglacials.

Milanković's discoveries were greeted with uncertainty by other scientists, then gradually dismissed as unprovable until the late-twentieth century. In early 1968, Wallace S. Broecker, the Columbia geophysicist who coined the term *global warming* seven years later, found that the Milanković hypothesis was "supported by precise dating of coral reefs and deep-sea sediments."[9] According to Harris and Faraday, "When paleoclimatologists met in 1972 to discuss how and when the present warm climate would end, it was expected that rapid cooling would lead to the coming ice age." Satellite monitoring of the biosphere then confirmed Milanković's solar-glacial cycles. "These data sets may be used to serve as a signal for the coming ice age."[10]

Four years later, *Science* magazine published a virtual validation of Milanković's work in "Variations in the Earth's Orbit: Pacemaker of the Ice Ages." Authors John Imbrie, James Hays, and Nicholas Shackleton announced a correlation they uncovered between climate data obtained from ocean sediment cores and Milanković's Earth-sun relationship. Combined, "the results indicate that the long-term trend over the next 20,000 years is towards extensive Northern Hemisphere glaciation and cooler climate."[11]

Today, Milanković's explanation is, as *Pravda* asserts, "the predominant theory to account for Ice Age causation among climate scientists."[12] Their reconsideration of his proposals in the 1970s was prompted by growing concern for climate deterioration generally and an understanding of its mechanism. A 1974 issue of *Time* magazine reported that "38 ships and 13 aircraft, carrying scientists from almost 70 nations, are now assembling in the Atlantic and elsewhere for a massive 100-day study of the effects of the tropical seas and atmosphere on worldwide weather."[13]

Observers from various scientific fields participating in the Global Atmospheric Research Program (GARP) found that a mere 1 percent decrease in the amount of sunlight striking the surface of Earth could tip the climatic balance sufficiently to cool temperatures, and precipitate an ice age in a very short time. They learned, too, that temperatures have been as high as they are now in only about 5 percent of the last 700,000 years. In other words, our climate has been enjoying an anomalous warm phase that cannot last much longer.[14]

While GARP researchers were endeavoring to determine just when the next glaciation might take place, others at Climate Long-Range Investigation, Mapping, and Prediction (CLIMAP) hauled up deep-sea core drillings going back over the past half a million years to discover that the coming and going of ice ages closely followed Milanković's cycles of precession, orbital shape, and rotational wobble. The ocean-bottom cores also showed that glaciation sometimes began and ended with great suddenness.

The so-called Younger Dryas, also referred to as the Big Freeze, was a brief 1,300-year cold snap that afflicted the world about 12,000 years ago. Within a single decade, temperatures plummeted worldwide. Increased snowfall blanketed every mountain range on Earth, all of Scandinavia's forests were reduced to tundra, and drought overcame the Levant. In North America, numerous animal species went extinct, while the Clovis culture—an early society of Paleo-Indians—entered a steep decline from which it would never survive.

The respected editor of *New Scientist* magazine, Nigel Calder, was sufficiently alarmed by these disclosures to declare in the July 1975 issue of *International Wildlife:* "The facts have emerged, in recent years and months, from research into past ice ages. They imply that the threat of a new ice age must now stand alongside nuclear war as a likely source of wholesale death and misery for mankind."[15]

Climate research into the following decades confirmed and deepened the worst suspicions about glaciation. Greenland's Ice Core Project of 1987 sent an improved drilling apparatus nearly 2 miles beneath Earth's surface to retrieve samples formed over the last quarter of a million years. The specimens revealed that every ice age within that time parameter began abruptly.

The British scientific journal *Nature* reported in 1999 that Antarctic ice cores collected at Lake Vostok demonstrated how glacial maximums alternate with warm periods known as interstadials in recognizable patterns, yet again confirming Milutin Milanković's hypothesis. *Pravda* added that core samples retrieved from Lake Vostok show how "today we are near to the end of a warm interglacial, and the Earth is now due to enter the next Ice Age."[16]

Its expected arrival seems at odds with concerns for global warming caused by industrial pollution. While debate still rages over civilization's impact on the natural environment, any questions regarding climate deterioration due to modern human's interference may be knocked into a cocked hat by Earth's own rotational cycles responsible for initiating glaciation in recurring patterns. Some scientific observers argue, however, that human meddling in the biosphere does play a direct role in fostering ice-age conditions.

Reid A. Bryson at the University of Wisconsin (Madison) and other climatologists point out that dust and other particles released into the atmosphere as a result of farming and fuel burning block more and more sunlight from reaching and heating the surface of Earth to foster cooler, wetter conditions that allow for ice ages. His conclusions prompted geologists Gillford H. Miller and Anne Vernal to ask, in a 1992 issue of *Nature,* "Will Greenhouse warming lead to Northern Hemisphere ice-sheet growth?"[17] They were answered that same year by climatologists Ken Caldera and James Kasting, who revealed the "suspectibility of the early Earth to irreversible glaciation caused by carbon dioxide clouds."[18]

At his death in June 2008, Bryson was widely recognized as "a towering figure in climatology and interdisciplinary studies of climate, people and the environment."[19] Among his notable achievements was discovery of the jet stream in 1945. According to his obituary by Terry Devit, he "pioneered the use of computer models in climate science . . . was among the first to explore the influence of climate on humans and human culture and, in turn, some of the human impacts on climate. He was an early developer of simple computer models to study the causes of past climate change, comparing those simulations with records of paleoclimate and human culture."[20]

John Kutzbach, University of Wisconsin-Madison professor emeritus of atmospheric and oceanic sciences, said of Bryson: "His interdisciplinary interests and knowledge of these topics allowed him to see connections that others missed and to initiate studies that are still at the cutting edge of climate research."[21] Given his recognition as "the pioneer of climatology," Bryson's belief in human contribution to prospects for a new ice age deserves serious consideration. Interestingly, he was less a proponent of either global warming or cooling than of climate destabilization, in which extremes of both increasingly hot and cold conditions irregularly alternate with each other.

Like virtually all of his colleagues, Bryson concluded that the present Holocene Epoch of mild temperatures that have characterized Earth's climate over the past 5,000 or more years is about to end soon. Just when is a question scientists are beginning to answer with growing certainty. "The fact is that ice ages recur in a dependable, predictable cycle that's about to repeat itself," according to Robert W. Felix, author of *Not By Fire, But By Ice*. "The next ice age could begin in our lifetimes."[22]

In 2008, Habibullah Abdusamatov, head of Russia's Pulkovo Observatory space research laboratory, told the RIA Novosti Press Agency, "Earth has passed the peak of its warmer period, and a fairly cold spell will set in quite soon, by 2012. Real cold will come when solar activity reaches its minimum, by 2041 . . ."[23]

Abdusamatov's statement that "a fairly cold spell will set in quite soon, by 2012" ominously coincides with the Mayas' prediction for that year. They did not indicate that our Fifth Sun would terminate in a glacial event, although the abundant astronomical and solar imagery surrounding 4-Ollin is coincidental to Earth's rotational cycles responsible for recurring ice ages. The sudden onset of catastrophically frigid conditions may not result in the extinction of humankind, but civilization would not fare as well.

With at least the entire upper third of the Northern Hemisphere buried under ice, the stresses of mass migrations in the direction of warmer, southern areas, coupled with loss of farmlands and unbearable overloading of every form of energy production, would cause famine and strife on an unprecedented scale. If the next ice age is comparable to the last one, all of New England will be covered by fifteen-story-high glaciers. They will additionally cover the entire Great Lakes Regions down to the tip of southern Illinois, the northern half of Missouri, eastern Nebraska and South Dakota, most of North Dakota, plus the northern regions of Montana, Idaho, and Washington. All of Canada and Russia will be uninhabitable. In Europe, Scandinavia, the British Isles, Poland, the Baltic, most of Germany and the northern Balkans will be covered by ice.

Population displacement alone could shatter the foundations and framework of organized society. Those fleeing beyond the reach of the ice will not be spared its consequences, however. With all but some of the Northern Hemisphere's crop regions lost, a crippled agriculture will not be able to feed seven billion people suddenly confined to about two-thirds of their previous living space. Merely being able to breathe will become increasingly difficult, because the oxygen-producing forests of the north will have disappeared. These projections are based on the most recent glaciation, which was far milder and spread over much less territory than previous ice ages. A repitition of the glaciation that accompanied or immediately followed the extinction of the dinosaurs about 65.5 million years ago was at least twice as ravaging and appears to have been a truly global affair.

Challenges presented by the next ice age, regardless of its severity, will be inevitably sorted out in the way humans invariably respond to social dislocation: through war and other forms of mass murder. Bolon Yokte will reign over Earth for the next 100,000 years, until Xolotl shall have conveyed most of humankind—perhaps all of it—into the bowels of Mictlán, never to return.

None of this should come as a surprise. We like to think of ourselves as immortal in at least some way, but the biological history of Earth is an unbroken chronicle of extinction. The Cretaceous-Tertiary event is the most famous for its sudden annihilation of the dinosaurs, when 70 percent of all life on Earth was the victim of sudden mortality. Previous catastrophes of this kind were sometimes responsible for much higher death rates. The Ordovician-Silurian, Late Devonian, Permian-Triassic and Triassic-Jurassic events exterminated virtually every kind of creature in the world. As such, there are far more species that have flourished and forever winked out of existence than are alive today.

We ourselves have already lost innumerable members of the human genus—Neanderthal man, *Homo habilis, Homo erectus,* and so forth.

Modern humans, such as the ancient Egyptians, Sumerians, Babylonians, Etruscans, Trojans, Olmec, Aztecs, Anasazi, Incas—not to mention the Atlanteans and many other peoples—are no longer with us. In consideration of their passing, we early-twenty-first-century Earthlings must not imagine that our admittedly fragile civilization is immune from the same forces—historical or natural—that purged them and our nonhuman predecessors from the planet.

If an impending ice age is the next agent of extinction, what might be its connection to the Mayan calendar? Robert Felix concludes that glaciation's geological trip mechanism is Earth's magnetic field, because it "holds tectonic forces in check. But when the field weakens during a reversal, that balance disappears. Suddenly unleashed, underwater volcanoes heat the seas and excess moisture rises into the sky. Then the moisture condenses and falls to the Earth as giant snowstorms and great floods."[24] He believes that underwater volcanism triggered by a geomagnetic flip—not Earth's rotational wobble—is responsible for ice age conditions. In any case, glaciation is invariably accompanied by such polar reversals.

A March 2005 issue of the *India Times* reports how geophysicists and astrophysicists cooperated with private research and analysis company computer experts to make projections for the magnetic field's behavior during the twenty-first century. Their combined efforts in the so-called Hyderabad Computer Model indicated that "Earth and Sun both will go through a process of magnetic pole reversal in 2012. Earth's magnetosphere will weaken and cosmic radiation from the Sun will increase many fold, making radiation hazards like cancer and so on inevitable."[25] The *India Times* underscored Felix's theory, "Earth's crust will experience increasing volcanoes, tectonic movements, earthquakes and landslides."[26]

Yet does our planet's magnetic field actually have some bearing on tectonics, glaciation, and recurring extinction patterns? According to Dr. David E. Loper, professor emeritus of geological sciences, Florida State University (Tallahassee), "There is evidence that climate, volcanism, and magnetic reversals may all be correlated."[27] He is seconded by professor of

Earth and environmental sciences at Columbia University (New York), James D. Hays: "The possibility that here is some connection between reversals, climate change, and extinctions cannot be ruled out."[28]

As long ago as 1964, the Australian archaeo-biologist I. K. Crain suggested a "possible direct causal relation between geomagnetic reversals and biological extinctions."[29] Building on his research ten years later, climatologists C. G. A. Harrison and J. M. Prospero detected "reversals of the Earth's magnetic field and climate changes."[30] Their colleagues Thomas J. Crowley and Gerald R. North went further in 1988 to find evidence for "abrupt climate change and extinction events in Earth history."[31] They were seconded by David M. Raup, who wrote in *Nature* magazine of "magnetic reversals and mass extinctions."[32]

It would appear the Maya left no opening for escape from 4-Ollin and its terminal consequences. They made no mention of a Sixth Sun or promised any future cycles of destruction and renewal. All we are told is that the descending Clenched Fist of Tonatiuh will strike on the winter solstice of 2012 with a rebellion of the Earth.

Even so, the Maya indirectly offered a faint glimmer of hope to late Fifth Sun humankind. They insisted that existence rested upon balance, and that all forms of energy were not only interchangeable, but also actually nothing more than variations of the same impulse. In this, they prefigured modern physics by at least 2,000 years.

Imbalance anywhere, they reasoned, must invariably generate exponentially amplifying distortion and physical consequences all along the energy spectrum. The human victims of Earth's previous four catastrophes—4-Ocelotl, 4-Ehecatl, 4-Quihuitl and 4-Atl—deserved their fate, because they had tampered with the cosmic equilibrium of their world. The imbalance they created through unnatural lifestyles, attitudes, and behavior set up a swelling frequency around the universe that recoiled on them ten thousandfold. They could have escaped the cataclysmic verdict that fell upon them, however, if the imbalance they were responsible for setting in motion had been corrected in time to damp down sufficiently its gathering resonance, thereby depriving it of its vibrational destructiveness. That, in essence, is what the ancient Maya cosmologists would probably most want us to understand. They, the great masters of calendrics, might warn us that there is still time, although admittedly precious little, to mitigate, if not altogether to avoid, the worst of 4-Ollin by a revision of human behavior as universal as it is radical.

At the last conceivable moment, we can swerve narrowly to miss a collision with fate through an ethical about-face. To side step a global calamity, we require no less than a global reorientation, *vis-à-vis* our fundamental relationship with nature. Whether that foretold event or humankind's ability to evade it is inevitable will stand revealed only after December 21, 2012. If, as a species, we have not sufficiently altered our self-destructive conduct before that date, what might we expect? The arrival of a new ice age—or a dramatic resumption of the Pleistocene Epoch that never really left us—seems to be the most likely scenario.

That most recent glacial period began gently approximately 100,000 years ago, although it soon lapsed into violent change. Geologist Geneviéve Woillard at the Université Catholique de Louvain tells how a warm phase (the Eemian Period) immediately preceding the last ice age ended "in less than twenty years."[33] Her European colleagues at the Greenland Ice Core Project further concluded from contemporary samples they retrieved nearly 2 miles beneath the surface of Earth's largest island that the latest glaciation began "catastrophically." W. F. Ruddiman and A. McIntyre wondered about the "severity and speed of Northern Hemisphere glaciation pulses" in the 1982 *Bulletin of the Geological Society of America*.[34]

Felix mentions that "worldwide temperatures plummeted twenty degrees Fahrenheit almost overnight."[35] Summarizing the environmental transition revealed by the Greenland ice cores, science reporters for Washington State's *Journal American* explained, "It was as though the climate of Nome, Alaska, suddenly descended on San Francisco."[36]

A 2004 movie titled *The Day After Tomorrow* dramatized sudden glaciation sweeping across the Northern Hemisphere within a day or so—but is such a rapid change likely to occur again? "When we looked at the records of past temperate intervals," Woillard writes, "we found abrupt shifts in forest composition at the end of all previous interglacials."[37]

Though not all climatologists may agree with Felix's conclusion that "every ice age began fast," periods of geological upheaval appear to have punctuated at least the early stages of glaciation whenever it took place. As such, we might expect the next ice age to begin no less violently.

Would the Maya have placed such emphasis on the demise of our Fifth World and surrounded it with such apocalyptic imagery merely to mark the end of one calendrical era and the start of another, as some observers insist? Or did they know something that we are only beginning to suspect?

THE
SUPER SOLAR STORM

Though the onslaught of a new ice age might coincide with the end of the Mayan calendar, another natural event offers perhaps an even more likely possibility. In January 2009, geophysicists at the U.S. National Academy of Sciences announced that a super solar storm could catastrophically effect our world sometime during 2012, when sunspots will become particularly numerous and active. Although the dotlike phenomena appear as mere "spots" from our perspective 93 million miles away, they are not benign blemishes on the photosphere, but instead are roiling hurricanes of incomprehensible size. During early 2008, astronomers observed two sunspots, each one as large as the planet Jupiter, or 318 times larger than Earth. Concentrations of intense magnetic activity, sunspots eject far into space solar flares thousands of miles long, together with coronal masses of plasma—charged high-energy particles.

How vulnerable has our increasing electronic technology become to exceptionally powerful solar storms? This was the question that concerned members of the National Academy of Sciences in May 2008. Funded by the National Aeronautics and Space Administration (NASA), their paper told how "the workshop brought together representatives of industry, the government, and academia to consider both direct and collateral effects of severe space weather events and contemporary society's vulnerability to space weather."[1]

They found that civilization is at a higher risk to solar storms than at any other time in its history, because modern society runs on electicity. A billion-ton plasma fireball striking our planet's atmosphere would violently distort its magnetic field, thereby inducing tremendous surges of current throughout the electrical power grids of the Northern Hemisphere. As Michael Brooks explained in *New Scientist* magazine, "The greatest danger is at the step-up and step-down transformers used to convert power from its transport voltage to domestically useful voltage. The increased DC current creates strong magnetic fields that saturate a transformer's magnetic core. The result is runaway current in the transformer's copper wiring, which rapidly heats up and melts."[2] Incapable of absorbing such a sudden and colossal burst of electricity, the entire power grid overloads and fries. The transformers are shorted, because all of them are strung together like extension cords plugged into one another: Californians receive their electricity from Oregon, Floridians get theirs from Pennsylvania, and so forth.

National Academy of Sciences (NAS) scientists stress that the effects of a sun storm on our interconnected network are not theoretical, and they point to historical examples. In March 1989, an only slightly stronger than usual gust of solar wind generated an electromagnetic surge across Quebec, superheating and melting its power lines to plunge six million Canadians into darkness for nine hours. That incident was nothing compared to the Carrington event of 130 years earlier. In a sun storm lasting 8 days, "the entire Earth was engulfed in a gigantic cloud of seething gas, and a blood-red aurora erupted across the planet from the poles to the tropics," according to Stuart Clark, a British writer for the European Space Agency.[3] "Around the world, telegraph systems crashed, machines burst into flames, and electric shocks rendered operators unconscious. Compasses and other sensitive instruments reeled as if struck by a massive magnetic fist."[4] For the first time in recorded history, people throughout the Caribbean were treated to spectacular displays of the Aurora Borealis. Its glow was so brilliant across the Rocky

Mountains that gold miners, assuming that morning had already come, awoke to prepare breakfast. This remarkable phenomenon was named after astronomer Richard Carrington, who discovered that a solar disruption caused these events just before noon on September 1, 1859.

Its effects were relatively harmless, owing to electricity's low level of application in the mid-nineteenth century. But if a super sun storm of equivalent magnitude were to occur today, its impact would be far more serious. "In 1859, the technology was quite low in comparison to today's technology," says Bruce Tsurutani of NASA's Jet Propulsion Laboratory. The telegraph had been invented just fifteen years before. "However, the technology that we rely on today is much more vulnerable."[5] According to the NAS paper, "Electric power is modern society's cornerstone technology on which virtually all other infrastructures and services depend."[6] It goes on to report that within 90 seconds after three hundred key transformers overload and melt down, a cascade effect will surge through the grid network to which they are all connected, cutting power to one hundred-thirty million Americans. Europe, Russia, China, and Japan would be likewise impacted.[7]

John Kappenmann, a power industry analyst with California's Metatech Corporation (Goleta), says that water distribution will be affected "within several hours; perishable foods and medications lost in twelve to twenty-four hours; loss of heating/air conditioning, sewage disposal, phone service, fuel re-supply and so on."[8] While lights go out around the Northern Hemisphere, water taps will run dry for anyone residing in high-rise apartment buildings, because electrically powered pumps will cease to function. People living at ground level can count on enough water left in the pipes for another twelve hours, but nothing thereafter. Subways and every form of electrically powered public transportation will cease to operate. With no electricity for fuel pumps, private cars and delivery trucks will be limited by how much gas they happen to still have in their tanks.

All Internet systems will go down, and many computers unfortunate enough to have been operating at the moment the sun storm hit our magnetosphere will have been fried. Every bank and most businesses—certainly the larger corporations—will stop operating, together with the elevators in their office buildings. We will not be able to access Automated Teller Machines (ATMs), which rely on orbiting relay stations. The economic foundations of the United States—already badly cracked by a chronic recession and the collapse of its financial institutions—will totter to a fall.

Aircraft in flight at the time will be especially vulnerable, because they navigate largely by avionics. Many will simply lose all power and crash. Only the lucky ones will be able to force land at the nearest opportunity. Televisions and radios will fall dark and silent; our telecommunications satellites will have been knocked out by the solar storm. Backup generators will be able to keep vital services going only until the fuel to run them expires. According to the NAS report, hospitals strictly limiting themselves to essential care would be able to function for 72 hours, but not therafter. Phamaceuticals would be among the first industries to collapse as perishable medications succumb to production, storage, and distribution shut-downs, thereby dooming many individuals—especially the elderly and diabetics—who depend on drugs to keep them alive. Kappenmann points out, "In the U.S. alone, there are a million people with diabetes,"[9] and all will die without insulin.

Even wider health hazards will arise when the nation's sewer treatment facilities are terminated. After supermarkets have been emptied, food will become increasingly scarce, because the trucks that are used to supply them run out of gas. What food happens to be on hand in our refrigerators will spoil within the first week. Save for those who have adequate, working fireplaces or woodstoves and large stores of kindling to see them through the winter, Americans will not be able to heat their homes, because most natural gas and fuel piplines need electricity to function. Nuclear power stations will not be able to be depended upon, because they are programmed to shut down when the grid is overloaded, and they cannot be restarted until it is operating again.

With all hydrants inoperable, conflagrations everywhere will rage out of control, reducing firemen to little more than monitors. Even more disturbing—especially for urban residents—will be the drastically reduced capabilities of law enforcement agencies. Hampered by a massive communications shut-down and rapidly dwindling fuel reserves, police officers will find their normally onerous duties virtually impossible to fulfill. America's rising crime rate will skyrocket as street criminals take advantage of the situation, just as they did during New Orleans' Hurricane *Katrina*. That natural disaster caused damages of $125 billion.

"If a Carrington Event happened now," concluded Paul Kintner, a plasma scientist at New York's Cornell University in Ithaca, "it would be like a Hurricane *Katrina,* but ten time worse."[10] NAS geophysicists argue that a severe geomagnetic storm could result in $2 trillion worth of damages. Further, given the federal authorities' infamously incompetent response to the 2005 New Orleans hurricane, the scope of chaos to ensue would be beyond our present comprehension. "A contemporary repetition of the Carrington Event would cause . . . extensive social and economic disruptions," the NAS reports warn.[11]

According to the Uniform Crime Reports of the Federal Bureau of Investigation for January 2009, no less that one hundred thousand "known" gang members infest the United States. The real number is estimated to be higher by approximately twenty thousand armed criminals. The reports go on to point out that, given consistent trends since the early 1990s, these figures could double by mid-century.[12] By way of comparison, the mighty German 6th Army that surrendered at the Battle of Stalingrad in 1943 numbered ninety thousand men. America's more than one hundred thousand gang members can be counted upon to avail themselves of the social disruption caused by a major solar event. How a largely unarmed, unprotected populace could cope with such a threat suggests a potential for social implosion in a kind of civil war that, by comparison, would make the American mid-nineteenth-century Civil War a calm affair.

Clearly, replacement transformers would be most urgently needed before conditions reached that stage. "Within a month," Kappenmann says, "the handfull of spare transformers would be used up. The rest will have to be built to order, something that can take up to twelve months."[13] Yet the NAS paper puts recovery time at four to ten *years*. The chaos that would reign during such a period could preclude all attempts at reconstruction. Michael Brooks, a reporter for *New Scientist,* believes "It is questionable whether the U.S. would ever bounce back."[14]

To be sure, recovery would not only be a matter of building and setting up new transformers, but also of trying to do so in the midst of extreme economic and social chaos. Just the demographic nightmare of many millions of people escaping on foot from colder regions of the north for warmer southern climes would radically reconfigure the continental United States, imperiling its political existence. The collision of mass migrations with settled populations already stressed by disintegrating conditions might lead to the kind of violence that topples civilization.

These postulated results for another Carrington event are not alarmist fantasy. "I don't think NAS is scare-mongering," said Mike Hapgood, chair of the European Space Agency's weather team.[15] "Scientists are conservative by nature, and this group is really thoughtful," stated James Green, head of NASA's planetary division. "This is a fair and balanced report."[16] "We're moving closer and closer to the edge of a possible disaster," according to Daniel Baker, the University of Colorado's space weather expert at Boulder and chair of the NAS committee that issued the controversial paper.[17] "It could conceiveably be the worst natural disaster possible," Kappenmann adds.[18] "If it happens anytime soon," observes science writer Robert Roy Britt, "we won't know exactly what to expect until it's over, and by then some modern communication systems could be like beachfront houses after a hurricane."[19]

Earth's only current defense against geomagnetic storms is a fading space probe launched as long ago as 1997. Locked in an orbit between our planet and the sun, the Advanced Composition Explorer (ACE) transmits information regarding the direction and velocity of solar winds and is able to provide a 15- to 45-minute warning of any highly charged particles heading our way. The window of opportunity it offers power companies, however, appears more like a narrowing slit. It may be too much to ask that an alarm sounded by ACE from outer space could filter down to Earth through the electric companies' chain of command in time to disengage the nation's transformers before a plasmic bombardment strikes our magnetosphere. If a sun storm of the magnitude of that in 1859 were to target us today, it would speed past ACE's position and collide with our planet in less than 15 minutes. A coronal mass ejected from the solar photosphere normally requires 3 or 4 days to reach Earth, allowing at least some time to sound a warning. But to cover the 93 million miles from the sun, the Carrington event took just 17 hours and 40 minutes. "It arrived faster than anything we can do," according to Hapgood.[20] Moreover, an in-coming solar flare on the order of the Carrington event would probably saturate and roast all sensors carried by the probe before it had an opportunity to fire off a single signal. Baker notes that the Advanced Composition Explorer "was built to look at average conditions, rather than extremes."[21]

In any case, ACE's on-board detectors, weakening after more than a dozen years of continuous operations, are not expected to last much longer. Nor are there any plans to launch a better replacement. "Not to have a spare," says Baker, "or a strategy to replace it if and when it should fail, is rather foolish."[22] In fact, a back-up robotic solar probe was in place for almost nineteen years. Directors at NASA and the European Space Agency terminated *Ulysses* on June 30, 2009, even though its transmitter "kept operating, sending important science information about an extraordinarily quiet year for the sunspots and solar wind."[23] Considering the effect of a super sun storm on modern civilization, *Scientific American* magazine concludes that "the cost of such an event justifies more systematic solar monitoring and beefier protection for satellites and the power grid."[24] When ACE dies, Hapgood says, "we will largely lose the early warning capability."[25] NASA's Solar and Heliospheric Observatory, along with one or two other satellites keeping tabs on the sun, are inferior early-warning pickets, because they transmit only a fraction of the information ACE provides and take at least twice as long to do so.

Yet how likely is it that another Carrington event will happen? According to *Scientific American,* "ice cores suggest that such a blast of solar particles happens only once every five hundred years."[26] That should give us about another 350 years to make suitable preparations.

Geophysicists point out, however, that ice-core dating reveals no discernable pattern or 500-year cycle for super solar storms, which are, in any case, generated perhaps by the sun's imperfectly understood gravitational mechanisms. Tsurutani believes Earth's next super sun storm "could very well be even more intense than what transpired in 1859. As for when, we simply do not know."[27]

Though a replay of the nineteenth century's geomagnetic hurricane in 2012 is uncertain, far more probable is the occurrence of a squall not as powerful as the Carrington event, but stronger than the solar wind that blacked out Quebec in 1989. These lesser incidents of space weather take place roughly every 50 years, give or take a decade or more. On May 15, 1921, a glob of coronal plasma ten times more potent that its Canadian successor lit up Earth's magnetosphere. As the *New York Times* reported,

> at 7:04 a.m., the entire signal and switching system of the New York Central Railroad below 125th Street was put out of operation, followed by a fire in the control tower at 57th Street and Park Avenue. Telegraph operator Hatch said that he was actually driven away from his telegraph instrument by a flame that enveloped his switchboard and ignited the entire building at a loss of $6,000. Over seas, in Sweden, a telephone station was "burned out," and the storm interfered with telephone, telegraph and cable traffic over most of Europe.[28]

These disruptions were relatively innocuous, because industrialized society was far less dependent on electricity than it has come to be, and Earth's angle relative to the incoming angle of the sun storm favored escape from most of its worst effects. Now that virtually every aspect of civilization runs on electricity, a repetition of 1921's geomagnetic gale colliding with our atmosphere at a more dangerous angle of attack would impact the modern world almost as severely as a Carrington event, if only because of the grid's national and even international connectivity.

Nowhere throughout the one hundred thirty-two pages of the

National Academy of Sciences' report will readers find so much as an allusion to the end of the Mayan calendar. Nor can this mention be found among any of the statements made by so many scientists in their serious discussions of the super sun storms that threaten to overturn human life. These scientists nonetheless concur that the next most favorable opportunity for a potentially disastrous encounter with the solar wind will arise when sunspot activity increases and proliferates in 2012. That scientific projections for a global calamity caused by our sun should coincide with ancient predictions of solar demons ravaging the world in the same year must at least give us pause.

THE COMING
OF THE BLUE STAR

The sacred fifth numeral of Atlantis and the deluge that overwhelmed this Bronze Age civilization are crucial components of the Aztec Calendar Stone, but they are not the only outside influences apparently at work on the monumental almanac. Depicted at the Stone's center, the ferocious expression of the sun god Tonatiuh is the mirror image of the Lion, a facial exercise practiced by the followers of hatha yoga.

Derived from the Sanskrit *yuj* for "union" or "yoking," yoga is an ancient spiritual discipline of physical and mental procedures still used to focus on purification of the physical body as a prerequisite for purifying the mind. Goals range from improving bodily and emotional health to achieving liberation from all worldly suffering, particularly from the cause of all misery: the cycle of birth and death.

The yogic Lion exercise calls for the extension of the tongue to its limits, the tensing of all facial muscles, widening of the eyes, and stretching of the fingers to resemble a lion's claws. This posture is identically displayed by the sun god on the Aztec Calendar Stone, including his talons. The hatha yoga exercise signifies the relief of tension, an ending, or completion, just as 4-Olin marks the end of a tension-filled epoch, our present Fifth Sun. The yogic Lion and Tonatiuh's face are, in fact, physically and symbolically indistinguishable from each other.

Although the oldest surviving references to yoga are found in the Brahmanas (written commentaries on the proper performance of rituals), circa 900 BC, cylinder seals from the first Indus Valley civilization at Harappa depict figures in yoga postures going back nearly 2,000 years earlier. Yoga was and still is the dominant spiritual discipline of Asia, particularly identified with ancient India generally and Buddhism specifically.

The appearance of hatha yoga's Lion face at the center of the Aztec Calendar Stone is not the Eagle Bowl's only curious connection with ancient India, however. According to Kenneth Caroli, the Mayas' 5,150-year cycles "certainly fit the traditional Hindu dates for Krishna and the juncture of Davpara with the Kali Yugas. If one accepts 2012 as the juncture of these two 'great years,' as it seems to be with respect to the Winter Solstice galactic alignment, the current 'great season' began around 10,959 B.C., very close to the sudden onset of the Younger Dryas stadial, the final cold phase of the last Ice Age."[1]

In Hinduism, the Kali Yuga signifies the end of the universe, the last of four *yugas*, just as the Maya knew four suns. Both sets are "world ages" subject to cycles of creation, destruction, and renewal. The Aztec Calendar Stone's 4-Ocelotl, 4-Ehecatl, 4-Quihuitl, and 4-Atl parallel the Hindu Satya Yuga, Treta Yuga, Dwapara Yuga, and Kali Yuga. Beginning in 3112 BC, the start of the Kali Yuga is a mere 2 years later than the start of the Mayas' Fifth Sun in 3114 BC. The Maya believed the demise of the Fifth Sun would be brought about by Macuilli-Tonatiuh, the god of destruction, portrayed on the Aztec Calendar Stone as the enraged face of a man with his tongue extended in the yogic Lion grimace. So, too, the Hindu Kalki Purana describes Kali, the demon of universal annihilation (as distinguished from the goddess Kali) who terminates the Kali Yuga in global upheaval, with a large, lolling tongue. The violent end of both the Mesoamerican Fifth World and the Hindu Kali Yuga are presided over by the same god of destruction. As Caroli observes, "Clearly, the Maya thought in similar terms to the Hindus and early Buddhists at least in so far as their scale went."[2]

Suggesting a variant of the Atlantean sacred numeral, Kali was the tenth avatar, or incarnation, of the beneficent deity Vishnu, just as the Aztec Calendar Stone's Tezcatlipoca was the malevolent twin of Quetzalcoatl. In his guise as Kali, Vishnu declares in the Bhagavad Gita (Book IV, Sutra 5, 7, 8), "Whenever there is a withering of the law and an uprising of lawlessness on all sides, then I manifest myself. For the salvation of the righteous and the destruction of such as do evil, for the firm establishing of the Law, I come to birth, age after age."[3]

Recalculations arrived at by some modern Hindu scholars have shown that the vast spans of time separating the four yugas (1,728,000 years; 1,296,000 years; 864,000 years; and 432,000 years) are not to be taken literally. Instead, these otherwise unmanageable parameters, if understood in symbolic terms, indicate that the present Kali Yuga will be catastrophically brought to a close in 2012.

The Hopi Indians of the American Southwest likewise tell of four "worlds," or ages, all ending in natural disasters instigated by the imbalanced behavior of humankind. They predict a Day of Purification, when "Saquasohuh Kachina dances in the plaza and removes his mask." In other words, modern civilization will be shattered as "the Blue Star appears in the sky." In the Hopi language, *qatsina,* or, literally, "life bringer," refers to anything in the natural world or cosmos, including natural phenomena, whether good or evil. As Hopi Nation elder Dan Evehema stated, "We are in the final stages now, so our prophecy says."[4]

Saquasohuh Kachina cannot be positively identified with any particular "Blue Star," although Sirius, the Dog Star, is sometimes suggested for its blue-white color shift. If so, its relationship to the controversial winter solstice seems unclear. At 8.6 light years from Earth, we should not anticipate the appearance of Sirius in our skies by 2012 or at any other time. The Hopi's Blue Star is more likely a large meteor or asteroid that could approach the orbit of our planet.

In any case, their Saquasohuh Kachina prophesy was supposedly an ancient oral tradition shared with Presbyterian minister David Young by White Feather, a terminally ill elder of the Bear Clan, during the summer of 1958, and published 5 years later by the historical writer Frank Waters in *The Book of the Hopi.* Dr. Allen C. Ross, a Santee Dakota educator and

Lakota language scholar, relates that the same prophesy was uttered during the most important Hopi ceremony, the Wuwuchim, at least as long ago as early 1914. It may, in fact, predate even this early-twentieth-century instance by many years, perhaps generations.[5] In part, it forecasts:

> You will hear of a dwelling-place in the heavens, above the Earth, that shall fall with a great crash. It will appear as a blue star. Very soon after this, the ceremonies of my people will cease. These are the signs that great destruction is coming. The world shall rock to and fro. There will be many columns of smoke and fire such as White Feather has seen the white man make in the deserts not far from here. You will hear of the sea turning black, and many living things dying because of it. Turtle Island could turn over two or three times, and the oceans could join hands and meet the sky.[6]

Unlike the Maya, the Hopi are less definite regarding the arrival of these earth-changing events, although at least some tribal elders have occasionally implied that an undisclosed section of the Wuwuchim ceremony does indeed specify the winter solstice of 2012 for the appearance of the Blue Star. They are more willing to describe the last catastrophe that brought our present world into existence by destroying a former one. This former world, our ancestral homeland, was a large island in the Sunrise Sea, which one day rose up over the people, drowning most of them. Some were saved by the flood hero Kuskurza, who directed them to the back of a giant turtle. It carried them westward across the ocean, eventually coming to rest on the shores of a new land, which the survivors named after their means of rescue: Turtle Island.

Joining Kuskurza and his followers was a pair of antediluvian holy women, the Huruing Wuhti, today venerated as mother goddesses, because they greatly increased the number of survivors. The Hopi version of the deluge states in part, "Down on the bottom of the seas lie all the proud virtue, and the flying *patuwvotas,* and the worldly treasures corrupted with evil, and those people who found no time to sing praises to the Creator from the tops of their hills."[7]

The ancient Scandinavians were no less indefinite than Hopi Indians regarding the exact moment when we might expect the next global cataclysm. Yet the Norse were not unlike Native American or Hindu cosmologists in their belief that the world had been destroyed several times over and would be again. Ragnarok, literally the Ending of the Gods, was also referred to as *aldar rof,* the "destruction of the world," and in Germany as the Goetterdaemmerung, or Twilight of the Gods. In every case, it was not a unique event, but a global catastrophe that has occurred throughout the past again and again and will continue to do so in the future. With each repetition, the world is virtually destroyed, but a handful of survivors—sometimes no more than a single man and woman—escape to renew the cycle of life.

Ragnarok appears in the "Gylfaginning," or "Tricking of Gylfi," the first part of the *Prose Edda,* a collection of Norse myths by the early-thirteenth-century Icelandic historian Snorri Sturluson. He describes the coming of a cosmic wolf, its eyes and nostrils spouting flames, reminiscent of the Aztec Tonatiuh. Fenrir's gaping mouth is so huge that it swallows first the sun, then the moon. Accompanied by a celestial snake, the wolf plunges out of heaven to attack Earth. The sky splits in two, allowing the sons of Muspell—the region of flames—to fall on the world. They set it on fire, led by their chief, Surtr, who wields an immense sword brighter than the sun: "Already the stars were coming adrift from the sky and falling into the gaping void. They were like swallows, weary from too long a voyage, who drop and sink into the waves."[8] The seas rise up, deluging the land. "Mountains will tumble, the Earth will move, men will be scoured by hot water and burned by fire," relates "The Tale of the Mountain Dweller," a thirteenth-century Norse poem. "What will remain after heaven and Earth and the whole world are burned?" Gylfi asks at the beginning of chapter 52. "All the gods will be dead, together with the *Einherjar* [mortal heroes], and the whole of mankind."[9]

Sturluson depicts the popular storm god, Thor, as a protector of Earth, furiously defending it from the cosmic serpent. He kills the monster but is himself slain in combat. Their last hope gone with Thor's death, people everywhere despair as they behold a gigantic dragon flying across the sky with millions of corpses in its mouth. Earth sinks into the sea; obscuring billows of steam rise and flames shoot toward the heavens. The world has been destroyed and virtually all life has been extinguished.

Ragnarok's astronomical character seems obvious, as does its Aztec-like fiery demise. The cosmic wolf, serpent in the sky, and flaming "sons of Muspell" are standard metaphors for destructive comets and meteor falls. Interestingly, both the Norse Ending of the Gods and Aztec Nahui-Ollin are global conflagrations caused by fire gods from above.

According to Norse legend, these calamitous events will be immediately preceded by a Fimbulvetr, literally the Great Winter. Stanzas 40 through 58 of "Voeluspá," a poem in the *Poetic Edda,* reads, "Black become the sun's beams in the summers that follow, weathers all treacherous. A wind age, a wolf age—before the world goes headlong."[10] The first sign of Fimbulvetr will be three continuous winters without spring, summer, or autumn. In the resulting hardships, many wars of especially intense savagery will break out: "[B]rothers will kill brothers, sons their fathers."[11]

Some commentators conclude that the concept of a Fimbulvetr occurred to the Norse because they inhabited areas of northern Europe that were undergoing dramatic climate change from warmer to colder conditions starting around AD 1250. This interpretation is challenged, however, by not only Norse but also Persian allusions to the Great Winter long before the so-called Little Ice Age took place in the West. With roots in eighth-century Iran, the Bundahishn, or Primal Creation, dealing with Zoroastrian cosmology, likewise forecasts 3 years of unrelieved wintery conditions just prior to the end of the world.

Fimbulvetr eerily presages the ice age catastrophe associated with the winter solstice of 2012. Though Norse cosmology did not set a precise future date for this Great Winter, its role in another version of the Ending of the Gods foreshadows climatologists worst fears: "A long time ago, Creation was all ice. Then one day, the ice began to melt, and a mist rose to the sky. Out of the mist came Ymir, a frost-giant, from whom the Earth and the heavens were made after the gods slew him. That is how the world began. And that is how the world will end. Not by fire, but by ice. The seas will freeze, and the winters will never end."[12]

More specifically than Norse prognostication for a frigid Ragnarok, the ancient Chinese Book of Changes, like the Mayan calendar, indicated that the end of time would take place in 2012. The I Ching is a system of symbols (*jīng*) believed to discern order or patterns from the apparent chaos of random occurrences as a means of determining the future. It is based on the constancy of change, the dynamic balance of opposites observed in nature, and the progressive evolution of events—one conditioning its successor—as part of an interrelating process. The I Ching text comprises oracular interpretations for sixty-four abstract line arrangements known as hexagrams. These are made up of six stacked horizontal lines forming sixty-four possible combinations. A hexagram is said to be "cast" when a stick is thrown in its direction.

Although the I Ching was preceded by the visionary experiences of Fú Xī in the early third millennium BC, the sixty-four hexagrams upon which the system is based stem from another legendary emperor, Yǔ, whose reign began in 2194 BC. This date illuminates our investigation, because it indicates that he ascended the throne just one year before the second global cataclysm that occurred in 2193 BC.

The virtually perfect coincidence of these two events suggests that the Chinese of Yǔ's time were recipients of an oracular tradition already developed elsewhere, from whence it was carried by refugee culture bearers expelled from their homeland ravaged by natural catastrophe. The same familiar sequence of events was repeated on the other side of the world, when the natives of Yucatán received their prophetic almanac at the hands of flood survivors from the first worldwide disaster 921 years before.

Despite apparent dissimilarities between China's I Ching and Maya time measurement, both were, in fact, calendars, as ethnobotanists and mathematicians Terrence and Dennis McKenna found when they made a comparison of the I Ching's hexagrams. They learned that the sixty-four, six-line figures virtually matched the number of days in thirteen lunar months. In other words, one day multiplied by 64, multiplied by 6 equals the 384 days in thirteen lunar months. Building upon this discovery, the brothers multiplied the thirteen lunar months by 64 to arrive at 67 years, 104.25 days—the length of six minor sunspot cycles, each comprising 11.2 years. When multiplied by 64, the 67 years (104.25 days) amount to the +4,306 years that make up one pair of zodiacal ages. The +4,306 years multiplied by 6 equal 25,836 years, or a single precession of the equinoxes, one Baktun.

Indeed, this revelation of the Book of Changes as a solar-zodiacal almanac makes it seem far less traditionally Chinese than identifiably Mayan. Moreover, its essential reliance on 6, one of the two Atlantean sacred numerals, connects the I Ching origins with the same sunken civilization from which Mesoamericans received their system for measuring time.

If, as the brothers found, the I Ching was a kind of celestial almanac, they presumed there must be an end date, like all calendars. They set out to find it by composing a table of differences from one hexagram to the next. Over this table was superimposed a historical timescale indicating civilization's high and low points as peaks or troughs on a graph. Extraordinary periods of change in the past, referred to as "novelty," corresponded to differences among the hexagrams—so much so that the timescale lay upon them as a virtual template.

Tracing these parallels with all sixty-four hexagrams, the brothers observed that "novelty" attains its maximum potential for the first and only time when something unprecedented for its effect will occur and the I Ching terminates on December 22, 2012, the day after the controversial winter solstice. Applying this end date backward in time based on thirteen lunar months, they discovered that 1.3 billion years from 2012 brought them back to the beginning of life on Earth.

Does their calculation mean that December 22, 2012, will correspond with the end of life on our planet? It could signify "the dissolution of the cosmos in an actual cessation and unraveling of the natural laws, a literal apocalypse," according to the McKennas.[13] Yet they also theorized an alternate possibility wherein 2012 could represent "the culmination of a human process, a process of tool-making, the dream of a union of spirit and matter"[14]—in other words, the total transformation or replacement of our materialist civilization by something radically different.

Dennis and Terrence McKenna were not influenced by growing popular interest in the Mayan calendar's prophecy for 2012. Their work on the I Ching was completed by the early 1970s, at least 15 years before they learned of the Mayan calendar's prediction, which was not generally well known, even to scholars, until the early 1990s. The publication of their findings in the original 1975 edition of *The Invisible Landscape* neither mentions nor references the Maya.

According to physicist Claude Swanson, the credibility of a prophecy increases when it is at least basically repeated by different sources unrelated to each other. As such, Chinese, Mesoamerican, Hopi, Hindu, Persian, and Norse prognostications share a generally similar conception that suggests the prophecy is at least fundamentally valid. Resemblances particularly between the Mexihcah 4-Ollin and Hindu Kali Yuga are so close in some important details that one appears to have been directly influenced by the other, despite India's location half a world away from Middle America. More probably, both the Olmec or Maya and their distant contemporaries of the subcontinent separately inherited the same, calendrical tradition—as did the Chinese—from a common, outside source. This is the long lost point of origin from which they and so many postdeluge peoples derived their cultural impetus: Atlantis.

THE INCA CALENDAR

Although the Mayan calendar is receiving attention these days because of its upcoming end-date in 2012, far less well known is the Inca calendar. While its Mesoamerican counterpart was far more complex, the two systems nonetheless shared some fundamental similarities, suggesting both may have derived from a shared contributor.

Archaeologists believe little or no direct communication existed between the peoples of pre-Columbian Middle and South America, but either calendar was divided into astrological and historical halves: the Maya version for the prediction of coming developments; the Inca for the commemoration of past event-horizons. Moreover, the Aztec Calendar Stone offers no chronologies for its various "ages."

Immediately after the Spanish Conquest, conquistadors and friars got to work dismembering the Inca Empire, plundering all its gold and purging its traditional belief-system with monotheistic Christianity. Fortunately, at least the historical half of the Peruvian calendar was saved by a native convert to Catholicism, Felipe Guaman Poma de Ayala.

Born in Huamanga, in the central Andes Mountains, his father had been a provincial nobleman serving as emissary of the Inca Guascar to Francisco Pizarro when the conquering Spaniard was headquartering at Cajamarca. After receiving intense ecclesiastical indoctrination from local priests, de Ayala enthusiastically demonstrated his religious fervor by combating any perceived form of "idolatry." To assist him in doing

God's work, he collected everything the natives told him about pre-Christian spirituality, all the better to extirpate it.

Between 1583 and 1613, de Ayala amassed an enormous collection of myths, folklore, and religious ideas in a twelve hundred-page manuscript entitled, *Nueva corónica y buen gobierno,* or "New Chronicle and Good Government." His chief intention was not to preserve the Indians' cultural legacy, but to familiarize himself with it in his campaign against the faith of their fathers. In so doing, however, de Ayala saved a great deal of the Incas' oral tradition, including their calendar, from otherwise certain oblivion.

Remarkably, it reflects not only current Andean archaeology, but coincides with a global catastrophe that may have destroyed the Motherland of civilization and dispersed its survivors throughout the world. The historical calendar comprises five ages, or "Suns," each roughly separated by one thousand years. The first belonged to the Wari Wiracocha Runa. Their name signifies "cross-breed"—referencing the camellid, offspring of a llama with an alpaca—since the Wari Wiracocha Runa were themselves the result of unions between native South Americans and the Viracochas. These were the followers of "Sea Foam," the creator who traveled from his kingdom in the far west across the Pacific Ocean, and made landfall in coastal Peru during the ancient past. Because they were remembered as bearded, red-haired, fair-complected "giants," the Incas similarly referred to all modern Europeans as "Viracochas."

The Wari Wiraocha Runa were primitives who knew only a rudimentary culture. According to de Ayala's native sources, they emerged as a people around 2800 BC. This date matches the onset of an archaeological period known as the Pre-ceramic Phase, when various Andean tribes began to coalesce into the fundamentals of organized society. De Ayala compared the Wari Wiraocha Runa to the pre-Flood people in Genesis, because their era ended in a natural catastrophe reminiscent of the deluge from which Noah escaped with his family.

The Wari Wiraocha Runa were followed by the Wari Runa around 1800 BC, when these more advanced Peruvians, likewise described as

"Viracochas," introduced the benefits of agriculture. Two hundred years later, their era came to a sudden close, when it, too, was terminated by a catastrophic deluge. Here, as well, de Ayala's chronology matches some important event horizons.

1800 BC sparked the so-called Initial Period, a vital transition from Pre-Ceramic primitivism to pottery manufacture and the rise of village life. The global flood cited by the Inca calendar circa 1600 BC coincides with the eruption of Thera, a volcanic explosion that devastated the eastern Mediterranean in 1628 BC. The black cloud above Thera, known today as Santorini, sixty miles north of Crete, filled with sixty thousand miles of ash, rising twenty-three miles into the sky.

It was the accumulation of seven cubic miles of rhyodacite magma ejected from a thirty-cubic-mile hole, its crater nearly fifty square miles in area. Multi-ton boulders were ejected into the stratosphere, and some have been found as far away from Thera as the Black Sea, seven hundred miles from the blast-center. More than seventy miles to the east, over a foot of ash fell on the islands of Kos, Rhodes, and Cyprus. Phaistos, Minoan Crete's second city, as though struck by the shockwave of a hydrogen bomb, had been carbonized in a flash.

This truly cataclysmic event was not limited to the Aegean Sea, but part of a global disaster geophysicists, volcanologists, oceanographers, and scholars in related fields of study suspect may have been triggered by meteoric debris colliding with seismically sensitive areas of our planet. At the international convocation of professional researchers at Fitzwilliam College (cited in chapter 2) they determined that the near miss of a comet in the early seventeenth century BC set off a chain-reaction of seismicity and volcanism expressed in monstrous tsunamis and unprecedented rainfall around the world.

While Thera erupted with the force of two hundred five hundred-megaton atomic bombs, New Zealand's Taupo Valley volcano simultaneously exploded, generating two hundred-foot-high walls of water that traveled several hundred miles per hour as far as the Arctic Circle. Additional tsunamis were sent careening back toward the southwest by the contemporaneous eruption of Akiachak volcano in Alaska. Islands standing in their way were overwhelmed and swept clean of every obstruction. Whole archipelagoes vanished or were utterly depopulated.

The Klamath Indians of south-central Oregon and northern California believe that Kmukamtch, a shining demon from the sky, endeavored to destroy the Earth with his celestial flame, followed by a worldwide deluge. This self-evident reference to the comet associated with the Lemurian catastrophe is underscored by the appearance of the lost Motherland's name in "Kmukamtch."

To another California tribe, the Modoc, Kmukamtch means literally the "ancient old man from Mu," the creator of mankind. According to New Mexico's Ute Indians, "the Sun was shivered into a thousand fragments, which fell to Earth causing a general conflagration." Their name for this heavenly explosion was Ta-wats, who ravaged the world "until at last, swollen with heart, the eyes of the god burst, and the tears gushed forth in a flood which spread over the Earth and extinguished the fire."

It was this 1628 BC catastrophe that may have been responsible for the final destruction of Lemuria, a high culture spread over the same island chains spanning the south-central Pacific Ocean. Also known as Mu, Kahiki, Hiva, Horai, Marae Renga, and many other names, it is memorialized in the oral traditions of numerous peoples throughout the Pacific realm, where the enigmatic ruins of Nan Madol, Kuai, Guam, Easter Island, and many other archaeological zones testify to its former existence.

The Lemurians were consistently portrayed as the possessors of an extraordinarily sophisticated civilization, who passed on its greatness to other peoples after calamitous events of the early seventeenth century BC. Their story seems reflected in the Incas' historical calendar, which cites a contemporaneous flood that closed the age of the Wari Runa.

They were followed by the Purun Runa, or "Wild Men," who applied the deluge-survivors' advanced technology. Mining for precious metals—particularly gold and silver—was undertaken, and jewelry manufacture became an art. But these luxuries engendered greed that soon led to strife and even warfare. The Purun Runa's "Sun" was supposed to have dawned around 800 BC, a critical moment in Andean archaeology, when the Initial Period turned into the Early Horizon.

This phase is most important for the founding of Chavín de Huantar. Located one hundred fifty-five miles north of Lima, the site is the first stone city of its kind in Peru, and came to typify the entire epoch. De Ayala does not tell us how the age of the Purun Runa came to its close, suggesting perhaps that transition to the next epoch was peaceful.

In any case, the Auca Runa who followed in 200 AD instituted a decimal system; built mud-brick fortifications called *pucaras,* and worshipped *guaca bilcas,* translated by de Ayala as "supernaturals." They also invented the *ayllu*s. These were social, religious, and ritual organizations that exerted political power through a combination of kinship and territorial ties. Once again, the Inca calendar accurately reflects crucial archaeological transition, when, during the Early Intermediate Period, the Moche civilizers began building cities along Peru's northern coast around 200 AD.

The Moche, like the Auca Runa, operated the first *ayllus,* erected *pucaras,* employed a decimal system as the basis of their construction projects and astronomical calculations, and, instead of confining their worship to variations of Viracocha, venerated a pantheon of "supernaturals." Although their day ended around 700 AD, the peoples who came after them—the Huari, Chimor, Llacuaz, Chachapoyas, et. al.—all at least fundamentally upheld and carried forward the cultural principles created by the Moche. Once again, de Ayala does not explain how or why the Auca Runa vanished, although the extensive warfare he implies through the construction of *pucaras* did typify those centuries leading up to the rise of the Incas.

The final "Sun" arose in 1200 AD, when the first *Sapa Inca,* or emperor, founded the Kingdom of Cuzco, the imperial capital. This last age did not end with the execution of Atahualpa, the last *Sapa Inca,* in August 1533. The Spanish Conquest only terminated an initial phase of an epoch that includes our own time. It is scheduled to climax in the next one hundred ninety-two years, around the turn of the twenty-third century. If the Incas made any prediction for the conclusion of the fifth

Sun, de Ayala did not include it in his *Nueva corónica y buen gobierno.*

More certainly, the Andean calendar demonstrates that the Incas understood their history with at least a fundamental accuracy that went back some forty centuries before their own time. This record-keeping feat is made all the more remarkable, when we realize that they kept no written documents; the only aids to memory they relied upon were devices such as *quipu,* knotted cords signifying numerical units.

No less impressive, each of their five "Suns" closely corresponds to the major event horizons of Andean archaeology, including an early-seventeenth-century BC global catastrophe that appears to have destroyed the Pacific Ocean Motherland of Civilization. It was, in fact, from a Lemurian kind of island kingdom that Viracocha and his followers were said to have escaped by sailing to Peru from the west.

The Inca calendar is testimony to the power of oral tradition, which is able to preserve the historic legacy of a people with surprisingly high levels of accuracy over the course of millennia. As such, it is proof that enduring myths are neither mere fables nor unreliable legends, but, on the contrary, important truths enshrined in the national memory of a folk that may no longer exist.

DOOM NUMBER

Our times are bracketed by two specific dates—September 11, 2001, and December 21, 2012, respectively—the greatest single act of terrorism committed against the continental United States and the end of the Mayan calendar. If, as some observers suspect, something more than a coincidental relationship exists between these two events, its explanation must lie beyond the powers of ordinary human reason and in the world of numbers.

The relationship between human destiny and numbers was recognized when the sixth-century BC Greek philosopher Pythagoras observed that, "all is number." This dictum means that all existing things can be ultimately reduced to numerical relationships. He regarded numbers as the expression of those relationships and the universal spiritual force connecting every one of them in a network of energy laid over the whole breadth of creation.

In the *Epinomis,* Plato expanded upon the Pythagorean concept of numbers as keys to the synchronous interconnectedness of all phenomena: "All geometric constructions, all systems of numbers, all duly constituted melodic progressions, and the ordered scheme of all celestial revolutions disclose themselves through the revelation of a single bond of natural interconnection."[1]

The sacred character of numerical synchronicity was recognized by ancient Egyptian sages who regarded the universe as a composite whole, in which every part is related to every other part. To them, this universal entity represented a cosmic consciousness expressing its will in a hierarchy of levels. What humans perceived as "matter" was the materialization of that will, just as "mind" was awareness at a higher, and therefore invisible level. The Pythagoreans sought to unlock the mysteries of cosmic consciousness through their study of numerical inter-relationships, because they believed that number is the expression of function.

But only traumatic, widely recognized events—referred to by Terrence McKenna as "novelty"—are potent enough to compel awareness of any relationship between destiny and numbers. The most recent example was the destruction of New York's World Trade Center in 2001. It took place on the eleventh day of the ninth month, or, as is commonly expressed: 9/11, the same digits used as a general emergency telephone number. Whether or not the attackers deliberately chose these numbers is unimportant; no one escaped the parallel between the date of the event, its disastrous character, and the emergency number.

Additionally, the numeral 1 features prominently in the Twin Towers disaster. For example, $9/11 = 9 + 1 + 1 = 11$. September 11th is the 254th day of the year: $2 + 5 + 4 = 11$. After September 11, 111 days were left to the end of the year.

The Twin Towers, standing side by side, resembled the number Eleven. The combined windows in the Twin Towers numbered 21,800, or $2+1+8=11$. The first jetliner to collide with them was Flight 11. On board Flight 11 were 92 passengers: $9 + 2 = 11$. The other suicide aircraft, Flight 77, carried 65 passengers: $6 + 5 = 11$.

When President George W. Bush visited the ruins of the World Trade Center, he was photographed beside a fireman wearing a helmet emblazoned with the number, 164: $1 + 6 + 4 = 11$.

At 1:11 on the morning of September 11, 2001, Geminorum-13, one of forty-eight stars in the constellation of Gemini, appeared inside the crescent moon. Gemini signifies the twins while the crescent moon is the emblem of Islam. And Mohammed's birthday is celebrated on the eleventh day of the ninth month.

Thirty years before the suicide attacks on the towers, numerologist

Maria Valla wrote that persons associated with the number Eleven "can destroy anything that it touches, including self. You will conquer others, but in so doing, destroy yourself."[2] Among folk traditions around the world, the number Eleven is traditionally associated with political instability and violence, lack of self-restraint, destructive transition, danger, and revolution.

These traits are generated by the removal of the number One from the cosmic order, as personified in the number Twelve (the twelve houses of the zodiac, Christ's twelve apostles, the twelve hours of the day, the twelve months of the year, the human body's twelve pairs of ribs and thoracic vertebrae), and the imbalance created when 1 is added to the patriarchal number Ten, which signifies political power or civilization (i.e., Plato's ten kings of Atlantis; the ten patriarchs of the Hindu god Manu; the original ten patriarchs in the biblical Genesis; the Babylonians' ten world rulers before the Flood, etc.).

In the Pythagorean system, Eleven signified chaos because it was a cardinal number separating humanity or civilization—associated with Ten—from the cosmic order embodied in the number Twelve.

The troubling nature of Eleven was introduced in the west after the Greek geometrician Pythagoras studied the mystical significance of numbers at the ancient Egyptian mystery school of Heliopolis, meaning "City of the Sun." Could the early astronomers there have known about the sun's eleven-year sunspot cycle, the basis for the number Eleven's association with chaos?

Sunspots are cooler regions on the surface of the sun, which seriously disrupt electronic communications and interfere with normal human thought processes. They discharge abnormally large concentrations of electronically charged particles. These *photons* interface with radio, telephone and television transmitters and receivers, as well as the neural network of our brains, overloading artificial and organic systems with power surges beyond the design limits they were engineered to withstand.

During the early fourteenth century, the inexplicable disappearance of sunspots was coincidental with a relatively brief, worldwide drought climatologists refer to as the Little Ice Age. They suspect that the eleven-year sunspot cycle was linked to the advance and retreat of glaciation over the last half-million years.

Our Sun also changes its magnetic polarity every eleven years, inter-facing with Earth's own magnetic field to cause worldwide breakdowns in all forms of electronic communication. But disruption is not confined to radio and television. From the mid-twentieth century, parapsycholo-gists have traced a correlation between the solar flips and upsurges of emotional disturbances in human behavior.

A study published in the December, 1979 issue of *Psychology Today* reported that residents of U.S. day-care centers, nursing homes, and psy-chiatric wards all experienced an abnormally high frequency of anxiety attacks and erratic behavior during the apogee of the Sun's eleven-year polar reversal. This May 1979 event also precisely defined an unusual upswing in violence and its precipitous decline experienced by prison populations across the United States and Mexico, according to the same *Psychology Today* article.[3]

Other mammals, even fish, appear to be effected. Writing for *Natural History* magazine, Dr. Dennis Duda described a five-year study of whale vocalization undertaken by Cetacean behaviorologists at the University of Oregon beginning in 1976. To their astonishment, they discovered that the leviathans sang original songs during a solar magnetic reversal, but the unique sounds had not been made before nor were heard since.[4]

As recently as 2006, marine biologists from Chicago's Shedd Aquarium observed the disruption of lake trout spawning patterns cor-related with the Sun's polar flip. Researchers speculate that the bioelec-tric field of many creatures is directly influenced by the sun's eleven-year cycle.[5] If so, modern science and ancient mysticism begin to compliment each other—and applies no less well—to the close of the Mayan calendar on December 21, 2012.

As mentioned in chapter 2, the ecliptic of our star will intersect with the galactic ecliptic on the morning of that year's Winter Solstice. The Sun at that moment will be one degree above the horizon at the equa-tor (73 degrees west). Why did the Maya regard this cosmically unique event as the end of their calendar? The number Eleven may provide an answer.

The Mayan calendar terminates precisely on the morning of 2012's winter solstice at 11:11 U.T.C. (Coordinated Universal Time). Millennia before the Christmas holiday, which usurped it, the winter solstice was mankind's greatest festival, the annual conquest of darkness, the original New Year's Day. Thus, it may signify the close of our chaotic, dark times with the onset of human enlightenment.

The Maya were more explicit, however, if not entirely clear in explaining the termination of their calendar. It had begun with one catastrophe—the *Hun yecil,* the Great Flood—and would close with another they said would be known as "The Rebellion of the Earth."[6]

In both the magnitude and speed of deterioration, climate change continues to take natural scientists by surprise. Dr. George McKendry, director of the Massachusetts Institute for Earth Studies, stated in the year 2002, that just ten years remain for the implementation of major, international improvements to head off "an irrevocable alteration in the life-support systems of our planet."[7]

If decisive, preventive measures were not in place after that period, he stated, not even the most radical solutions would be able to deter exponentially developing global instability. Increasing frequency and destructiveness of super-storms—particularly hurricanes and tornados—together with unusually dry conditions for major outbreaks of brush- and forest-fires, would more and more typify our world in the twenty-first century.

Whether or not Dr. McKendry was aware that his deadline corresponded to the end of the Mayan calendar, it is a dire prognostication underscored by the reappearance of the number eleven in our uncertain times.

HOW COULD THEY
HAVE POSSIBLY KNOWN?

If the Maya were truly aware of some future catastrophe—a new ice age, perhaps—how could they have possibly learned of it? They possessed none of the deep-space telescopes, interplanetary satellites, or super computers that have enabled modern astronomers to make some of the discoveries with which the Maya and their predecessors were already familiar thousands of years ago.

Without these sophisticated technologies—relying entirely on their powers of observation with the naked eye over many generations—what abilities allowed them to see, from the perspective of at least 200 BC, that the southern end of our galaxy's dark rift at midpoint in the Milky Way will form a perfect alignment with the winter solstice sun on the morning of December 21, 2012?

The Maya and their Olmec or Atlantean predecessors did not make such an incredible observation simply because they were wise. This calendrical achievement especially cannot be explained away by the mere fact of their obvious genius. Something as difficult to ascertain in deep prehistory as 2012's geo-solar-galactic alignment could have been determined only through simple observation with the assistance of modern-like technology, or through psychic abilities. Each alternative seems more unacceptable than the next.

Fig. 11.1. Mexico City's National Museum of Anthropology illustration of an Atlantean Bacab supporting the sky atop Chichén Itzá's Pyramid of the Feathered Serpent, as the Mayan calendar cycles overhead toward its close in 2012.

To predict such an alignment so far into the future with pinpoint accuracy unaided by outside support of any kind seems impossible. It is understandable that the Maya could forecast, even by millions of years, the correct positions of Venus and other planets, stars, or constellations based on the regular cycles of these luminaries across the night sky. The 2012 event, however, is not cyclical in the same sense, because such a galactic eclipse occurs every 26,000 years. Simple observations of precession would have required the passage of at least three such periods and uninterrupted preservation of their notation over the course of 78,000 years.

No society in human history has endured for more than a fraction of that time. The world's oldest, continuous civilization, the Chinese, has been punctuated over the course of its final 4,000 years by anarchy, invasion, tyranny, natural catastrophes, book burnings, and other cultural revolutions that have all too often consigned its science and literature to oblivion. Human nature has repeatedly proved itself incapable of governing a society strong enough or resilient enough to endure 78 or more millennia of unbroken stability.

If the Maya did not make their calculations for 2012 by naked-eye observation alone, could they have possessed supertechnologies that allowed them to see into the heavens, as we do now? Did they operate some third-century BC forerunner of the Hubble space telescope? If Maya astronomers had such an instrument at their disposal, no scrap of it has been found to date, nor has anything of the kind been so much as alluded to in their lengthy hieroglyphic texts or portrayed in temple art.

Notwithstanding a lack of evidence, ancient-astronaut theorists believe extraterrestrial benefactors descended from outer space to tell the Maya about the heavens and 2012. As material proof, they cite Palenque, where the Maya ceremonial center's Temple of Inscriptions contains a stone sarcophagus lid, the underside of which is adorned with a splendid bas-relief carving purportedly showing a seventh-century ruler—K'inich Janaab' Pakal, also known as Pacal II, the Great—at the controls of a spaceship. In *Chariots of the Gods,* the famous Swiss author Erich von Däniken describes the scene: "In the center of that frame is a man sitting, bending forward. He has a mask on his nose, he uses his two hands to manipulate some controls, and the heel of his left foot is on a kind of pedal with different adjustments. The rear portion is separated from him; he is sitting on a complicated chair, and outside of this whole frame, you see a little flame like an exhaust."[1] Von Däniken's interpretation seems complemented by glyphs around the edges of the lid, which represent the sun, moon, Venus, and various constellations. On closer inspection, however, Pacal is clearly depicted descending into the jaws of Xibalba, the underworld—appropriately enough, because his body was entombed in this very sarcophagus. Moreover, the representation of a deity guarding the underworld appears to await the dead ruler's imminent arrival.

Equally as far-fetched as arguments on behalf of ancient astronauts sharing their celestial wisdom with Yucatán natives are prospects for psychic power that the Maya perhaps employed to ascertain the significance of the winter solstice of 2012. Unacceptable as such a consideration might be to some serious investigators, it is, after all, the only conceivable method the Maya could have used to forecast accurately the rare astronomical events transpiring on the morning of a single day more than 2,000 years beyond their time.

The specific modus operandi they probably chose to make such a long-distance observation was their equivalent of a practice known in the Western world since the late twentieth century: remote viewing. Introduced by Stanford Research Institute laser physicist Harold Puthoff and parapsychologist Russel Targ in 1974, it refers to the acquisition of information about distant or unseen targets through extrasensory perception. Remote viewing is by no means the fantasy of New Age dabblers in the occult. As early as World War II, the U.S. government began funding paranormal researchers in the hope of turning them into psychic spies. These early programs lapsed after the cessation of hostilities, but resumed with special interest after intelligence officers learned that similar programs were under way in the USSR and Red China.

In 1972, Puthoff was approached by representatives of the Central Intelligence Agency's (C.I.A.'s) directorate of science and technology, who put him in charge of a $50,000 project called Stargate, following his successful remote viewing experiments. The results of his and Targ's investigations were published in *Nature,* and in the proceedings of a symposium on consciousness sponsored by the American Association for the Advancement of Science. John McMahon, who headed the C.I.A.'s Office of Technical Service and later became the agency's deputy director, enthusiastically supported their work. With the Watergate scandal, however, the C.I.A. was under pressure to disassociate itself quickly from anything unconventional, and in the late 1970s, it turned over Project Stargate to the Air Force under the Foreign Technology division.

Meanwhile, the U.S. Army's Intelligence and Security Command took up its own remote viewing research under the command of General Edward Thompson as chief intelligence officer. He learned that contemporary investigations into the military application of paranormal abilities were receiving better funding and government support in the USSR and the People's Republic of China. At his urging, Project Stargate eventually moved from research into field operations with some notable successes. These included the remote viewing of a monster crane operating at a Soviet nuclear research facility; locating the crash in Africa of a Red Air Force bomber referred to by President Jimmy Carter in several speeches; and the discovery made by three psychics of a secret, new class of Russian submarine. Thereafter, a special training program of military officers resulted in the formation of a military remote viewing unit based at Fort Meade in Maryland.

By the early 1990s, the utility of remote viewing was firmly established when U.S. Army colonel William Johnson spent several months running another remote viewing unit against military targets. Results were so positive that he insisted on the phenomenon's usefulness as an intelligence tool. With Republican control of House spending in late 1994, however, remote viewing was regarded as somehow irreligious, and the C.I.A. terminated the project in 1995. That same year, an article in *Time* magazine reported that three full-time psychics were still working on a $500,000-a-year budget at Fort Meade, but they were due for termination.

Contrary to results over the previous 25 years, C.I.A. spokesmen stated that remote viewing did not exist or could not be proved. Off the record, other government representatives confided that the phenom-enon was authentic enough, but its viewers were unreliable, their perfor-mance varying in effectiveness from day to day or lacking effectiveness altogether. Soldiers required a reliable weapon, they explained, one they could depend on in any eventuality.

Some veterans of Project Stargate, however, are not convinced by the C.I.A.'s public pronouncements. They believe that advanced research into remote viewing continues in secret, together with its military appli-cation and use in espionage. Having learned everything they needed to know from civilians such as Harold Puthoff or Russel Targ, the govern-ment operatives summarily dispensed with them and now pursue their own classified remote viewing agendas.

This very brief overview of the use of extrasensory perception in the U.S. military illustrates that it is a real phenomenon that is only just being understood and put to use in modern times by world governments. The same practices appear to have been far better known to the Maya, whose entire culture was not only open to psychic abilities, but also took them for granted as part of the human condition and embraced them. They and other ancient peoples around the world often spoke about the flight of the shaman, a tribal seer who extended his consciousness far beyond his own time and space to bring back vital information to his people from remote distances, the past, or the future. Majority skeptical opinion refuses to acknowledge the possibility of these paranormal abili-ties, because their existence would undermine fundamental ideas about causality, time, the function of the human mind, and other principles currently held by the scientific community.

Despite such fears, the Maya were serious in the application of their psychic abilities, which they nurtured over the course of many centuries, as is abundantly established by their surviving temple art. These pow-ers may have enabled them to project their consciousness far into the future, where they beheld the event of December 21, 2012, and returned to include it in the termination of their calendar.

PART TWO

The Seer

PLATO OR CAYCE?

If Jesus was asked what he thought of the Maya prophesy for 2012, he might answer, as he is quoted as having said in the Christian Scriptures (Matthew 24:35–36), "Heaven and Earth will pass away, but my words shall not pass away. But of that day and hour, not even the angels of heaven, nor the Son, but the Father alone."

Undeterred by the apparent finality of this pronouncement, Pope Leo X assured his fellow Christians: "I will not see the end of the world, nor will you, my brethren. For its time is long in the future, five hundred years hence."[1]

According to the pontiff, 5 centuries after he made his promise in 1514, the world would end—a mere 2 years after 2012—that is, if he meant exactly 500 years from the date on which he uttered his prediction. It would seem Leo X did not intend such precision, but nevertheless, he gave his flock to understand that the world would come to a close sometime around 2014, near enough to 2012. In any case, his prophetic statement very closely parallels the Mayas' more specific 4-Ahau 3-Kankin. Unlike them, however, the pope did not appear to base his prediction on any calendrical computations. As the highest priest in the Roman Catholic church, he appears to have spoken out of a kind of religious ecstasy.

Another spiritual figure who allegedly foresaw distant happenings—both backward and forward in time—was Edgar Cayce, the twentieth-century's Sleeping Prophet. While no one before Cayce's death in 1945 knew enough to ask him what he envisioned for the winter solstice of 2012, he came closest to commenting on such an event when he said that similar "awareness during the era or the Age of Atlantis and Lemuria or Mu brought, what? Destruction to man, and his beginning of the needs of the journey up through that of selfishness."[2]

Fig. 12.1. Edgar Cayce, the twentieth-century's Sleeping Prophet, stated that the consequences set in motion by the destruction of Atlantis are reverberating across the millennia into our time.

His trance-state utterance coincides with the moral underpinning for catastrophe stressed by Plato, the Mexihcah, Hindu tradition, Hopi elders, and other sources linking the violation of natural law to the horror of physical consequences forecast by the Mayan calendar.

The mystical meaning of the Atlantean sacred numeral was additionally recognized by Cayce. He stated that 5 "represents man in his physical form, and the attributes to which he may become conscious from the elemental or spiritual to the physical consciousness, as the senses, as the sensing of the various forces that bring to man the activities in the sphere in which he finds himself."[3] His definition of the mystical number certainly reflects its significance from Plato's sunken kingdom to Mesoamerica.

During the Roaring Twenties, the reincarnated memories of lost Atlantis began to surface for the first time in Cayce's "life readings." He would eventually leave behind 14,256 such stenographic records documenting his clairvoyant comments for some eight thousand different clients over a 43-year period. Most of his readings produced during deep trances were concerned with diagnosing spiritual and physical health problems, with no references to vanished civilizations. In fact, his uncanny accuracy in personal analysis impressed not only thousands of sufferers who benefited from his curative insights, but also the medical establishment. As early as 1910, Cayce's psychic procedures were substantiated in a report to Boston's Clinical Research Society by Dr. Wesley Ketchum.

The success of the Sleeping Prophet's work was complimented by Cayce's natural piety and disinterest in material wealth. He never made a fortune from his gifts that so greatly helped others. Indeed, his achievement is an ongoing process of verification, as people from around the world continue to study his collected remarks at the Association for Research and Enlightenment, in Virginia Beach, Virginia.

Until he was 47, Cayce's life readings of the people who approached him for assistance never sparked any memories of past lives among the Atlanteans. During 1922, however, he suddenly began recalling life in a place with which he was totally unfamiliar. Hugh Lynn Cayce knew his father "did not read material on Atlantis, and that he, so far as we know, had absolutely no knowledge of the subject."[4] The evocative, often verifiable detail of his readings where Atlantis was described is all the more astounding when we realize he knew nothing about the vanished culture during his waking hours. As his son wrote, "They are the most fantastic, the most bizarre, the most impossible information in the Edgar Cayce files. If his unconscious fabricated this material or wove it together from existing legends and writings, we believe that it is the most amazing example of a telepathic-clairvoyant scanning of existing legends and stories in print or of the minds of persons dealing with the Atlantis theory."[5]

Polychrome restoration of the Mexihcah Cuauhtlixicalli, House of the Eagle, Eagle Bowl, or Vessel of Time—better, if improperly, known as the Aztec Calendar Stone.

A stone disk engraved with apparent numerical notation may be the earliest known example of the Mesoamerican calendar predicting the end of time on December 21, 2012. The object was discovered outside the important Olmec city of Izapa, where a Mayan inscription referring to that terminal date has been found recently nearby.

Replica of the original, 8-foot
sun stone at the Coricancha,
or Enclosure of Gold, at the
Inca capital of Cuzco. Before its
destruction by the Conquistadors,
the disk was Peru's equivalent of
the Aztec Calendar Stone.

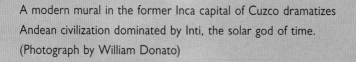

A modern mural in the former Inca capital of Cuzco dramatizes
Andean civilization dominated by Inti, the solar god of time.
(Photograph by William Donato)

The Bahamas' Bimini Road, 55 miles east of Miami, Florida, is an Atlantean ruin, according to American psychic Edgar Cayce, who predicted its discovery 24 years before the structure was found. (Photograph by William Donato)

The culture of Lemuria was spread across island chains spanning the south-central Pacific Ocean until its people were overwhelmed by a natural catastrophe prior to the final destruction of Atlantis.

Southern Wisconsin's thirteenth-century Pyramid of the Sun at the prehistoric ceremonial center of Aztalan, the Aztecs' ancestral city, from whence they migrated into the Valley of Mexico. Appropriately, the Wisconsin pyramid was oriented by its builders to sunrise of the winter solstice.

The step pyramid at Chichén Itzá, Yucatán's ceremonial center, was dedicated to Kukulcan, the Mayas' Feathered Serpent, a flood hero who escaped the destruction of his homeland across the sea.

Visitors to Mexico's Villahermosa Archaeological Park encounter an Olmec Sky Watcher statue originally dedicated to astronomer-priests in charge of the sacred calendar. (Photograph by Claudete Nicholls)

Visitors at Chichén Itzá's Great Ball Court, below the Temple of the Bearded Man, where the non-Indian profile of Kukulcan, the Mayas' Feathered Serpent, appears inside as a bas relief. (Photograph by Laura Beaudoin)

This jade mask depicts— as a basis for the Mesoamerican calendar—an Olmec priest in an altered state of consciousness, during which conventional understanding of time dissolves, enabling the human mind to glimpse several possible futures.

Model of an ancient Peruvian astronomer-priest of the kind who preserved a history of four global catastrophes associated with the rise of the Incas. (Photograph by William Donato)

Pachacamac, on the Pacific coast, 25 miles southeast of the Peruvian capital at Lima, was pre-Columbian South America's leading oracle. Here, astronomer-priests preserved the secrets of their prophetic calendar. (Photograph by William Donato)

A low stone circle near the shores of Bolivia's Lake Titicaca was erected long before the rise of the Incas by astronomer-priests. From it, they made celestial calculations that went into the Andean calendar. The tower in the background is a chullpa, a mausoleum for the privileged dead. (Photograph by William Donato)

Edgar Cayce's ignorance of the sunken civilization is not surprising. His formal education was meager, and his points of reference were more conventionally religious than historical or academic. His grasp of the past was biblical, not scholastic. It seems clear, then, that the subject was outside the purview of both his personal background and essentially Christian view of the world. Yet his pronouncements are self-evidently credible, because they often contain information that made little or no sense at the time they were uttered, but have since been verified by science. The objective reader cannot avoid the unmistakable impression that Cayce actually "saw" with his own inner eye a real place long since vanished.

Some important archaeological finds confirming Cayce's statements have come to light since he made them more than 60 years ago. In light of these fresh revelations, his life readings assume newer and greater significance; they are made current as our own civilization enters a new epoch of hitherto undreamed of exploration in both inner and outer space. The profusion of historic and geologic details and cultural correspondences—some of them unknown at the time he spoke of them—comprising the Edgar Cayce life readings confirm that he did indeed "see" Atlantis.

His clairvoyant utterances will be, therefore, all the more poignant and pertinent to a humankind in search of its origins. To realize where we came from is to know how we arrived at our present situation—and to understand where we may be headed.

Until the last decades of the twentieth century, most rational people would have deplored any attempt to combine serious research with the comments of a psychic. But times and perspectives have changed. Today, psychics are often called upon by law enforcement agencies around the world, often unearthing valid clues and even solving crimes when other, conventional methods failed.

Closer to the subject of this investigation, California's Mobius Society is a group of remote viewers who work hand-in-glove with professional archaeologists to find traces of lost civilizations. Their track record is remarkable, with perhaps their most spectacular discovery being the underwater Ptolemaic harbor of Alexandria, lost since an earthquake caused it to collapse into the Mediterranean Sea nearly 2,000 years ago. It seems fitting, then, that with America's greatest psychic as our guide, we should seek the first and grandest of such lost worlds. Edgar Cayce often spoke of these lost worlds during his deep sleeps. In fact, of the sixteen hundred people for whom he conducted life readings, about seven hundred clients described conditions in the vanished homeland of civilization. And comparing his recorded statements with what has been learned recently about Atlantis from archaeology and geology, we may obtain an unusually clear, detailed, even credible glimpse of an otherwise dimly remembered age.

Throughout his adult life, Cayce's predictions were as numerous as they were accurate. He even correctly foresaw the date of his burial on January 5, 1945. More relevant to our discussion here, however is the fact that his credentials as a genuine seer into the ancient past are revealed in two particularly outstanding readings, one of them concerning the Essenes. These were members of a small Jewish sect that began in the second century BC. They lived a severe monastic existence that focused on divine retribution for sin, while they proclaimed an impending last judgment that God would call down on an unrepentant humanity. When the Essenes' oft-repeated end of the world failed to materialize after nearly three centuries, their cult vanished.

Cayce mentioned the Essenes during 1936, when he envisioned a woman client's incarnation near Jerusalem: "The entity was what would now, in some organizations, [be] determined a sister superior or an officer of the Essenes. For the entity was associated with the school on the road above Emmaus near the road that goes down toward Jericho and towards the northernmost coast of Jerusalem."[6] At the time of this life reading, scholarly opinion held that all Essene groups were exclusively male. Fifteen years later, however, the remains of Kirbet Qumran, the site of an Essene community that Cayce precisely described, were excavated just where he said they would be found. Graves in the area yielded skeletons of women as well as men, thus proving that the religious community was not exclusively male after all. Perhaps one of the skeletons unearthed by the archaeologist's spade was once inhabited by the same woman whose past life Cayce described.

His belief in the doctrine of reincarnation is evident in this instance. A lifetime of similar readings assured him of the human soul's immortality, its survival after physical death, and its inevitable rebirth in a new body. Rather than seeing reincarnation as a pointless recycling of the spirit, Cayce regarded it as part of the great moral order of the cosmos in which each material manifestation of life on Earth was conditioned by a previous life—sometimes to gain knowledge through experience, to resolve ongoing problems, or simply to serve. In any case, it reaffirmed each individual's sense of purpose and destiny. The reincarnation theme appears again in this remarkable life reading: "For the entity was among those spoken of as a 'holy woman', first the entity coming in contact with those activities at the death and raising of Lazarus and later with Mary, Elizabeth, Mary Magdalene, Martha; all of these were a part of the experience of the entity as Salome."[7]

The only Salome mentioned in the Christian Scriptures describes her as a witness to the Crucifixion, but not present at the raising of Lazarus. In 1960, however, the Associated Press released information confirming the identity of Cayce's "entity" during a past life. Published in Long Island's *Newsday* for December 30, the Associated Press dispatch reported that Dr. Morton Smith, an associate professor of history at Columbia University, discovered the copy of a letter written by St. Mark. Scholars at the Society of Biblical Literature and Exegesis established its authenticity and ascertained that the document belonged originally to Clement of Alexandria, one of the Christian church's most important founding fathers in the third century. The copy attributes the story of Lazarus to St. Mark, an account previously found only in the Gospel according to St. John. St. Mark's version is virtually the same as that of John, save for a minor detail coinciding with Cayce's life reading: Clement of Alexandria's copy states that a woman witness to the miraculous rising of Lazarus was called Salome.

These two verified examples underscore Cayce's glimpse of the world 2,000 years ago, but his vision extended many centuries earlier, to a place far more remote in time. The earliest known person to describe it is also one of European civilization's leading intellectual figures. Together with Socrates and Aristotle, Plato is still generally regarded by classical scholars as among the most influential thinkers in the early history of the Western world. Declared the prominent twentieth-century metaphysician Alfred North Whitehead: "The safest general characterization of the European philosophical tradition is that it consists of a series of footnotes to Plato."[8] It is impossible to imagine a more credible source for Atlantis as fact.

Many historians believe Plato traveled to Egypt himself, perhaps to verify personally the account inscribed on a memorial column at the temple of the goddess Neith in the city of Sais, located near the southernmost end of the Nile Delta. The existence of this temple record was documented by two other influential thinkers. The last major Greek philosopher, Proclus, wrote 800 years after Plato, but in his *In Platonis theologiam* (Platonic Theology) he cited the credibility of Atlantis by pointing out that Egyptian columns inscribed with the story were visited and identically translated more than half a century after Plato's death in 347 BC.[9]

They were examined by yet another influential thinker, Krantor of Soluntum, who went to Sais as part of his research for Plato's first biography. Proclus writes that Krantor found the Atlantis story preserved exactly as described in the Dialogues. The enormous temple of Neith was demolished down to its foundations on the orders of Christian authorities determined to purge every manifestation of paganism from Egypt. In the fifth book of *Historia Ecclesiastica,* written less than 50 years after the destruction in AD 391, church historian Socrates Scholasticus told how, "At the solicitation of Theophilus, Bishop of Alexandria, the Emperor issued an order at this time for the demolition of the heathen temples in that city; commanding also that it should be put in execution under the direction of Theophilus."[10]

First on the agenda was pulling down the Great Library of Alexandria and the incineration of its million or so texts on medicine, botany, philosophy, astronomy, geometry, architecture, irrigation, agriculture, and virtually every aspect of classical civilization. "Thus this disturbance having been terminated," Scholasticus continued, "the governor of Alexandria and the commander-in-chief of the troops in Egypt assisted

Theophilus in demolishing the heathen temples."[11] Among them was the temple of Neith and all its original documents, including the history of Atlantis inscribed on its memorial pillar. With the wholesale obliteration of ancient source materials, it should hardly come as a surprise that Plato's two Dialogues represent the only record of Atlantis still available to us. The wonder is that even the *Timaeus* and *Kritias* survived into modern times. Yet they may represent no other report from pagan Europe so firmly supported by men of such stellar credentials as Solon, Plato, Proclus, and Krantor.

Aristotle's only known comment about Atlantis—"he that created it also destroyed it"—is regarded by some skeptics to mean that Aristotle believed Atlantis was merely a fable concocted by Plato, who also invented its cataclysmic conclusion.[12] Aristotle's "he," however, might have just as likely referred to Poseidon, the sea god in Plato's account who laid the foundations of Atlantis and was responsible for later sinking it to the bottom of the ocean at the command of Zeus.

If Aristotle did regard Atlantis as fantasy, he was virtually alone among his scholarly contemporaries, who affirmed the veracity of Plato's report. The geographer Statius Sebosus was cited by the Roman scientist Pliny the Elder for his detailed description of Atlantis. Predating both Aristotle and Plato, Dionysus of Mitylene wrote *A Voyage to Atlantis,* circa 550 BC. Born around 50 BC, Diodorus Siculus was a Greek geographer who described the Atlantean War. The first-century Alexandrine theologian Philo Judaeus taught that Plato based his allegorical story of Atlantis on historical reality.

Ammianus Marcellinus, a fourth-century Roman historian, classified the destruction of Atlantis as a *chasmatiae,* a natural disaster in which seismic violence broke open great fissures in Earth to swallow large tracts of territory during a single event. The famous Roman biologist Aelian reported in his third-century *The Nature of Animals* that "the inhabitants of the shores of the Ocean tell that in former times the kings of Atlantis, descendants of Poseidon, wore on their heads, as a mark of power, the fillet of the male sea-ram [perhaps frigate birds, whose habit of diving into the ocean may have inspired such a name], and that their wives, the queens, wore, as a sign of their power, fillets of the female sea-rams."[13]

Contrary to a general consensus of ancient Old World scholars affirming the veracity of Plato's account, modern skeptics, particularly archaeologists, are convinced Atlantis was only a legend. They fail to consider that, beyond his position as the seminal philosopher of Western civilization, Plato based his entire body of thought on uncompromising pursuit of the truth. The *Timaeus* and *Kritias* cannot comprise a fictional allegory for his notion of the ideal state, as some critics insist, because the Atlantis he portrayed was far removed from his utopian conception as presented in the *Republic*. It seems likely, however, that had Plato completed the Dialogue, he would have used the rise and fall of Atlantis as a historical example illustrating the fatal consequences of civil degeneracy. In the *Kritias,* he did not inexplicably change from philosopher to historian. Instead, it appears more probable that he intended citation of corrupt Atlantis to provide a factual basis for the Dialogues.

Unlike Plato, who relied chiefly on a Greek translation of Egyptian temple records, Edgar Cayce's source of information was a kind of spiritual record he reviewed while experiencing an altered state of consciousness. Yet his descriptions of the doomed civilization seem to some researchers a mix of the credible and the fantastic. For example, his portrayal of the migration of Atlanteans to the Nile Valley following the destruction of their empire is entirely convincing. Many otherwise obscure names of people and places that he associates with the Atlantis experience likewise seem to reflect real events.

For someone of no formal education, Cayce's grasp of archaeology and geology was extraordinary, even prophetic. When he said in the 1930s that the Nile River flowed across the Sahara Desert to the ocean in early Atlantean times, no scientist in the world would even have considered such an apparently outlandish possibility. Yet in 1994, nearly half a century after his death, a satellite survey of North Africa discovered traces of a former tributary of the Nile that, in prehistory, connected Egypt to the Atlantic Ocean at Morocco.

Perhaps most impressive of all, obscure, even fleeting references he made to Atlantis during the early 1920s were sometimes repeated only once, but within an exact same frame of reference, even after more than two decades. Cayce mentioned almost as an afterthought that old Jewish documents, unknown to the outside world during his lifetime, but disclosed around the turn of the next century, would provide evidence for the former existence of Atlantis. In 2000, a Dutch science writer, Auguste Helaine, described an obscure Hebrew treatise on computational astronomy dated to AD 1378–1379. It appears to be based on or even to paraphrase an earlier, lost Islamic work about Atlantis, opening with a reference to the known inhabited regions of Earth and the Atlantic Ocean: "Some say that they start at the beginning of the western ocean and beyond. For in the earliest times, there was an island in the middle of the ocean. Scholars were there, who isolated themselves in philosophy. In their day, that was the longitude of the inhabited world. Today, it has become sea, and it is ten degrees [about 300 miles] into the sea [i.e., west from Gibraltar]."[14]

Persuasive elements of Cayce's life readings such as these even give skeptics pause. Further, they encourage many investigators, regardless of their spiritual beliefs, to reconsider everything Cayce had to say about Atlantis. Yet some are troubled by his unmanageable chronologies, which make the lost capital to have been tens of thousands of years old, even going back to the early evolution of modern humans. No less disturbing is Cayce's repeated characterization of the Atlanteans as the inventors of a technology superior to twentieth-century accomplishments. He describes them as the builders and operators of aircraft and submarines who mastered all manner of electrical and chemical energies, including nuclear fission. Many serious researchers balk at Cayce's life readings when [to them] they begin to verge on science fiction, but they still feel that completely condemning his work for its apparent excesses would be throwing the whole Atlantean baby out with the fantasy bathwater.

Critical investigators striving to understand a credible Atlantis within the context of the documented past may accept his vision *cum grano salis,* finding it especially useful for his commonly convincing insights, which personalize Atlantis's participants and make the lost civilization come alive, as no one else has been able to achieve. They may not embrace all Cayce's statements without reservations, but they carefully examine each one, putting aside—but not discarding—those that do not currently fit into the hugely complex Atlantean puzzle, while selecting those that, after close scrutiny, correspond to other pieces of information. To the surprise of honest skeptics, this careful comparative process more often validates Cayce's portrayal of Atlantis. Because he was correct in at least some important details, other Atlantologists believe he was telling the whole truth, however difficult it may be for us to grasp at the moment. He is the chief guide in all their research and is held in at least as high regard as Plato.

Regardless of the response Cayce continues to elicit, an important part of his legacy is the Association for Research and Enlightenment, operating in his former home at Virginia Beach. It maintains the largest library of its kind in the world, featuring not only all of his life readings, but also many hundreds of books, papers, feature articles, and reference materials about the lost civilization.

Plato and Cayce do not disagree with each other about Atlantis. On the contrary, their discussions are complementary, at least in their general outlines. The American psychic fleshes out the story with real-life individuals, putting a human face on the Atlanteans presented by the Greek philosopher in their broader cultural context. Plato himself was not adverse to extrarational means of ascertaining the truth, as he made clear in his post-Atlantis dialogue *The Laws:* "The ultimate limits of the human mind are surpassed only by what the spirit may learn."[15]

Together, Plato and Cayce more fully present ancient civilization's greatest drama. While no important discrepancies contradict the two versions [separated by 24 centuries], they do feature some nonexclusionary differences. The most important are the Atlanto-Athenian War and ancient technology: the former plays a central role in Plato's report, but Cayce does not even allude to it, while the latter, which never appears in the Dialogues, is a recurrent theme throughout the life readings. How can we reconcile these apparently major inconsistencies?

The answer seems to lie in the narratives themselves: both speak of the same civilization but at different periods in its very long life. By all accounts, Atlantean history spanned not centuries, but millennia. Cayce was concerned primarily with its early to middle years of internal religious strife, when its colonizers were traveling throughout much of the world. Plato's Dialogues focus on its last period of overseas military involvement and final destruction. In other words, the two versions describe Atlantis in different epochs, separated by thousands of years. Plato and Cayce agree that during the millennial interim, Atlantean civilization entered a decline from its former greatness, a degeneration that could have conceivably lost an earlier, higher technology, just as today we speak of lost arts from bygone cultures and eras.

That the story of Atlantis should have as its supporters the greatest philosopher and the greatest psychic in the Western world says much for its credibility—but if Plato's Dialogues had failed to survive the collapse of classical civilization and the long Dark Ages that followed, Atlantis would be known today only in the enduring myths of various peoples effected by it and through Cayce's life readings. This is at the core of what the great Scottish Atlantologist of the early twentieth century, Lewis Spence, called "the problem of Lemuria."

No great thinker narrates the story of that earlier and parallel civilization described in widely scattered folk traditions from Malaysia and China to Polynesia and British Columbia and beyond to California and South America. Punctuating this profuse if fragmented oral evidence are the sunken ruins recently discovered in Japanese waters and other ruins found on dry land in Micronesia, on Easter Island, and in Peru.

The Sleeping Prophet reconstructs them all, and brings back to life a people predating Atlantis, but who were perhaps even closer to us in our own New Age spirituality. Edgar Cayce's provocative views of life in Atlantis and Lemuria, here updated in the light of new discoveries, are not merely valuable as history. They uncover an even more disturbing parallel between the catastrophic fate of a once richly powerful society and the modern world's similarly global and materialistic civilization.

America's preeminent visionary lifted the dark veil concealing our ancient Atlanto-Lemurian origins and identity. Perhaps, if we look beneath the raised curtain, we may gaze into a mirror reflecting, to our surprise and even dismay, something of the image of our own times.

LOST MOTHERLAND, DROWNED FATHERLAND

No two peoples could have been more different from each other than those that dominated the Pacific and Atlantic Oceans. It is fitting that the Lemurians pervaded the Pacific, in view of their gentler society. The Atlanteans were politically extroverted and militaristic; the Lemurians, introverted and pacifist, so the two sea-borne civilizations were separated by more than thousands of miles. Their inhabitants were far from unaware of each other, however. On the contrary, limited contacts had always taken place.

Cayce offers abundant examples of Atlanto-Lemurian relations, all of them cordial, some of them intimate, which more often occurred when Lemurians and Atlanteans happened to meet in overseas lands they both visited, especially Yucatán. He spoke of a time "when the people had come from Lemuria" to Atlantis "for the indwelling of the various activities."[1]

The Lemurians were self-indulgent sexual activists whose family ties were loose and not clearly defined—shocking behavior to the devout Edgar Cayce, who shook his head at their perceived immorality. He condemned a "very much perverted activity by those from Mu."[2] (The Lemurians are still remembered as the "Mu" by Hawaiians and Tibetans.) Such libertine attitudes were part of the legacy passed down to their mixed descendants, the Polynesians, whose sexual behavior was likewise branded licentious by Christian missionaries. Freed from the necessity of working to survive because of the superabundance of food, and inhabiting a very hot climate where anything more than seminudity was less than practical, the Mu developed a sensible, guiltless sexuality that was regarded merely as an aspect of physical life.

It was in the spiritual arts, however, that the Mu most excelled, even surpassing the skilled adepts of Atlantis, according to Cayce. The Atlanteans achieved "the highest or the greatest advancement in the earthly sojourning of individual entities or souls at that particular period—or the highest that had been save that which had been a part of the Lemurian Age."[3] The soul-practitioners of first Mu and then Atlantis engaged in mass-meditation sessions involving hundreds, thousands, and occasionally millions of participants.

The psychic power generated from these single-minded assemblies was beyond anything comparable before or since. Levitation of otherwise immovable objects, psychokinesis, communal telepathy, remote viewing, metaphysical healing, the shifting of space and time, prophesy, interspecies communication, interdimensional travel—the whole gamut of known psychic phenomena, and far more than guessed at present were supposedly developed by the Lemurians and later refined by the Atlanteans. Cayce told a client in 1935 that he once dwelled "in Atlantis during a higher state of civilization, teacher of psychological thought and study, especially that of transmission of thought through ether."[4]

Mass mental telepathy took place in "a great congress" shortly before the final destruction of Atlantis:

In the period when this became necessary, there was the consciousness raised in the minds of the groups, in various portions of the Earth, much in the manner as would be illustrated by an all-world broadcast in the present day of a menace in any one particular point, or in many particular points. And the gathering of those that heeded, as would be the scientific minds of the present day, in devising ways and means of doing away with that particular kind or class of menace.[5]

The Atlanteans were adepts at what would now be called channeling, or, in the nineteenth century, spiritualism, because they applied "the concentration of thought for the universal forces, through the guidance or direction of the saints (as would be termed today)."[6] They were masters too of astral projection: "Through the concentration of the group-mind of the Children of the Law of One, they entered into a fourth-dimensional consciousness—or were absent from the body."[7] The Atlantean initiates had psychokinesis—the ability to influence physical objects by thought processes—literally down to a science, as Cayce revealed to a client who lived "in Atlantis before the second upheavals, a priestess in the temple through which mystics studied those tenets of the application of spiritual laws to material things."[8]

Common to his readings, which describe these abilities, are references to regular group activity: "concentration of thought for the use of the universal forces," "the consciousness raised in the minds of the groups,"[9] and so forth. The implication here is that the coordinated mental exertion of perhaps thousands of people, disciplined and working together at the same moment, concentrating all their psychological strength on the same object, generated powerful psychic energy. When focused into their "great, terrible crystal,"[10] the amplification of this energy must have been potent beyond measure—enough, perhaps, to destroy an entire civilization "in a single day and night," as Plato described it, if misappropriated by the Sons of Belial.

Cayce's readings suggest just such a psychic cause for the destruction of Atlantis: "In the Atlantean period those peoples gained much in understanding of mechanical laws and application of the nightside of life for destruction."[11] It was particularly because of these alleged paranormal powers that both Atlantis and Lemuria figure into our discussion of 2012. If, as seems likely, the rational science that went into the Mayan calendar was carried to Mesoamerica by adepts from Atlantis, who themselves inherited it from their Lemurian forebears, the kind of spontaneous prognostications made by the likes of Pope Leo X or Edgar Cayce appear to have had their ancient origins among a different people more reliant on a subtler intuition of the human subconscious.

Until the late-twentieth century, professional archaeologists were virtually unanimous in their conviction that Mu (or Lemuria) was an unrealistic fantasy. Even scholars such as the well-known science-fiction author L. Sprague de Camp, who conceded at least to the possibility of a factual Atlantis, perhaps confusing it with Minoan Crete or coastal Spain, were adamant that the existence of a Pacific Ocean counterpart was beyond all possibilities. The accidental find made by a diving instructor near Yonaguni, last in the southern chain of Japanese islands, during 1985, however, reopened scientific debate concerning Lemuria.

Kihachiro Aratake's discovery of a stone "citadel" 75 feet beneath the surface of the Pacific Ocean attracted the serious attention of certified researchers from around the world. With a few notable exceptions—among them, Boston University's Dr. Robert M. Schoch of Great Sphinx fame—most geologists agree with Professor Maasaki Kimura, commissioned by the University of the Ryukyus to survey the "monument," that the underwater anomaly is not only man-made, but also is at least 3,000 years old. Others, such as Canberra's Australian National University Dr. Kurt Lembeck, believe the structure is much older, going back some 12,000 years to allow for a 75-foot rise in sea levels. Both investigators have dared to use the still controversial, formerly anathematized L-word, describing the sunken citadel as Lemurian.

The ruin is not an anomaly, however, because islands scattered throughout Polynesia, Micronesia, Macronesia, and Melanesia are replete with physical evidence in the form of arches, columns, statues, and pyramids—on land, as well as underwater—testifying to a high culture that long ago spanned the Pacific. This abundant, hard proof

Fig. 13.1. Divers investigate a sloping wall at the base of Japan's sunken "monument" off the island of Yonaguni.

is richly supported and elucidated by the islanders' own oral accounts. They uniformly recall a huge, prosperous, and powerful kingdom that long ago dominated the ocean until it slipped beneath the waves, and its survivors became culture bearers to foreign lands.

A consistent theme threading these folk traditions stresses the spiritual disciplines mastered by this lost people. They are still often remembered as "sorcerers," adept in using unseen powers for healing, building monumental structures, remote viewing, or envisioning the future. On the Macronesian island of Pohnpei, native explanations for the off-shore city of Nan Madol claim its 250 million tons of magnetized basalt were levitated through the air and stacked into place by a pair of brothers—Olisihpa and Olsohpa—magicians from their drowned homeland, Katau Peidi.

Lemuria was known by many different names wherever its representatives influenced the outside world. On Easter Island (Rapa Nui), it was remembered as Marae Renga. To the Japanese, it is Horai. Native Hawaiians refer to it as Kahiki. These appellations and all the rest were nothing more than various cultural inflections on the same motherland. More important, various oral traditions among outside cultures emphasized the extraordinary paranormal abilities exercised by the Mu, as they continue to be remembered in Tibet and, almost half a world away, on the Hawaiian island of Kauai.

Other than these persistent myths preserved over generations by folkish memory keepers, the ruins of Nan Madol or Yonaguni are mute witnesses to the special powers allegedly applied in Mu. Our only other possible source for information about them lies with the man who was himself part of that psychic otherworld known only too well to the lost Lemurians.

EDGAR CAYCE'S
DREAM OF LEMURIA

According to Edgar Cayce, "the Andean, or the Pacific coast of South America occupied then [in predeluge times] the extreme eastern portion of Lemuria."[1] When he made this statement more than 70 years ago, oceanographers knew little of what lay beneath the Pacific. Only recently could they confirm that a subsurface archipelago connected to the Peruvian coast as dry land until it sank sometime within the last 10,000 years.

With the collapse of the Soviet colossus and the consequent end of the Cold War, hitherto secret U.S. Navy surveys of the world's sea floor were declassified and made available to the general public for the first time. California's renowned Scripps Oceanographic Institute at La Jolla used the ex-military data to compile the most detailed and up-to-date series of maps, graphically revealing more than ever before what lay on the bottom of Earth's oceans.

The maps revealed several startling features. Among the most compelling of these was a sunken archipelago identified as the so-called Nazca Ridge. This is a more or less contiguous group of former islands extending in a straight line for some 275 miles southwest from the Peruvian coast at the town of Nazca, south of the capital at Lima, and adjoining another group known as the Sala y Gomez Ridge. It bends almost due west for approximately another 350 miles in the direction of Easter Island. Both ridges were known before the new maps were released, but what the Scripps' charts reveal is that they are part of a sunken archipelago that stood as dry land above the ocean in the recent geologic past. In fact, part of the Nazca Ridge is in shallow water, its topmost sections only 100 feet or less beneath the surface.

Oceanographers now believe that, at least until the close of the last ice age some 10,000 years ago, a large archipelago of closely connected islands stood not far from the shores of Peru, extending into the Pacific for more than 700 miles. With the discharge of melting ice at the close of the Quaternary Phase, the latest interval of geologic time, sea levels suddenly rose, deluging the entire archipelago. This appears to be precisely the sunken landmass Edgar Cayce said was part of Lemuria, nearly 70 years before it was identified by science.

Although not a continent in a strict geological sense, Mu was indeed "continental" in its far-flung influences and vast cultural extent. The Pacific civilization was variously known as Lemuria and Mu, and both names appear interchangeably throughout world mythic traditions.

James Churchward, who first popularized the subject in his series of books about Mu in the 1920s, wrote that the aristocracy of Lemuria was ruled by a white race. Indeed, Polynesian legends still speak of white-skinned, fair-haired culture heroes who fled to the Pacific islands after their homeland sank into the sea. The Chumash Indians, whose previous name for today's Santa Cruz Island was Limu, displayed many anomalously Caucasian characteristics, such as full beards, not shared with other indigenous Americans. Moreover, these native tribes of white people told of their ancestral arrival from an island that sank into the sea. It also appears that a black population was in residence on Mu, descendants of which migrated westward into Micronesia, where they became today's Negritos. Other black Lemurians journeyed to the Americas, where they participated in Mexico's Olmec civilization and became memorialized by its ancient sculptors. These are the famous stone heads, eleven of which still survive, on display at La Venta's Villahermosa Museum, near Veracruz, in eastern Mexico.

Cayce tells us that some Lemurians belonging to a brown-skinned race were the first of the great horde of strangers to reach Peru. They appear to have been Lemuria's native majority population, whose descendants are modern Polynesians, despite significant influences from Asia, India, and the Americas. Churchward, who published decades before the Cayce material was generally known, likewise stated that a brown race resided in the motherland.

He wrote that Mu was subject to a white aristocracy, while Pacific island traditions imply that a theocracy prevailed in the sunken kingdom. In speaking of a client who brought Lemurian political ethics to South America, he said, "The entity gave the peoples those principles of self-government that have gone to the best rule through many, many ages."[2] Later, Cayce addressed another past life in a similar vein: "The entity established much of help and assistance to the peoples in that period, giving much understanding of division in a proper manner among the workers and the shirkers, among the well and the ill, the strong and the weak."[3]

From these utterances, Vada F. Carlson, the well-known writer of Native American subjects, concluded in her 1970 book, *The Great Migration,* that Mu was a democratic society not much different from what is supposed to be our own, modern version. Yet equating modern democracy with Lemurian government, for whatever reasons, is a mistake.[4] Clearly, the political leadership that Cayce describes for Mu, was a religious oligarchy or theocracy to divide "the workers and the shirkers, among the well and the ill, the strong and the weak"—more reminiscent of Incan socialism. Idealizing the past, especially through the lens of our own politically correct preferences, is to debase it and lose the truth. We cannot cast some admired, deeply ancient people in our own image without risking the most vulgar kind of self-flattery.

Cayce went on to say that the Pacific civilization predated Atlantis, but both shared a fundamentally common fate: "Then, was that portion, then the South Pacific, of Lemuria, began its disappearance—even before Atlantis, for the changes were brought about in the latter portion of that period, or would be termed ten thousand seven hundred light years, or earth years, or present setting of those, as by Amilius, or Adam."[5]

Cayce seems to be referring to a solar calendar ("light years, or earth years"), rather than the speed of light itself. The destruction of Mu begins to date, then, from around the year 8700 BC, but this date, too, is troublesome. If, in fact, a civilization existed at that time, it flourished in a vacuum, utterly cut off from both southwest Asia and Pacific coastal America. There, archaeologists cannot detect the merest trace of high cultural influences until much later.

Theosophists in the late-nineteenth century insisted that civilization flourished on Earth at a time when humankind had not yet evolved beyond homo erectus. Their Mu included saber-toothed tigers battling psychically endowed Lemurian giants with eyes at the backs of their heads. Such fantasies paraded with a straight face by people more interested in the occult than science do little for serious investigators, who are lumped together with Madame Blavatsky by skeptics of early civilization in the Pacific.

At the time that Mu supposedly went beneath the waves, 107 centuries ago, its survivors left no impact on contemporary Peru, where the first known ceremonial center was not built for at least another 5,200 years, a period roughly contemporary with the earliest civilized stirrings in China and Thailand. If archaeologists' understanding of Asia and America (to say nothing of the Pacific islands) in the ninth millennium BC is correct, then either Cayce was wrong or we have not understood him properly. To accept his date at face value, we would have to acknowledge that our conception of the world 10,700 years ago is wildly inaccurate and woefully incomplete. Geologically, however, Cayce's time frame is more credible. Scientists believe the seas rose suddenly with the end of the last ice age at levels sufficient to have drowned the stone monument discovered during 1986 near Yonaguni at the southernmost end of the chain of Japan's Ryukyu Islands.

We can return for a closer look at his life reading: Cayce said, "Lemuria *began* [author's italics] its disappearance" in 8700 BC. It is entirely conceivable—and, in fact, far more likely, geologically—that the process of total submersion took millennia to complete, longer than some sudden natural upheaval. Indeed, a gradual inundation is reflected in the Yonaguni ruins, which stand in relatively good condition. They evidence no signs of catastrophe, implying a slow burial beneath the surface of a continually rising ocean. If we acknowledge this interpretation of Cayce's date, together with the archaeological evidence at Peru and Yonaguni, then Lemuria emerges as possibly the world's first civilization, perhaps antedating Atlantis, with whom it was at least partially contemporaneous.

"According to Churchward," Carlson writes,

> Mu was a continent in the Pacific. There were, he writes, four great cataclysms, the first taking place in the Miocene era, about eight hundred thousand years ago; the second and less violent episode about two hundred thousand years ago; and the greatest about eighty thousand years ago. A fourth and final event was the catastrophe of twelve thousand years ago that sent Mu and millions of her people to the depths in a "vortex of fire and water."[6]

Carlson here confuses the Theosophists of Madame Blavatsky, Scott-Elliot, and so forth, with James Churchward, who, while a colonel with the British Army in India during the early 1870s, learned from native sources about *The Lost Continent of Mu,* as his first book on the subject was entitled. In it, he relates that the motherland was destroyed around 10,000 BC, when some sixty-four million inhabitants perished in a natural catastrophe of tremendous violence.

If taken at face value, however, as Churchward seems to have done, his date parameters for the destruction of Mu are even more incredible than Cayce's. His prime sources were Hindu monastery inscriptions, the literal translation of which he used for the basis of his conclusions. Almost certainly, those prime materials were written originally by chroniclers whose conception of time was not the same as ours. Very often, they possessed lunar or sidereal calendars and understood lunar years to count months or star years to count for longer or shorter passages of time.

We do not know on what kind of time scale Churchward's Indian documents were based. Accepting the 12,000-year-old date as literally true places Mu at the end of the last ice age, when the tropical conditions Churchward describes did not exist. Not a trace of anything dating to that time and remotely suggesting civilized life has been found anywhere, least of all in the Pacific.

Interestingly, Plato wrote that Atlantis was destroyed 11,500 years ago, allegedly five centuries after Churchward's Mu. Cayce always said that Lemuria was destroyed before Atlantis, but he never indicated by how many years, and investigators have long suspected that the doom of both was somehow related through a common catastrophe.

Cayce tells us the Lemurians were unlike the aggressively imperialistic Atlanteans and may have been reluctant to assert themselves in foreign lands. Their self-imposed isolation could have been part of Mu's cultural personality, much like that of the introverted feudal Japanese up until the mid-nineteenth century. In fact, the Lemurian impact on Japan was profound and indelible. The gated monument beneath the surface of the Pacific Ocean off Yonaguni has already been mentioned. It is joined by at least dozens of otherwise unaccountably megalithic sites across Honshu and is dramatized by sea-side ceremonies commemorating the arrival of Lemurian survivors performed today by tribal members of the Ama. Not without cause is a Mu Museum located in Japan.

Comparisons of the archaeological record and oral tradition with Edgar Cayce's life readings do more than establish the Sleeping Prophet's credibility. They demonstrate that lost Lemuria was a real place, the motherland of humankind, as it was earlier characterized by James Churchward.

HE SAW ATLANTIS

In a 5,000-year-old Sumerian epic known as *The Epic of Gilgamesh,* the teller of the tale, Utnapishtim, is described early in the prologue: "He was wise. He saw mysteries and knew secret things. He brought us a tale of the days before the Flood."[1]

The same might be said of Edgar Cayce, who told of three major periods of inundation that afflicted Atlantis. The single natural disaster described by Plato represented a final destruction that came after the upheavals cited in Cayce's life readings, which appear to focus on the late-fourth millennium BC cataclysm. A combination of the Plato and Cayce material restates, therefore, the four global catastrophes defined by the Mexihcah, Hindu, Persian, and other traditions. A typical life reading exemplifying these various epochs of upheaval took place in 1933, when Cayce told a client that the client once dwelled "in the Atlantean land before the third destruction."[2]

Researchers since then have discerned three decisive geologic episodes in the history of an Atlantic island that originally comprised a land mass that in area was roughly the size of modern Spain. The first seismic unrest dropped much of its territory beneath sea level, followed several millennia later by renewed geologic violence, which sank the remaining dry land, save for the tops of its tallest mountains. These volcanic peaks became known in historic times as Madeira and the Azores and Canary Islands, together with Atlas, on which the city of Atlantis arose. The

140

ultimate destruction took place when Mount Atlas detonated and hollowed itself out with ferocious eruptions, then collapsed into the sea.

Present interpretation of this evidence confirms the accuracy of Cayce's clairvoyant view of the Atlantean catastrophe. As he said, "the destruction of this continent and the peoples was far beyond any of that as has been kept as an absolute record, that record in the rocks still remains."[3]

Cayce's account of major geologic upheavals in ancient times was verified by a 1958 Ph.D. dissertation to the Association for Research and Englightenment (A.R.E.) entitled "Earth Changes." After comparing to modern knowledge of Earth science fifty representative examples of Cayce's life readings dealing with planetary upheavals, the report concludes:

Most of the readings on prehistorical subjects were given in the 1920s and 1930s, and were all on file before 1945. It is thus clear that the majority of the psychic statements antedate nearly all of the striking discoveries recently made by such youthful fields of scientific endeavor as deep-sea research, paleomagnetic research and research on the absolute age of geologic materials. Whereas the results of recent research sometimes modify or even overthrow important concepts of geology, they often have the opposite effect in relation to the psychic readings, in that they tend to render them more probable.[4]

Atlantologists have also had to catch up to Cayce's visionary grasp of the lost civilization's geologic past. His clairvoyant understanding of ancient Earth changes and their specific bearing on the fate of Atlantis explain the mass migration of its refugees across North Africa into Egypt. Skeptics long contended that such migrations through the vast expanse of the Sahara Desert would not have been possible, but Cayce said, "What is now the Sahara was an inhabited land and very fertile."[5]

At the time of this utterance, in 1932, geologists were certain the Sahara Desert was at least several million years old, and that living conditions there were no less hostile than at present, precluding any form of human habitation. Yet by 1955, the first extensive subsurface testing in the desert retrieved core samples proving the Sahara was indeed fertile enough to support herds of cattle as recently as 3000 BC. Only in the centuries following did North Africa begin to lose its battle with the inexorable sands.

Almost simultaneous with these geologic revelations, archaeologists discovered the first evidence of a nomadic people who inhabited the Sahara and shared numerous points in common with the dynastic culture of Egypt. These civilized desert dwellers, or travelers, appear to have been the pharaonic Egyptians' own immediate ancestors migrating eastward into the Nile Valley from the seismic chaos of their Atlantean homeland, just as Cayce described.

No pyramids have yet been discovered in the Sahara—nor are any likely to be found there, because the wandering refugees from Atlantis probably recognized that the gradually desiccating conditions were increasingly unsuited to permanent habitation. During the late-fourth millennium BC, the desert was winning its struggle over the retreating, fertile plains, with a consequent decline in the herds of bison and cattle that once roamed its grasses.

Yet the passing Atlanteans left their mark here, too. Illustrations at Jabbaren and Aouanrhet, painted with the same red ochre the Egyptians used in their temple wall murals, show women wearing wreaths and headdresses identical to those of their Nile counterparts. The girls pictured with Egyptian facial features and blond hair at Tassili-n-Ajjer, in the Oran Province of Libya, wear Egyptian robes, including Wadjet tiaras. (Wadjet was a cobra goddess, protectoress of the Lower Nile.) The figures are poised with worshipful gestures (their hands with raised palms, in the Egyptian manner) before animal-headed deities commonly represented throughout the Nile Valley. The deities portrayed most often are the lion, falcon, and cow, which sports a lunar disk between her horns. In Egyptian religion, these beasts were Sekhmet, the goddess of fiery destruction associated by twentieth-dynasty Egyptians with the Atlantean disaster; Heru (or Horus), the god of kingship, personifying pharaoh's royal soul; and Mehurt. This trio comprised a most ancient set in the Egyptian pantheon, all of them predynastic and said to have arrived "from the West." Interestingly, Mehurt's name means, literally, "the Great Flood."

The Pastoralists, as archaeologists have come to refer to these Atlanteans in transit across the Sahara, practiced deformation of cattle horns, a curious custom shared only with the Egyptians, and employed animal breeding procedures used along the Upper Nile. Clearly, these refugees were the people Cayce envisioned when he spoke of the Sahara as fertile and inhabited by survivors migrating from the destruction of Atlantis into the Nile Valley.

Dynastic Egypt itself began quite suddenly with the arrival of (as the pioneering British archaeologist W. B. Emery defined it) a master race from the west. Known as the Semsu-Hr (Followers of Horus), and the Mesentiu (Harpooners), they came equipped with all the features of a full-blown civilization. Previous to their momentous arrival, the Nile Valley was sparsely populated by Neolithic tribes of indifferent farmers and artless potters who dwelled in mud-thatch huts and eked out a subsistence living on the riverbanks. Their lands were transformed virtually over night by the construction of monumental architecture, the creation of complex, massive irrigation systems, a government hierarchy, divisions of labor, an institutionalized religion, visual arts of a high order, navigation, a written language, astronomy, geometry, surveying, a standardization of weights and measures—in short, all the elements of a culture that had already witnessed a long period of development elsewhere.

The advanced society that rapidly took root in the sands of Egypt was not merely some transplanted civilization, however. It was instead the outcome of native cultures blended with the genius of the arriving Followers of Horus and the Harpooners. This standard view of dynastic beginnings as a synthesis of foreign and domestic influences interacting during the late-fourth millennium BC is illustrated by a life reading Cayce made for a client who was "in Egypt at a time of coalition of natives, king, priest, Atlanteans, etc. Entity among natives in authority as counselor to various groups and historian of that to be preserved, native and Atlantean."[6]

The seafaring Semsu-Hr and Mesentiu are echoed in the life reading of a client who was "among those who came from Atlantis to Egypt in command of the fleets or ships, explored along waterways."[7] The beginnings of the Harpooners' civilizing efforts are clear when Cayce read for a man who was "among Atlantean who came into Egypt for preserving records and promises of Atlantean development."[8] The guiding leadership of the Followers of Horus and the Harpooners appears in a later reading: "Before that, the entity was in the Egyptian land among the Atlanteans who came in with those peoples in authority. For there the entity was one who personally cared for the records that were brought by the leaders of that people [the Atlanteans] for preservation in that portion of man's experience in the Earth."[9]

In his 1984 examination of Egypt's Great Pyramid, researcher William Fix stated that its internal chambers are places for rites of passage and initiation into the mystery religion of the human soul's rebirth after death. More than 50 years before, Edgar Cayce spoke of "the pyramid of initiation, where the opening of the records would come, that are as copies from the sunken Atlantis."[10] In 1941, he addressed another client as "the entity in the Atlantean and Egyptian lands—among those who came into the Egyptian experience for preserving the records of those activities—became a supervisor of the excavations—in studying the old records and in preparing and building the house of records for the Atlanteans, as well as a part of the house of initiate—or Great Pyramid."[11] Cayce told another client in 1942 that he once "aided the priest in the preparation of the manner of building the temple of records that lies just beyond that enigma that still is the mystery of mysteries to those who seek to know were the manners of thought of the ancient sons who built the man-made beast."[12] Cayce's reference to "that enigma" and the man-made beast describe the Great Sphinx, an identification made all the more clear by its position "just beyond" the Great Pyramid, "the temple of records."

Even here, we find revealing details in Cayce's readings that point out the reality and accuracy of his statements. In a 1933 session with a client, he spoke of "the Sphinx, that was set later as the sentinel or guard."[13] In fact, the Egyptian word for Sphinx was Hu, or "guardian." Of course, Egypt was not the only land settled by immigrants from Atlantis: "With the realization of the Children of the Law of One that there was to be the final breaking up of the Poseidian-Atlantean lands, there were the emigrations with many leaders to the various lands."[14]

A life reading of Cayce in 1934 told how his client "set sail for Egypt, but ended up in the Pyrenees in what are now Portuguese, French and Spanish lands."[15] The same period of eastern migration is again described for another client who lived "in Atlantean land of Poseidian peoples when there was the breaking up of the land, among those who came first to the Pyrenees and then to Egypt, active in preserving records."[16] These migrations to the Pyrenees took place after the earliest geologic upheavals: "With this also came the first egress of peoples to the Pyrenees."[17]

The Pyrenees are mentioned in Cayce's life readings more often than any other area settled by the Atlanteans: "Evidences of this lost civilization are to be found in the Pyrenees"; "Among Atlanteans who first came to Egypt, journeyed to what is now a portion of Portugal or the Pyrenees, where some Atlanteans had set up temple activity, aided in decorations of temple"; "in Atlantis at time of disputes when many sent to many lands, a mathematician, came to Pyrenees"; "Came to Egypt from Pyrenees land, hence came with latter portion of those from the Atlantean land."[18]

Cayce sometimes identified Atlantis by an unusual name—Og. He could hardly have known in his waking state that Og had been used in different cultures to describe Atlantis, including the Scotch-Irish Tir-na-Og, which caused a world-class flood; or Homer's Ogygia, an Atlantean isle visited by the hero, Odysseus; King Ogyges, the deluge-survivor in Greek myth; even the Hebrew Scripture's Og, who clung to the superstructure of Noah's Ark during the Flood.

The sheer number of Cayce's insights into the destiny and even precise location of the lost civilization have convinced many of its leading investigators that he was absolutely prophetic in 1941, when he said that it will "rise again" near the small Bahamian island of Bimini. It was there, in fact, that a 1,250-foot-long, organized arrangement of squared, pillowlike stone blocks running along the ocean floor just 19 feet beneath the surface of the Atlantic and 55 miles due east from Miami, Florida, was accidentally found long after the Sleeping Prophet's death. Attempts to dismiss the so-called Bimini Road as nothing more than a natural formation of beach rock have been thoroughly undone by more than 20 years of on-site investigations led by underwater archaeologists William Donato (Buena Vista, California) and Dr. Gregory Little (with the Association for Research and Enlightenment, Virginia Beach, Virginia). They unquestionably established the configuration's man-made identity by revealing the stones' unnatural relationship to Bimini's shoreline; retrieving core samples from some stones demonstrating they are not native to the Bahamas; discovering Bronze Age anchor stones at the site; showing the artificial placement of one block upon another; comparing the site's close resemblance to a typical Bronze Age harbor works in the Eastern Mediterranean Sea, although absolutely unlike any known natural formation of beach rock; and so forth.

These archaeological finds show that the so-called Bimini Road was actually a walled breakwater or quay belonging to a docking facility of the kind built to accommodate ships in the ancient Old World, 3,000 and more years ago. Stylistic comparisons to Bronze Age maritime engineering are supported by Bimini geology, which indicates that lower sea levels during the middle- to late-second millennium BC were shallow enough for the site to have served as a harbor. These discoveries strongly suggest that Bimini was the last landfall for sailors in need of provisions and particularly fresh water available in abundance on the limestone island during round-trip voyages from Europe to North America.

In 1933, long before these disclosures came to light from the late 1980s to the early twenty-first century, Edgar Cayce spoke of "the sunken portion of Atlantis, or Poseidia, where a portion of the temples may yet be discovered under the slime of ages of sea-water . . . near what is known as Bimini, off the coast of Florida."[19] Eight years later, he told how "Poseidia will be among the first portion of Atlantis to rise again. Expect it in '68 and '69. Not so far away."[20]

A civilian pilot on a routine flight from Nassau happened to pass over the northern point of Bimini just as the sun's rays, instead of reflecting off the surface water, as they usually do, momentarily penetrated the depths to reveal what appeared to him a paved highway going across the bottom of the Atlantic Ocean. After landing in Miami Beach, he filed his report, inadvertently setting in motion the first of numerous diving expeditions to the Bimini Road. The year was 1968.

THE TERRIBLE, MIGHTY CRYSTAL

Among Edgar Cayce's most controversial life readings are those describing a high technology developed and used by the people of Atlantis. Mainstream scholars are adamant that nothing resembling the modern physical sciences existed during preindustrial times, to say nothing of the ancient world. While praising the material greatness of the Atlanteans, Plato has nothing to say about any futuristic powers they may have possessed.

Cayce, nonetheless, tells of an electronic quartz crystal technology developed and mastered in Atlantis: "There were those destructive forces brought through the creating of the high influences of the radial activity from the rays of the Sun, that were turned upon the crystals into the pits that made for the connections with the internal influences of the earth."[1] And later, he mentioned "the principles of the stone upon the spheres . . . these brought destructive forces."[2] "Both constructive and destructive forces were generated by the activity of the stone."[3] "It was in the form of a six-sided figure," he said,

> . . . in which the light appeared as the means of communication between infinity and finite; or the means whereby there were the communications with those forces from the outside (outer space?).

Later, this came to mean that from which the energies radiated, as of the center from which there were the radial activities guiding the various forms of transition or travel through those periods of activity of the Atlanteans.[4]

The building above the stone was oval, or a dome, wherein there could be or was the rolling back, so that the activity of the stone was received from the sun's rays or from the stars; the concentrating of the energies that emanate from bodies that are on fire themselves—with the elements that are found in the earth's atmosphere.

The concentration through the prisms or glass, as would be called in the present, was in such a manner that it acted upon the instruments that were connected with various modes of travel, through induction methods—that made much the character of control through radio vibrations or directions would be in the present day; through the manner of the force that was impelled from the stone acted upon the motivating forces in the crafts themselves.

There was the preparation so that when the dome was rolled back there might be little or no hindrance in the application directly to the various crafts that were to be impelled through space, whether in the radius of the visioning of the one eye, as it might be called, or whether directed underwater or under other elements or through other elements. The preparation of this stone was in the hands only of the initiates at the time.[5]

Cayce spoke of "a crystal room" in Atlantis, where "the tenets and the truths or the lessons that were proclaimed by those that had descended to give the messages as from on High" were received by the initiates of a mystery cult. They "interpreted the messages that were received through the crystals."[6] "The preparation of this stone was solely in the hands of the initiates at the time."[7]

Cayce explained, "in Poseidia [Atlantis] the entity dwelt among those that had charge of the motive forces from the great crystals that so condensed the lights, the form of the activities—in conveniences of the body, as television and recording voice."[8] He described another client as "active in recording messages and directing those forces. These were not only the rays from the sun, amplified by crystals, but were the combinations of these."[9]

None of this made scientific sense in the 1930s, nor could it have until the advent of the crystalline silicon chip, nearly 50 years later. International Business Machine's (I.B.M.'s) 1989 second quarter stockholders' report echoes Cayce's life readings on the Atlantean crystals: "A crystal 'memory chip' has recently been invented by a German firm that contains more than four million bits of information."[10]

Referred to also as the "firestones," the crystals of Atlantis were supposed to have had certain curative powers: "Through the same form of fire the bodies of individuals were regenerated; by burning—through application of rays from the stone—the influences that brought destructive forces to an animal organism. Hence, the body often rejuvenated itself."[11] Cayce spoke too of the "high influence of radial activity from the rays of the sun that were turned on the crystals." These produced "the super cosmic ray that will be found in the next twenty-five years."[12] As he predicted, lasers were invented [reinvented?] around 1960. An article at the time in the *Physical Review* described the basic principle of the laser in almost Atlantean terms: "The amplification is achieved by storing up energy in a small insulating crystal of special magnetic properties. The release of energy is triggered off by an incident signal, so that the crystal passes on more energy than it receives."[13]

The crystals of Atlantis themselves were beyond good and evil: "About the firestone—the entity's activities then made such applications as dealt both with the constructive as well as the destructive forces in that period."[14] In the hands of well-meaning initiates, they were repositories for important information and survival tools for healing. Yet Cayce said Atlantis in its final days was torn by internal discord. Struggle between two factions eventually focused on possession of the powerful crystals. Somehow, the Sons of Belial wrested them from their keepers, the followers of the Law of One, probably through seductive appeal to materialist weaknesses, and, as Plato wrote, "human nature got the upper hand."[15]

Cayce, in fact, said his client was

> . . . in Atlantean land during those periods when there was the destruction or separations of the land during the period of the first destruction—among those aided in the preparation of the explosives or those things that set in motion the fires of the inner portions of the Earth that were turned into destructive forces. Improperly used for purposes of exploitation and domination, it became the terrible, mighty crystal; much of this brought destruction.[16]

So too, in our time, the laser is at the center of a life-and-death controversy. In the hands of a dedicated surgeon, it represents a wonderful healing power. To the military man, however, it is a laser cannon, a modern-day weapon of mass destruction. Like our Atlantean antecedents, we are nearing a decision of worldwide consequences for the future of our species regarding proper or improper use of such a "super cosmic ray" envisioned decades ago by the Sleeping Prophet.

NORTH AMERICA'S ATLANTO-LEMURIAN LEGACY

Oral traditions of the North American Indian are replete with folk memories describing the arrival of flood survivors from both Mu and Atlantis on the western and eastern shores, respectively, of Turtle Island. Tennessee's Cherokee believe Atali was an ancestral homeland in the Atlantic Ocean overwhelmed by a catastrophic deluge that ended a golden age of prosperity and power.

In recounting Hokan-Siouan origins, mythographer Joseph Wherry tells how, "In the dim and distant past, the forebears of many California Indians lived on an island somewhere in the Western Ocean. This island was Elam, and they worshiped the powerful god named Mu."[1] Cayce's trance-state insights throw an especially illuminating light on these abundant and enduring native accounts. He states:

In the Atlantean lands, during those periods when there were the beginnings of the exodus, owing to the destructive forces that had been begun by the Sons of Belial, the entity was among the princes of the land that made for the separating of those influences wherein there might be established the journeying to other lands, with the

keeping of the records, with the permanent establishments of activities that have become a part of that you call civilization in the present time.

Hence we find the entity making for the establishments in the
Yucatán, in what became the Inca, in the North American land, and
in what later became the land of the Mound Builders in Ohio; also
the establishments of those activities in the upper portion of what is
now the eastern portion of the land.[2]

Each of the cultures Cayce mentions—Mesoamerican, Andean, and
North American Indian—were rich with accounts of light-skinned visitors from across the sea who arrived following a terrible flood, yet stayed
to rebuild civilization in cooperation with the native peoples. Like him,
they told of technologically endowed foreigners making various landfalls
along both the Atlantic and Pacific shores of the Americas: "Hence these
places partook of the earlier portions of that people called the Incal;
though the Incals were themselves the successors of those of Og, in the
Peruvian land, and Mu in the southern portions of what is now called
California and Mexico and southern New Mexico in the United States."[3]
Cayce's linking of Mu to southern California and New Mexico is especially pertinent, because these states offer some of the best evidence for
Lemurian influences in the Americas.

Cayce describes overseas influences in pre-Columbian America
arriving from the Gobi Desert, among the most inhospitable places on
Earth and utterly disassociated from civilization, ancient or modern. Yet
he tells us that a great people once flourished there long ago, before the
intolerable conditions for which it is now infamous overwhelmed a formerly fertile land: "There the entity was the priestess. And there may be
seen some of those activities that are a part of the awareness to some in
that land of Ohio, where there were those plans for such, in the mounds
that were called the replica or representative of the Yucatán experience,
as well as the Atlantean and the Gobi land. All of these are as open consciousness in the entity's activity."[4]

Natural upheavals did not alone trigger the mass movement of ancient peoples. According to Cayce, "Those in Yucatán, those in the adjoining lands as begun by Iltar, gradually lost in their activities, and came to be that people termed, in other portions of America, the Mound Builders."[5] He correctly recounted the movement of Maya culture-bearers from Yucatán to territories above the Rio Grande River, where they were much later recognized as the Mound Builders. A growing number of archaeologists conclude that around AD 900 a large-scale exodus of civilized peoples did indeed leave the lowland regions of Middle America, finally settling in the Mississippi Valley. Here, they re-created their temple pyramids in soil, because stone was not as plentiful. They reinstituted astronomy, agriculture, social organization, and an organized priesthood.

America has always been a cultural melting pot, even in prehistory. As Cayce explains, "peoples came that were known as the Lost Tribes, as well as from Atlantis, Yucatán, the Inca, and the land of On (?)."[6]

A burgeoning richness of physical evidence supports so-called diffusionist researchers, who believe the Americas were impacted by numerous peoples from various parts of the world millennia before Columbus arrived here. Though Atlantean influences predominated in the early or formative periods of pre-Columbian civilizations, later epochs were touched by much smaller bands of Jews who arrived in North and Middle America sporadically, as refugees from their numerous enemies. In the second century, after a failed rebellion led by Simeon Bar Kochba, "the Hebrews fled across the sea to a land unknown to them before."[7] These belonged, in a general sense, to the same people Cayce loosely characterizes as the lost tribes. The so-called Bat Creek Stone discovered in Tennessee during the 1950s is believed by some investigators to be a remnant of the Bar Kochba revolt, wherein the leader is referred to in the Hebrew inscription as "a star for the Jews."

The "On" Cayce mentions is a reference to Egyptians from a cult center known to the Greeks as Heliopolis, or City of the Sun. Cayce tells us here that survivors of Atlantis, Mayas from Yucatán, travelers from South America, Lower Nile Egyptians, even lost tribes Hebrews, contributed to the mound-building culture of North America. These different influences, with their arrivals widely separated in time, explain the various phases through which that culture passed. Each one of North America's pre-Columbian periods parallels the alien forces melded with local influences that Cayce tells us took place in North America:

> They were portions of the entity's peoples that were a part of the experiences there of those peoples. For while confusions arose from the tenets of the Hebraic as well as the Atlantean, as well as the Inca, these became centralized or localized in the expressions of those peoples and those groups in that particular period of their activity. Yet the greater blessings that the entity in its activity rendered the people in that experience were in the building of individual homes.[8]

Cayce was particularly insightful in mentioning the corn-growing activities of the later Mound Builders:

> The entity was in the land of the present sojourn [Pennsylvania] during the early activities of a peoples that had been banished from Atlantis. The entity was among those of the second generation of Atlanteans who struggled northward from Yucatán, settling in what is now a portion of Kentucky, Indiana, Ohio, being among those of the earlier period known as Mound Builders. Then the entity was among those who supplied to the peoples the fruits of the soil, learning how to crack corn, wheat and grain, that it might be prepared into foods through cooking—though much in those periods was taken raw.[9]

Cayce singled out the Iroquois as "the pure descendants of the Atlanteans."[10] Indeed, virtually every Indian tribe throughout the Americas has its own account of a great flood from which their forefathers arrived in a new land. Yet prehistoric influences reached California shores from a Pacific civilization, as well. In 1934, Cayce informed a client that she once lived:

. . . in that land now known as the American, during the periods when the Lemurian, or the lands of Mu and Zu, were being in their turmoils for destruction. And the entity was among those that—in what is now not far from that land in which the entity in this sojourn first saw the light, that must in the near future fade again into those joinings with the land of Mu—established a temple of worship for those that escaped from the turmoils of the shifting of the earth at that particular period.

The entity, in the name Oeueou, established near what is now Santa Barbara, the temple to the sun and the moon, for the satellite of the moon had not faded then, and there was enjoined as to the entity in the worship as the goddess to the moon and the sun.[11]

The Zu Cayce mentions was one of the closely associated islands in a string of Pacific archipelagoes that comprised Lemuria. His association of the southern California islands and a Lemurian temple to the sun and moon is extraordinarily poignant, because the Santa Cruz area was known as Limu to the Chumash Indians, who dwelled in the area. They shared many aspects of their culture with those of the Mu, not least of all their worship of the heavenly bodies, particularly the sun and moon, as they were portrayed in surviving rock art and accurately described by Cayce.

In another reading, he told of a past life

. . . during those periods when the changes that had brought about the sinking of Mu or Lemuria, or those peoples in the periods who had changed to what is now a portion of the Rocky Mountain area: Arizona, New Mexico, portions of Nevada and Utah. The entity was then among the princesses of the land that established there the teachings of the Law of One, from the activities in the land which had brought destructive forces through the separations from those things that made for the love of the individual for the gratifying of selfish motives.

Then the entity established what may be called the home life in that land, as each home became then as the castle or place of worship—or activities that were separated, yet united in one as for purposes. The name then was Ouowu.[12]

This reading is especially significant, because the states Cayce includes in connection to immigrants from Mu—Arizona, New Mexico, Nevada, and Utah—are those same areas where the most dramatic oral traditions about Lemuria are preserved among the Navajo, Paiute, and Shoshone Indians.

Here Cayce shows the continuing impact made on Native American spirituality, which is rooted in the Lemurian arrival:

Uzld was in the land of Og, now known as that of the American plateaus, or in the northern portion of New Mexico and such. The entity was among the peoples who first gave to those people the home and home's influence. The entity was in that land now known as the American during the periods when there were the sojourn-ings of those from the Land of Mu, or Lemuria. The entity was then among the first of those that were born in what is now portions of Arizona and Utah, and among those who established the lands there for the building up or growing up of that civilization [the Anasazi?] in those experiences, and was in the name Uuluoou. The entity led many to a greater understanding of how there might be made the closer relationships with the material things and the spiritual thoughts of the people.[13]

Eventually, culture bearers from both Atlantis and Mu met in North America. An Atlantean named Amelelia who "acted as a priestess in the Temple of Light" was one of those "who oversaw the activities of the communications between the various lands, as from Om, Mu, the hier-archy land in that now known as the United States, in that particular portion of Arizona and Nevada, that are as a portion of the Brotherhood of those peoples from Mu."[14]

Underscoring Cayce, Carlson points out: "The Kootenay Indians of

Washington and British Columbia have a legend stating that their fore-fathers came to America from 'The Land of the Sun.' 'Land of the Sun' and 'Empire of the Sun' were common names of Mu before its submergence."[15] The Pacific Northwest features a majority of native folk traditions describing ancestral arrivals from Mu. Cayce told a client that the client "was in that land known as Mu, or the vanished land of the Pacific, the Peaceful, and was among those that journeyed from Mu to what is now Oregon, and there may still be seen something of the worship as set up, in what was the development from that set up by the entity's associates, as the totem, or the family tree. Then the women ruled, rather than the men."[16]

Churchward appears to have correctly interpreted the destruction of Mu from recurring features on several so-called totem poles raised by the Haida Indians of British Columbia. These tall, carved pillars of wood do not actually function as totems, because the animals often portrayed are not worshipped. Instead, they are memorial or heraldic devices that preserve and relate in images the mythic-historical past of a particular household or tribe. Sometimes, an eagle attacking a whale is symbolically used as a kind of heraldry to designate the earliest beginnings of a family whose current members can boast that their ancestors arrived along the Pacific Northwest coast after the flood that destroyed their tribal homeland.

Both Churchward and Cayce agreed that at least some of these totem poles symbolically depict the demise of Mu (the whale) brought about by the judgment of the Great Spirit (the eagle). Their common supposition is strongly suggested by the totem pole's internal evidence. For example, the Haida still speak of the Steel-Headed Man, their founding father, who arrived on the shores of Canada after a terrible flood that ensued when the whale, Namu, was killed by a sky god, the Thunderbird.

In the American Southwest, Cayce tells of a postdeluge civilization still shrouded in mystery: "The entity was among the first that have become known as the cave or cliff dwellers, in that portion now known as Utah, Arizona, Colorado and New Mexico. In those environs and places did the entity make for its activities, in the name, then, Uramm."[17]

Cayce's cliff dwellers were the Anasazi, or the Ancient Enemies, as they were referred to by the Jicarilla Apaches, Navajo, Southern Paiute, and other Southwest tribes. Beginning about AD 1200, the Anasazi built cities high up in the recessed areas of mountains or in remote valleys, such as Colorado's Mesa Verde. Although their immediate origins are obscure, their *kivas*—circular, ceremonial structures—embodied numerous features of the Omphalos religion practiced in Atlantis. Chief imagery of this Earth Mother mystery cult was the Navel of the World, represented by a natural cave or a subterranean temple signifying the Sacred Center of existence. Enacted in this sanctified precinct were rituals for the eternal rebirth of the human soul. Perhaps like no other building of its kind to have survived from prehistory, the kiva typifies these esoteric principles first enumerated in Atlantis. The Anasazi (or, at any rate, their shamans) might have had some Atlantean blood still flowing through their veins, and were yet able to preserve the old mysteries. Or they may have learned them from an even earlier people who had come into direct contact with adepts from Atlantis. In any case, more than a thousand years separate the final destruction of Atlantis from the moment the Anasazi began building their kivas and cliff dwellings.

Cayce shed some light on another archaeological mystery far to the north:

We find the entity there made use of the metal known as iron, or the combinations of iron and copper—which have long since been removed from use in the present, or copper so tempered by the use of same with a little of the iron, or in its formation in such a way and manner as to be hardened to the abilities for same to be used much in the way that many of those combinations have been found in the Egyptian, the Peruvian, and portions of the Chaldean lands—and more will be found in the Indo-China city yet to be uncovered.[18]

Plato describes the Atlanteans as great miners and metalsmiths whose national wealth largely depended on the world's highest-grade copper to produce extraordinary bronze. He refers to this superior bronze as *orichalcum*. Little known to the general public is America's greatest archaeological enigma: the excavation of at least half a billion pounds of copper ore in a stupendous mining enterprise that began suddenly in the Upper Great Lakes region of the Michigan peninsula about 5,000 years ago. Although the identity of these prehistoric miners is unknown, Menomonee Indian tradition remembers them as the Marine Men, white-skinned, bearded foreigners who sailed out of the East.

Coincidental with the Michigan operations, the Old World Bronze Age began: high-grade copper, never in plentiful supply in Europe, was combined with zinc and tin for the production of bronze. Both American copper mining and the Old World Bronze Age came to a sudden halt in 1200 BC—also the date for the final destruction of Atlantis, which lay between both continents.

In 1980, archaeologists stumbled upon what may be the world's oldest center for bronze-making in northern Thailand. Perhaps Bang Chiang is the place Cayce meant when he said that ancient, high-quality metalworking "will be found in the Indo-China city yet to be uncovered." But the process he described of combining copper with iron refers to the lost art of "hardened copper" developed both in the Near East and prehistoric Michigan. If his description of the process is correct, it could unlock a metallurgical secret lost for centuries.

MIDDLE AMERICAN CRUCIBLE

In one of his trance-state visions of the ancient past, Edgar Cayce told a client,

> Three thousand years before the Prince of Peace came, these peoples that were of the Lost Tribes, a portion came into this land, infusing their activities upon the peoples from Mu in the southernmost part of that called America, or the United States, and then moved on to the activities in Mexico, Yucatán, centralizing about the spots where the central of Mexico now stands, or Mexico City. Hence there arose through the ages a different civilization, a mixture again.[1]

Here, Cayce tells us that in about 3000 BC, Semitic visitors from the Near East arrived in the U.S. South—somewhere in the Gulf Coast region—before establishing themselves in what is now Mexico City. Since the middle of the last century, stone sculptures of men with distinctly Semitic countenances have been found associated with Mexico's earliest known civilizers. Outstanding examples of fork-bearded people with aquiline noses are on display at the Villahermosa Museum Park, in eastern Mexico and at prominent Olmec sites, including Monte Alban and La Venta.

The earliest surviving documentation of Israel is found in the military records of Merenptah, the twentieth-dynasty pharaoh who ruled Egypt around 1250 BC. It does not seem likely the Jews existed as a people much earlier than the thirteenth century BC, so their arrival in America 5,000 years ago is not credible. Yet archaic Hebrew writing has been found on widely separated artifacts in Tennessee (the Bat Creek Stone), Ohio (the Newark Decalogue Stone), Michigan (the Soper-Savage Collection of inscribed tables), Illinois (Burrows Cave), and New Mexico (Hidden Mountain, Los Lunas). These sites tend to confirm Cayce's statements describing something like lost tribes of Israel in prehistoric North America.

His statement that the Olmec may be traced to around the turn of the third millennium BC preceded by some 70 years scholarly reassessment of Mesoamerican civilizations beginning 5,000 years ago. Yet Israel did not even exist at this time, of course, and its tribes were "lost" for another 2,000 years or more. It appears instead that Cayce was using a better known name—the lost tribes—to identify a Semitic people that predated but may have been at least partially ancestral to the Jews.

The seafaring skills of the ancients combined with ocean currents acting as maritime highways to render America a meeting ground of diverse peoples long before the Statue of Liberty was erected at Staten Island. Although Atlanteans and Lemurians were the first and formative of the civilized peoples to impact our continent, they were followed by visitors from Bronze Age and classical Europe; medieval North Africa; and the Near East, Asia and India—centuries and even millennia before Columbus.

For example, Carlson writes that "Siguenza y Gongora, a Mexican of the 17th Century, may have been correct when he made the statement that all Indians of the New World were descendants of Poseidon [ruler of Atlantis] and that Poseidon was a great-grandson of Noah."[2] We can wonder what led Siguenza y Gongora to conclude that the natives of Mexico were descendants of Atlantis. It is conceivable that he heard Mexihcah oral traditions of Aztlán, in the Atlantic Ocean.

Sometimes, the racial tensions of a bygone epoch echo through successive lifetimes. In speaking of a client who experienced an otherwise unaccountable sense of identification with ancient Mexico, Cayce's characterization of the Aztecs as conquerors from the north is in accord with the archaeological record:

> We find the entity in that period when changes took place in what is now known as Mexican country, in the subduing of the peoples as came down from the north by those coming up from the south. The entity was then among those who were put in charge of the subdued people, from which arose that people now known as Aztecs. (They, the red race, were able to use in their gradual development all the forces as were manifest in their individual surroundings, passing through those periods of development.)[3]

Aztalan, or the Place Near Water in the language of the local Ho Chunk Indians, was southern Wisconsin's foremost ceremonial center during the thirteenth century. Three pallisaded walls interspersed at regular intervals with two-story watchtowers surrounded a trio of earthen pyramids oriented to the sun, moon, and planet Venus. The city of perhaps ten thousand residents led by astronomer-priests was also an important hub for commerce that supplied all of Mesoamerica with copper mined from the Upper Great Lakes region, beginning around AD 1100 until 1300.

East of Aztalan lies Rock Lake, with its own pyramids—including a delta-shaped platform 900 feet long on each side—lying at depths of 60, 40, and 20 feet beneath the surface. These stone structures are tombs flooded by a river that long ago spilled into the valley, thereby creating today's 3-mile-long, figure 8–shaped lake. Aztalan originally straddled both sides of the Crawfish River, although an archaeological park open to the public since 1960 covers only one half of the city on its western bank.

After some 200 years of occupation, the site was abruptly and entirely evacuated, its residents migrating *en masse,* according to Ho Chunk and Pottawatomie Indian oral traditions, disappearing forever toward the south. Aztalan's unique history suggests Aztec origins, for they were related to Spanish conquerors in the early sixteenth century. The Aztecs claimed to have originated at Chicomoztoc, the Place of the Seven Caves or Place of the Seven Wombs, a sacred lake in the far north, where seven related tribes formed a powerful coalition. It was from here that they left as a single group, eventually arriving in the Valley of Mexico, where they conquered the Mexihcah and absorbed the Mexihcahs' higher culture.

Chicomoztoc was symbolized in temple art as a spiral, signifying an infant's spiral descent from the womb. Pottery shards were similarly decorated with the sacred spiral motif at Aztalan, which was abandoned shortly before the Aztecs entered the Valley of Mexico, lending credence to the possibility of a northern homeland. Cayce was correct in characterizing the arrival of the Aztecs as "the subduing of the peoples as came down from the north by those coming up from the south."[4] The newcomers were indeed suppressed by all other tribes in the Valley of Mexico until they clawed their way to political supremacy, becoming the dominant power in Middle America toward the end of the fourteenth century.

Long before their ascendancy, according to Cayce, religious influences from Atlantis had permanently dyed the cultural fabric of Mesoamerican civilization. For example, he identified a female client of Atlantean background who "was then a princess in the Temple of the Sun, or the Temple of Light; though others have interpreted it as the Sun."[5] He implies that some worshippers venerated the sun as God incarnate, while initiates into the solar mysteries understood that the sun was only a metaphor for light or enlightenment of the universal consciousness that interpenetrates and orders the universe. Cayce related that these Atlantean temples functioned similarly on both sides of the ocean. He spoke of a woman client who "was in the Egyptian land when there were preparations of individuals for activities in other lands. The entity was among those who were prepared in the Temple Beautiful for those activities in what is now Yucatán."[6] This reading is revealing, because it shows that people arrived in Yucatán not only as colonists from Atlantis or refugees following the destruction of Poseidia, but also as Egyptians who traveled all the way to America for religious purposes.

Atlantean solar spirituality persisted among the Mexican people until the imposition of Christianity. Cayce told a client that, in a past life, she was

> . . . in Yucatán land, during those periods of the early coming in of those from the western shores, or during the Spanish periods. There the entity was a priestess to the sun-god, who attempted to bring into the experience of her peoples the closer relationships to those peoples through the ability of the entity to depict in drawings, in the markings, upon even the face of nature, as well as upon the walls, the buildings of the peoples, that as would bring awe—and yet an inspirational awe—to so pattern their lives, their activities, as to be acceptable unto the higher influences that are ever creative in the experiences of individuals.[7]

Here, Cayce describes a woman who served as a priestess of the sun cult in Yucatán at the time of the Spanish Conquest, during the 1520s. He might just as well have been speaking about a practitioner thousands of years before.

Atlantean and Lemurian influences on the formative development of Mesoamerica often surfaced in the life readings of Cayce's clients:

> With the leavings of the civilization in Atlantis [in Poseidia, more specifically], Iltar, with a group of followers that had been of the household of Atlan, the followers of the worshippers of the One— with some ten individuals—left this land of Poseidia and came westward, entering what would now be a portion of Yucatán. And there began, with the activities of the peoples there, the development of a civilization that arose much in the same manner as that which had been in the Atlantean land. Others had left the land later, others had left earlier.

There had been the upheavals also from the land of Mu, or Lemuria, and these had their part in the changing, or there was the injection of their tenets in the various portions of the land, which was much greater in extent until the final upheavals of Atlantis, or the islands that were later upheaved, when much of the contour of the land in Central America and Mexico was changed to that similar in outline to that which may be seen in the present.[8]

The late-nineteenth-century archaeologist August Le Plongeon spent decades among the jungle ruins of Yucatán, where he discovered many important Maya altars, one of which Cayce described in an Atlantean context:

The stones that are circular, that were of the magnetized influence upon which the Spirit of the One spoke to those peoples as they gathered in their service, are of the earliest Atlantean activities in religious service, as would be called today.

The altars upon which there were the cleansings of the bodies (not human sacrifice, for this came much later, with the injection of the Mosaic, and those activities in that area) these were later the altars upon which individual activities—that would today be termed hate, malice, selfishness, self-indulgence—were cleansed from the body through the ceremony, through the rise of initiates from the sources of light, that came from the stones upon which the angels of light, during the periods, gave their expression to peoples.

The pyramids, the altars before the doors of the varied temples' activities, were injections from the people of Mu, and will be found to be separate portions, and that referred to in the scriptures as high places of family altars, family gods, that in many portions of the world became again the injection into the activities of groups in various portions, as gradually there were the turnings of the people to the satisfying and gratifying of self's desires, or as the Baal, or Baalilal activities again entered the peoples respecting their association with those truths of light that came through the gods to the peoples, to mankind, in the earth.[9]

The circular stone altars, which Cayce said belonged to Atlantean religion, complement Plato's description of spiritually artistic and architectural designs throughout Atlantis, where concentricity dominated stylistic conventions. An altar precisely like the one Cayce describes was in fact discovered, not in Yucatán, but at a highly Atlantean site in western Italy, in a subterranean temple built 2,500 years ago by the Etruscans, near Lake Bolsena. Etruria is specifically sited in Plato's account as having been occupied by the Atlanteans, who brought the same kind of circular stone altars to Yucatán.

These artifacts belonged to a rich cultural legacy the Mayas inherited from Atlantis, according to Cayce, after the island kingdom had been obliterated by a global cataclysm. His vision was paralleled by the words of an oracular Jaguar priest in chapter 5 of the Book of Chilam Balam, a collection of calendrical, herbal, medical, astrological, cosmological, and historical texts: "The world was flooded and the sky fell upon the Earth. When the destruction and annihilation had been accomplished, the spirits of the Bacab began to re-organize the people of Maya."[10]

As described in chapter 2 here, the Bacab were pairs of long-bearded men supporting the sky with upraised hands. Hence, the spirits of these Atlas-like Bacab represented the Book of Chilam Balam's characterization of Atlanteans arriving in Middle America. Mexican archaeologists have associated the postdeluge appearance of the Bacabs in Guatemala with the foundation date of the Maya and the start of their calendar on August 10, 3114 BC.

That Cayce envisioned all this decades before mainstream archaeologists made their discoveries lends potent credence to his prophetic statements.

THE INCAS'
ATLANTO-LEMURIAN
HERITAGE

According to Edgar Cayce, survivors of the Atlantean catastrophe fled not only to Mexico, but also beyond, to South America:

> In the one life before this, we find the entity in the days of the peoples coming from the waters in the submerged areas of the southern portion as is now of Peru, when the earth was divided, and the people began to inhabit the Earth again. The entity was among those who succeeded in gaining the higher ground and then in the name of (which was changed afterward) Omrui, and changed to Mosases, for the entity became the ruler and the guide, or the patriarch of that age and gave much assistance to the few as were gathered about the entity.[1]

Cayce's description of immigrants from lost Atlantis seeking refuge in South America is also found in a native oral tradition recounted by the early-twentieth-century explorer Alexander Braghine: "The Paraguayan and Brazilian Guaranys possess a cycle of legends concerning their national hero, Tamanduare, who, with his family, was the only survivor spared by the catastrophe which destroyed 'The City of the Shining Roofs.'"[2]

The Inca themselves were proud to trace their lineage back to their own version of the Guaranys' Tamanduare: At-ach-u-chu, the tall, red-haired, bearded, fair-skinned culture bearer from a distant land in the east who arrived on the shores of Lake Titicaca after surviving some terrible deluge. He was remembered as the Teacher of all Things, who established in South America the arts of civilization, including agriculture, religion, astronomy, weights and measures, social organization, and government. At-ach-u-chu was the elder of five brothers who were known collectively as *wiracochas,* or "white men."

At-ach-u-chu is better remembered by his title, Kon-tiki-Wiracocha, or White Man of the Sea Foam—in other words, a foreigner who arrived by ship, "sea foam" being a poetic description of its bow wave. All features of this supremely important figure in Andean tradition, beginning with the *At-* at the beginning of his name, clearly define him as the leader of survivors from the final destruction of Atlantis who reestablished themselves by creating in Peru and Bolivia a hybrid civilization, a mix of local cultures and Atlantean technology.

At-ach-u-chu's resemblance to similarly fair-faced culture bearers appearing after a great natural disaster in the Atlantic Ocean is nothing more than an Andean version of the Aztecs' Quetzalcoatl or the Mayas' Kukulcan. These related founding heroes from over the sea apparently represent the impact native peoples experienced from the large-scale arrival of Atlantis refugees.

The South American At-ach-u-chu appears to derive from Atcha, known to the ancient Egyptians as a far-off, splendid, but vanished city echoing lost Atlantis. At-ach-u-chu could mean the Man from Atcha. In any case, Cayce seems to have had At-ach-u-chu in mind when he told a client that the client "was in the Atlantean land when there were those periods of the last upheavals, or the disappearance of the isles of Poseidia. The entity was among those groups into what later became known as the Inca. For the entity was then in the line of the house of Inca, and was the mother of an Inca in the Peruvian land, as called in the present."[3]

Cayce said of another female client that she "was in the Inca land when there had been the journeyings of the Atlantean peoples for setting up what later came to be known as the Incal activities. There the entity was a companion of the one that had acted in the capacity of a leader in setting up the customs, rituals and activities in that land following the destruction of Atlantis."[4] A year before his death, Cayce told a client that he "was among those that went from the Atlantean land to what is the Peruvian or Inca land."[5]

Yet the South American continent is also washed by the Pacific Ocean, which brought its own human influences to bear on the development of Andean civilization: "In this experience the entity was a priestess in those interpretations of what later became known as the Incals, the Lost Tribes, the people from the Atlantean land, and the people . . . from the Lemurian land."[6] We should find Cayce neither confusing nor vague when describing simultaneous influences in Peru from Atlantis and Lemuria. South America lay between these oceanic powers, which were, after all, contemporary, so detecting both Atlantean and Lemurian themes in Andean civilization is not contradictory or even surprising.

As he said of another client:

> The entity was among those that were to become the emissaries or the sojourners in what is now the Incal land, or the Peruvian land. Later from that sojourn the entity came to what is now the Central American land, aiding in the establishing not only of the tenets but the manners and the forms of worship during those sojourns. The entity was among the princesses of the land, not only of the Atlantean, but of the Ohlm and Og lands, and later Muri [Mu].[7]

This is a particularly interesting life reading, because Cayce, apparently oblivious to his own words, seems to be tracing the movements of "the entity" from Atlantis into Peru and beyond to Lemuria. It is a credible sequence of events that compliments everything known about these three ancient, interrelated civilizations. It also demonstrates the supposition, held by many investigators, that Atlanteans and Lemurians were not unknown to one another. For example, Churchward repeats a Lemurian tradition that the figure deified in Egypt as Osiris was actually a mortal Atlantean who journeyed to Mu, where he learned the esoteric principles associated with his name.[8]

Cayce said that a man who came to him "was among those that were the leaders of the Ohums [an earlier people, any one of the several cultures that preceded the Incas] where there was the breaking up of the deeps, and the land disappeared and reappeared."[9] Here Cayce implies a rise and fall of sea level, precisely the fluctuation that did indeed take place over thousands of years following the last ice age, when Cayce said Mu was lost and the underwater structures at Okinawa were covered.

Among the wonderful surprises found throughout the life readings are numerous, often small details, which are conspicuous for their accuracy. These little gems go far to establish that Cayce was indeed in contact with some alternative source of information beyond other human beings. A case in point is his reference to the Incas, who built "walls across the mountains."[10] Although their construction achievements were generally appreciated in Cayce's lifetime, no one knew of any walls they may have built in the Andes until more than 20 years after his death. During the late 1960s, the first reports of what newspapers immediately dubbed "the Great Wall of Peru" were published. Winding its way through jungle and around some of the highest peaks in South America, the stone structure has been dated by archaeologists to Inca builders in the mid-fifteenth century. Essentially intact, its full extent is still unknown, but investigators believe it may be at least several miles long.

The Incas also excelled in the production of textiles to a degree that was far greater than any other pre-Columbian people, a skill reflected in Cayce's life reading:

In the one before this we find [the entity] in the Peruvian country, now known, in the days of the first Incal, as known. [The entity was] then the one who gave the first of the draperies to the temples of that period, and the entity lost in that period of experience through self-aggrandizement of position held. The urge as is seen is the love of fine linen and as any work raised as figures on cloth, and the entity sees beauty in any raised figures in such, and often wonders why.[11]

As Cayce suggests, there was also a dark side to the intermingling of native Peruvians and the Atlantean newcomers:

Then, with these destructive forces, we find the first turning of the altar fires into that of sacrifice of those that were taken in the various ways, and human sacrifice began. With this also came the first egress of peoples to that of Pyrenees first, of which later we find that peoples who enter into the black or mixed peoples, in what later became the Egyptian dynasty.

We also find that entering into the Og, or those peoples that later became the beginning of the Inca, or Ohlum, that builded the walls across the mountains in this period, through those same usages of that as had been taken on by those peoples; and with the same, those that made for that in the other land, became first those of the mound dwellers, or peoples in that land. In the one [life], then, before this we find [the entity] in that land known as the Peruvian, and when there was the end of the Ohums and their rule over the land. The entity [was] then among those of the first people who brought in the sun worship to that land.[12]

He goes on: "The entity was among those that came from the Atlantean lands and gave the peoples much of the impulse of the added forces in a practical building up of the material things of life, as pertaining to court hangings, ritualistic forces, even to that of the offering of human sacrifice, for the entity was the first high priestess to the sun of that land, making the first human sacrifice in that period."[13]

Cayce's description of the Atlanteans as worshippers of a sun god is also found in the writings of a sixth-century BC Greek mythologist. Hesiod wrote that a previous civilization he referred to as an *oikumene* (from which our word *ecumenical* derives) established itself worldwide. It flourished in an age of gold, but the gold Hesiod mentioned was the gold of the sun, which was adored as a god. Like all religions, this solar cult had its esoteric and exoteric aspects. Though the uneducated masses believed the star around which our planet revolves was quite literally God himself, initiates into the solar mysteries understood that the sun was a metaphor for spiritual principles of enlightenment.

Yet the suggestion of human sacrifice adds an unsettling factor: "The one life before this we find in that land now known as the Peruvian, and the entity was then among those who—as a high priestess—led a people into a northern land now known as Yucatán, and the entity was the priestess in the temple as builded there. . . . In this experience the entity was rather the sun worshipper and the taker of blood."[14] There is no evidence, either in the Cayce readings or from more conventional sources, for human sacrifice in Atlantis itself. The practice was doubtless common enough among Native Americans long before the Atlanteans arrived. Though it reached monstrous proportions under the Aztecs, who degenerated into cannibalism, human sacrifice was far less prevalent among the Andean civilizations, especially under the Incas. They appear to have employed it on relatively rare occasions.

Prescott tells of an infrequent ceremony in which the most beautiful girl and boy were chosen from among all the children of the community, dressed in the finest clothes and precious ornaments, and paraded in public on raised thrones with great pomp and honor. Afterward, they were given a powerful narcotic, then they were ritually killed while deep in sleep, usually by a single blow to the head. In recent years, the preserved remains of Inca and possibly pre-Inca children or young adults have been found on the cold, dry mountaintops of the Andes, where they were deliberately exposed to death surrounded by rich offerings. The motives behind these human sacrifices, and those occurring in Mesoamerica are entirely different. The Incas offered to God the most precious things they knew—their loveliest children.

So too, the Aztec aristocrats employed the spectacle of ritualized human sacrifice—to overawe the Indian masses, to terrorize them into submission and obedience. The cosmic consequences of such unbalanced behavior, Cayce said—and the Maya would have concurred—were the precipitous downfall of pre-Columbian civilization and the virtual extermination of its peoples.

EDGAR CAYCE'S
ATLANTEANS AND
LEMURIANS

Historians and archaeologists can tell us much about Atlantis and Lemuria—the appearance of their temples and palaces, their wars, colonies, and final destruction—but what about the people, the individuals, great and small, who were part of this tremendous drama? They seem utterly lost to even the best scholars bent on resuscitating the vanished civilization.

Only Edgar Cayce restored them in the life readings of those who came to him for help with spiritual, personal, and emotional problems. He was able to show many of his clients that the roots of their difficulties lay in the deeply ancient past, among energies reverberating down through subsequent incarnations from Atlantean times. As such, his readings were in the nature of therapy, not history.

Yet in tracing these unsuspected influences from a former time so long ago, Cayce often described his clients in their lives as men and women of Atlantis and Lemuria. He thereby shed an absolutely unique light on the inhabitants—frequently the movers and shakers of society—who shared a great and terrible destiny. Nowhere else in all the twenty thousand books and magazine articles written about these lost worlds may we learn so much about the individual human beings who lived and died there or fled their violent demise as survivors in foreign lands, contributing thereafter not only to their own, subsequent incarnations, but also to the development of all humankind. In these personalized life readings, Edgar Cayce appears to fulfill the words of Roman emperor Claudius, in AD 54: "The men and women who laid the foundations of this world are gone, but their voices echo in the words of our great interpreters of the past."[1]

The following names Cayce recalled are heavily weighted toward Atlantis—because he described or mentioned far fewer Lemurians than Atlanteans, perhaps due to the more serious karmic consequences that he said were generated by the Atlanteans, which, more than historical concerns, interested him. Originally, the inhabitants of Atlantis, as both Cayce and Plato concur, were a virtuous people who developed several spiritual disciplines, and whose principles influenced the development of religions throughout the world, down to the present time.

The Atlanteans, however, eventually succumbed to the lure of self-indulgence and largely turned away from the gods. A reaction against this decline arose in the monotheist followers of the Law of One, who were opposed by the satanic Sons of Belial. In the midst of their confrontation, Atlantis suffered the sudden catastrophe that utterly destroyed the land. Individual decisions and actions produced by this drama resulted in effects reverberating down the millennia through numerous lifetimes.

The Lemurians had fewer soul-complexities to work out. They did not undergo the internal stress of religious turmoil, and the loss of their homeland was less traumatic. Their society did not decline and degenerate, because it was not progressive. Atlantis was an advancing, technological state cut in the style of modern Western civilization and therefore caught in the inescapable cycle of growth, strength, prosperity, stagnation, decline, degeneration, and extinction. The Lemurians were not bound by this cycle. They cared far less for material wealth or indefinite progress. Their chief focus as a religious society (similar to today's Tibetans) was spiritual enrichment. The gentler demise of their islands seemed less a cataclysmic judgment than a catalyst for the disbursement of their piety to other parts of Earth. As such, the Lemurians incurred less karmic debt, resulting in fewer confused souls for Cayce to heal.

The selected life readings that follow illuminate characters who played their roles in the separate but parallel dramas of the deep past. They likewise help to validate Cayce's vision through the myths and traditions of other peoples impacted by the Atlanteans and Lemurians. In calling upon these outside sources, that vision is brought into clearer focus through the otherwise forgotten men and women whose destiny contributed to our own.

A

Aahuen   An Atlantean religious scientist, he was "persuaded" by political leaders to assist in the misuse of spiritual energies for material purposes. The experiment was unsuccessful, culminating in the obliteration of Atlantis.

Aa-rr-ll-uu   An inhabitant of Poseidia, the western outpost of Atlantean civilization in the Caribbean, he lived at a time of intense foreign migrations and worked as an esoteric chemist (alchemist), who was not above abusing his powers at the expense of his clients. His name is very similar to a term used for a great, ancestral island described in a Babylonian account of the world flood.

In Babylonian tradition (circa 2100 BC), Arallu was a great, mountainous island in the Distant West, a kind of paradise where freshwater springs and a year-round temperate climate were enjoyed by the spiritually enlightened inhabitants. Arallu was the Babylonian version of Atlantis.

Aalu is ancient Egyptian for the Isle of Flame, descriptive of a large, volcanic island in the sea of the Distant West (the Atlantic Ocean), which physically matches Plato's Atlantis virtually detail for detail: mountainous, with canals and luxuriant crops and a palatial city surrounded by great walls decorated with precious metals, and so forth. Aalu's earliest known reference appears in *The Destruction of Mankind,* a New Kingdom history (1299 BC) discovered in the tomb of Pharaoh Seti-I, at Abydos, site of the Osireion, a subterranean monument to the great flood that destroyed a former age of greatness and described in the account. On the other side of the world from Egypt, the Apache Indians of the American Southwest claim their ancestors arrived after the great flood destroyed their homeland, still remembered as the Isle of Flame, in the ocean of the *east*.

The Hurrians were a people who occupied Anatolia (Turkey, in ancient times) from the early third millennium BC. Many of their religious and mythic concepts were absorbed by their Hittite conquerors, beginning after 2000 BC. Among these traditions was the story of Alalu, the first king of heaven, a giant god, who made his home on a mountainous island in the sea of the setting sun. His son, Kumarbi, was synonymous with the Greek Kronos, a mythic personification of the Atlantic Ocean through Roman times.

Ahajah   An important culture bearer from Atlantis, he landed in the Atlantean kingdom of Elasippos (modern Portugal) and traveled through Gadeiros (Spain), eventually settling in the Pyrenees Mountains. A virtuous diplomat, Ahajah did much to establish early civilization and the high-minded tenets of religion on the Iberian Peninsula through friendly collaboration with the natives. His legacy is associated with accounts of the Holy Grail, allegedly headquartered at a castle (Monsalvat) in the Pyrenees.

Ahasus   A princess who lived at a time of social unrest and geologic upheaval in Atlantis, she used her talent as a skilled practitioner in the Law of One mystery cult to pacify conditions through music. She and her fellow initiates believed the power of harmonics could bring an accord between humans and their environment. Her efforts were successful, and she presided over a period of spiritual and material greatness. Her philosophy of music was undoubtedly carried by Atlanteans to Greece, where precisely these same principles were expounded by later philosophers, particularly Plato and Aristotle.

Aian   An administrator at the Temple of the Sun, the most important solar powerhouse in Atlantis, who saved many lives through his personal and brave initiative during the final destruction. He escaped with them and other survivors to Egypt, where he was an early worker in the Temple of Sacrifice and the Temple of Beauty.

Ajax-ol   A statesman-historian who escaped the destruction of Atlantis and settled in Egypt, where he achieved even greater authority and helped direct the creation of the New Race, the wholesale intermarriage of Atlantean refugees with native Egyptians. Ajax-ol also supervised the placement of specially selected documents from lost Atlantis into a house of records that he commissioned and built near the Great Pyramid, which he likewise contributed to in a lesser way.

Ajxor   An Atlantean admiral, he successfully navigated his fleet from the catastrophe to the open sea, eastward across the Mediterranean, and finally to Lower Egypt. In his charge were some of the leading historians and statesmen of Atlantis, who became important culture bearers in the new land. Ajxor helped to develop Egyptian riverways for commerce, even exploring undiscovered reaches of the Nile, where he opened trade relations with new peoples, such as the Nubians. (See Istulo, on page 192).

Alpth   An extraordinary linguist, he was a translator who accompanied the leading Atlantean statesmen in Egypt during their culture-bearing mission through the Nile Valley. In time, he changed his name to its Egyptian equivalent, Ob-thet.

Alta   An Atlantean masculine name, it means "new life" and is associated partially with the eastern littorals of Florida. In 1993, the *Atlantis Organization* (Buena Park, California) launched Project Alta, a sonar investigation in the vicinity of the underwater Bimini Wall, believed by some researchers to be a remnant of Atlantean civilization.

Amaicaca   Remembered by the Carib Indians of Venezuela as a deluge hero who escaped some natural catastrophe in "a big canoe," which settled at the top of Mount Tamancu after the flood waters receded. Amaicaca resembles Edgar Cayce's Amaiur (see below) and the Colombian Amuraca. Scholars now believe it was from the native Amaicaca or Amuraca, not the first name of an Italian mapmaker (Amerigo Vespucchi), that the newly discovered continent of America actually derived its name.

Amaiur   The legendary first king of the Basque, he is equated in biblical parallels with Tubalcain, a grandson of Noah, the flood hero in Genesis. His name means Monarch of Maya, a kingdom referred to as the Green Isle, sunken in the Atlantic Ocean. In Greek myth, Maya was one of the seven Pleiades, daughters of the goddess Pleione and the Titan Atlas, and hence an Atlantis. See his resemblance to the Carib **Amaicaca** (above).

Amaki   A city in Poseidia, the Atlantean kingdom of the Caribbean, center for fire worship, a cult that spread into North America, at least as far as southern Wisconsin, where the remains of several pyramidal sites still survive.

Ambeno   This life reading describes the materially advanced state of Atlantean society in its last days, when its people were obsessed with the gimmickry and luxury afforded by technology. Ambeno was a princess who lived near

> . . . the great crystals that so condensed the lights (of the sun, moon and stars) . . . as to guide not only the ship upon the bosom of the sea but in the air and in many of those now known in the transmission of the voice, as in the recording of those activities . . . for television, as it is termed in the present." As a supporter of the Law of One, Ambeno believed in class collaboration, and rejected the "self-indulgences" of her time.[2]

Am-ee-lee   A high-ranking librarian, he lived in Atlantis during a period of serious civil disorder between adherents of the Law of One and the followers of Belial. Afraid the conflict would escalate to undermine civilization, Am-ee-lee organized and dispatched several missions to transfer vital religious, scientific, and historic records for safekeeping in other parts of the world, especially Egypt. He migrated to a retreat in the Pyrenees Mountains, but died frustrated because he never knew if his emissaries ever reached the Nile Valley with their precious documents.

Amia-ieou-lieb   A most important person (or would have been), and the last prince of the royal house, the successor to the throne, he was killed in the catastrophe that destroyed Atlantis.

Amiee   A queen of Poseidia, the Caribbean outpost of Atlantis, and infamous throughout the empire for her iron-heeled rule, which resulted in predictable civil unrest.

Amielee   Today's equivalent of a labor organizer, he was also a skilled agriculturist. Perhaps because of his success as a mediator among the working classes, Amielee was ordered to the Atlantean kingdom of Azaes (Yucatán), where his work in instituting garden-bed production of local crops survived him by many centuries in the farming policies of the Maya. In later life, he achieved a position of high authority, which he used with benevolence in establishing the religious principles of the Laws of One. These likewise carried over, at least partially, into subsequent Middle American belief systems.

Aneecl   Ruler of the Gate of Gold, a city in Poseidia, the Caribbean kingdom of Atlantis, whose application of the "nightside" of natural forces led to excesses of materialism, with subsequent cataclysmic results.

Aoun   The first man to cross the Atlantic Ocean (from Atlantis to Yucatán) in an aircraft. Thanks to the new technology of manned flight, Aoun traveled far beyond Mexico to Mongolia and Southeast Asia.

Apex-el   Sailing with his colleagues from the destruction of Atlantis, this scholar made for Egypt, but was blown far off course to land on the French coast. There they tried "to create a temple activity for the followers of the Law of One."[3] Though unsuccessful, they left "marks" (inscriptions?), which survived at least until 1934, in the chalk cliffs of Calais. After prolonged travels in France and Iberia, Apex-el and his followers finally arrived at the Nile Delta, where they found a new home among the large colony of surviving Atlanteans.

He subsequently played a seminal role in the rebirth of civilization by establishing a library in Lower Egypt that, over the course of centuries, grew to become the Great Library of Alexandria. Many documents pertaining to Atlantis were stored among its more than one million volumes, until they and the rest of this vast body of knowledge were lost when the Great Library was burned by a Christian mob in the fifth century. Had this catastrophe been avoided, we would have far more than the fragmentary accounts of Plato and Edgar Cayce to tell us about the civilization of Atlantis.

Apsa-Elarz   An Atlantean born in Egypt, he collected folk music of the various peoples who had settled along the Nile and served as a choral director in the Temples of Sacrifice and Beauty, where the power of sound (applied acoustics) was employed for physical healing and spiritual advancement.

Aptheno   While a young man in Atlantis, he abandoned himself to the excessive self-indulgence and crass materialism of Atlantis's final days. Although he survived the destruction, Aptheno utterly despaired for the loss of all his worldly goods. Only sometime after his arrival in Egypt with his fellow survivors did he begin gradually to undergo a process of personal enlightenment. His transformation came about through service in one of the early hospitals, where he eventually went into medical research and studied the use of sound in healing.

Arsth   A keeper of records in the Atlantean colony of Azaes (Yucatán), whose documents survived at least until 1944 and "may eventually be found again."[4]

At-o-tar-ho   In Iroquois myth, At-o-tar-ho was a female monster whose head was covered with writhing snakes instead of hair. This figure is known in the Western world as Medusa, appearing in Greek myth as one of the Pleiades—a child of the sea goddess Pleione, and a daughter of Atlas, an Atlantean.

The Iroquois preformative, At- in At-o-tar-h, implies the same Atlantean connection.

Asa-masa-me No longer a young woman, but still an active priestess in the Law of One religion, she escaped the destruction of Atlantis and sailed in company with many other survivors to the Nile Delta. She arrived in ill health, but recuperated enough to participate in the preservation of essential documents for the reconstruction of civilization in Egypt. Her task was mainly the translation of original Atlantean documents into Egyptian records. "These may be found," Cayce said, "especially when the house or tomb of records is opened, in a few years from now."[5]

Asme She was an Atlantean geneticist who, with her colleagues, conducted experiments on behalf of human physical perfection: outward beauty, and an accelerated internal capacity of the body to heal itself.

Asphar He was among the technicians who preserved the scientific knowledge of metallurgy from the destruction of Atlantis by resettling in the Nile Valley. Asphar used electroplating when working with precious metals and assisted in the electrical combination of copper, zinc, and tin for the production of bronze, so important in the ancient world. He also serviced a scalpel that generated coagulating energies for bloodless surgery in medical operations.

The electroplating techniques employed by Asphar found possible validation in the so-called Baghdad Battery recovered from an Iraqi archaeological dig and subsequently dated to Persia in the second century BC. Using citrus juice as an acid, it generated enough power to electroplate a statuette. Thirty years after Cayce described the Atlanteans' "electrical knife," just such a surgical tool was invented (reinvented?) by medical researchers in the United States.

Atso (or Gyatso) Tibetan for "ocean" and associated with the most important spiritual position in Bon Buddhism, the Dalai Lama. The Mongolian word for ocean is *dalai*, a derivative of the Sanskrit *atl* for "upholder," and is found throughout every Indo-European language for "sea" or "valley in the water" (as that created by high waves): the Sumerian

Thallath, the Greek *thallasa,* the German *Tal,* the English *dale,* and so forth. The term *dalai,* according to Tenzin Gyatso, the fourteenth Dalai Lama of Tibet, stems from the Tibetan word for "ocean" that forms his name. Although Dalai Lama has sometimes been translated as Ocean of Compassion or Wisdom, it really means Wise Man (Guru) of (or from) the Ocean, a title that appears to have originated with the pre-Buddhist Bon religion, which was partially absorbed by the creed introduced from India in the eighth century.

Atlantologists have speculated since the late 1800s that the history and religious tenets of Atlantis are still preserved in some of Tibet's secret libraries or even encoded in the very ritual fabric of Tibetan religion itself, although these suspicions have never been verified by documented evidence. Other investigators discern traces of the Lemurian mystery cults in Bon Buddhism, particularly the central importance placed on the doctrine of reincarnation. Tibetan sand mandalas designed to portray the celestial city, with its concentric layout of alternating rings of land and water, are powerfully reminiscent of Plato's sunken capital, even to the sacred numerals and elephants of Atlantis. These considerations seem underscored by Atlantean influences in the high-holy terminology of Tibetan just discussed: *gyatso, dalai,* and so forth.

Edgar Cayce spoke of an unnamed person from the land now known as Tibet who visited Atlantis at a time when Atlantean teachings were being disseminated. Perhaps this refers to the early spread of spiritual concepts to Tibet from Atlantis and accounts for the Tibetan Wise Man from the Ocean. In other life readings, Cayce mentions a correlation between Atlantean thought and Mongolian theology.

Ax-Tell   His name is mentioned more often than any other in the Cayce Atlantis readings. Ax-Tell's importance stems primarily from the large personal following he won in Atlantis and took with him into Egypt. He also preserved "those records of the Atlanteans as to the abilities for the use of the unseen forces."[6]

Ax-tent-na   Traveling from Atlantis to the Lower Nile Valley, he "was the first to set the records that are yet to be discovered or yet to be had of those activities in the Atlantean land . . . from the chambers of the way between the Sphinx and the pyramid of record [i.e., the Great Pyramid at Giza]."[7]

Ax-Tos   Not all the Atlanteans described by Cayce were great or powerful. Ax-Tos was a humble physician who administered to working-class patients during the imperial period of Atlantis, when the empire was aggressively spreading its control and influence over much of the world. He was also a priest of the Law of One (healers were invariably spiritual practioners, as well), who argued against the materialist Sons of Belial, then in control of society.

Ax-Tutem   A great leader among Atlantean energy technicians, he furthered the peaceful application of natural forces for private residences and public buildings, including heating and motive power. Although Cayce compares them to electricity, the precise nature of those forces is not disclosed.

B

Boob   As the early Atlanteans began to broaden their civilization to other lands, according to Cayce, they were confronted by masses of powerful and dangerous animals that threatened their expansion. Interestingly, the Aztecs had a similar tradition, known as Ocelatihu, wherein human beings took up counsel for a kind of war with these beasts for world domination. Cayce describes Boob as one of the counsel members, second in authority, who helped organize the successful defense of humankind against the rampaging animals.

Bus-Lu   The regent of Sus, an Atlantean city, where his obsession for the "misapplication of the truths"[8] found in science reduced him to becoming a narrow-minded technocrat.

C

Caphala   She was a companion to the leader of refugees from Atlantis during the city's early geologic troubles. Caphala arrived as a youngster in Peru and was so taken with the country's mountainous scenery, native ceremonial life, and abundance of gold that these impressions, according to Cayce, continued to resurface in subsequent lives, to her twentieth-century incarnation.

Checho   Even after the Sons of Belial succeeded in destroying Atlantis, they tried to reassert themselves throughout Egypt, the new Atlantean homeland. Among them was a refugee priestess who attempted to regain her former power by causing disturbances in the Nile Valley, but Checho failed because the Children of the Law of One now exercised supreme power through the Temple of Sacrifice, the religious and temporal administrative authority in Egypt.

Chi-Eloir   "Among the first of the off-spring of the Atlanteans in the Egyptian land,"[9] she grew up at a time when survivors from the Atlantis catastrophe were still arriving in the Nile Valley. Chi-Eloir was a dancer in the Temple Beautiful. But her performances would bear no resemblance to anything known in the West today, because all the arts, including dance, were strictly regulated by laws laid down according to a leading principle that all aesthetic expression was sacred.

Hence, Chi-Eloir's dances in the Temple Beautiful were regarded as spiritual experiences. About the only modern comparison may be found in the so-called Whirling Dervishes of Sufism, wherein the dancers, dedicating their revolving steps to Allah, enter altered states of consciousness in order to approach the divine. This originally Atlantean concept survived at least into classical Greek times, when the sacred or Apollonian dance was clearly distinguished from mundane or profane dances in the spirit of Dionysus.

D

Diu   One of the many simple peasants on the island of Atlantis, noted for his brotherly love expressed in the storing of food for less fortunate individuals. Interestingly, the name appears related to later developments in Greek and Latin (both at least impacted by Atlantean speech) for Deus and Deo, or God. Thirteen years later, Cayce spoke of another Atlantean, a recorder of messages, named Deui. Ignatius Donnelly, the founder of modern Atlantology, concluded in the nineteenth century that "the words we use every day were heard, in their primitive form, in their [the Atlanteans'] cities, courts and temples."[10]

Duo-She-Dui This name is chiefly interesting because it is one of the few instances where Cayce provided a direct translation from the original Atlantean into English. Duo-She-Dui means the "*duo* teaching," or the "dual life as one," and refers to the activities of a refugee in Egypt's Temple Beautiful, where he trained ministers from various lands in the tenets of both native and Atlantean theologies. As such, it appears to be more a title than a given name, and demonstrates how at least some Atlantean words have survived into modern English: our "dual" from the Atlantean *duo*. This appears to have been a convention invented by the civilizing Atlanteans to integrate their modes of thought with native beliefs still current in the Nile Valley. The eventual result was dynastic civilization, a harmonious synthesis of the two cultures.

This was Cayce's vision of pharaonic origins, and it is in perfect accord with both Egyptian myth and modern archaeology: the former recounted that seafaring foreigners (the Mesentiu Harpooners) arrived from the west to create the first dynasties; the latter, personified by the greatest specialist of the Archaic Period, W. B. Emery, claims evidence for the appearance of a master race that transformed the Nile Valley from a Late Stone Age conglomeration of loosely related agriculturists into a full-fledged civilization virtually over night.[11]

E

Ececo An early chemist, he was one of the investigators who helped develop the civilian use of explosives, a knowledge that would be lost with the destruction of Atlantis.

Donnelly also concluded that explosives were invented in Atlantis: "Having traced the knowledge of gunpowder back to the most remote times, we are not surprised to find in the legends of Greek mythology events described which are only explicable in supposing that the Atlanteans possessed the secret of this powerful explosive."[12]

Eesmes   Among the first generation of Atlanteans born in Egypt, her abilities as a writer (or, more probably, a scribe) served Eesmes well as a group organizer. The name has an anciently authentic ring, and may be a variation of Esses (better known by her Greek impersonation, Isis) or, more appropriately, Sheshat, the Egyptian Mistress of the House of Books, the divine inventor of writing and heavenly record-keeper.[13]

Elam   He was a worker who assisted in the operations of "the crystal, the mighty, the terrible crystal."[14] In his reading, we get a glimpse of Atlantean crystalline technology, which was superior to ours in at least a few respects. Cayce did, in fact, say that the Atlanteans "reached even a higher state of application of material things (hence called civilization) than even in the present day."[15] As such, Elam and his colleagues were busy "photographing from a distance;" they possessed "the ability for reading inscriptions through walls, even at a distance," and were capable of "overcoming of (termed today) the forces of nature or gravity itself (levitation?)."[16]

Elam is also the biblical name given to an important civilization in southwestern Iran, approximately equivalent in area to modern Khuzistan. Almost as old as Sumer, the first known civilization in Mesopotamia's Fertile Crescent (beginning about 3500 BC), Elam was a major, although distinct, Mesopotamian state that flourished as late as the Persian empire, where it formed a satrapy (or province) under King Darius I, after more than 2,000 years of existence. Given its profoundly ancient origins, Elam may have derived from the name of an Atlantean culture bearer or that of a refugee family from Atlantis.

Elam's Lemurian provenance is made clear in the Native American oral traditions of California's Washo Indians. Their flood story tells of a terrible natural catastrophe that engulfed a huge and magnificent kingdom whose leaders escaped over the sea to North America. Before its inundation, the ancestral island, known as Elam, was home to a primarily agricultural people, who called their chief deity Mu.

Elchi   An Atlantean navigator, his name is an intriguing parallel to the very ancient town of Elche, in southeastern Spain, on the Rio Vinalopo.

It was here that a polychrome stone statue known as La Dama de Elche (the Lady of Elche) was found during a nearby archaeological dig in 1897. Stylistically, the statue resembles nothing else of its kind but has suggested Atlantean provenance to many researchers, including the leading archaeologist in Spain during the 1920s, Elena Maria Whishaw.[17] Her conclusion is underscored by the statue's place of discovery in Alicante province, described 24 centuries ago by the Greek philosopher Plato as the location for a kingdom of Atlantis in Spain (Gadeiros, from which the modern Spanish city of Cadiz derives its name).

The name of the town appears to have remained phonetically unchanged over time, going back to the Arab Elix and the Roman Ilici, itself a derivation of a Phoenician version taken directly from the Atlantean.

Elem   A prince in the royal house of Atlantis, a son of the Most High, but he panicked "when the destructive forces came,"[18] and tried to save himself rather than help others, as his duty demanded.

Elie   "Worshiped by the peoples of a portion of the land," she was a famous if egotistical musician in the temple at Poseidia, where "sounds of all natures were produced upon the instruments of the day."[19]

The post-Atlantean, pre-Roman Etruscans were known to mount full-fledged orchestral performances, which appear to have been part of their legacy from Atlantis, where elaborate, large-scale musical ensembles, like those suggested in this life reading, were often heard.

Ellisy   A beautiful, manipulative priestess, who, against her will, was forced to leave Atlantis due to serious religious upheavals taking place in her homeland prior to its geologic destruction. Arriving in Yucatán, Ellisy moved on to Peru, charming her way to wealth as she went, leaving a swath of discontent behind her in the process.

Ellm   He "was among those in the temple worship of the period" who "were afterwards worshiped by the people." Here we learn that after their deaths, mortal human beings—if they had been particularly virtuous—were sometimes elevated as revered deities in Atlantis, perhaps equivalent to today's postmortem status of sainthood bestowed by the Catholic church on its most devout followers.[20]

Elmeur   The son of Atlantean ruler Ajax, at a very early period in the history of Atlantis, when the Law of One cult was just coming into being. His name appears to be a phonetic variant of Evenor, described by Plato as the first king of Atlantis.

Emesersea   A Law of One high priestess, she intuited the final, most violent destruction of the Atlantean lands, but, loving her homeland deeply, she was reluctant to leave it just because of a frightening premonition. "It was with foreboding, and with doubts and fears, that the entity almost by force was carried first into the Pyrenees land—or Spain and Portugal."[21] Emesersea finally settled in the Nile Valley, where her instinctive ability served in the early rebuilding of civilization.

Exina   She was the wife of Axel, an Atlantean ruler, who accompanied her husband to Egypt. There she personally engaged in the melding of the Law of One tenets with native beliefs in the Near East, particularly Assyria. Exina appears to have been memorialized and even deified in this part of the world as the very early Mesopotamian grain goddess Exinu.

H

Huloi   An Indian chieftain's daughter who lived and traveled around the American Midwest, from what is now Chicago to Terre Haute and Dearborn. Cayce describes the Iroquois as "the pure descendants of the Atlanteans." According to him, Huloi means "running water."[22]

Hy-Poc-Rax-El   Emery notes the sudden emergence of medical technology in the Nile Valley at the outset of dynastic civilization, during the late fourth millennium BC, while Cayce mentions the migration of a medical practitioner, Hy-Poc-Rax-El, from his Atlantean homeland to Egypt, where he was "very close to the one who headed the department of hospitalization (as would today be called), or the department of healing arts, or the application of the influences of nature into man himself."[23]

Cayce describes early Atlantean medical practices as surprisingly modern and holistic: "The study was then, as it should be now—that man is a part of that which was made—all that was made, and took upon himself a manifested part of same—through the mental expression that became crystallized in material forces. Hence, in the natural forces about man, added with the mental and the spiritual, there is that which will bring the connecting of man's relationship to his material environment."[24]

I

Iel   An Atlantean immigrant in Egypt, Iel taught "the art of weaving and making of heavier than the linens in the land but the coarser and heavier and finer arts of not only the decorations of the body but the weaving of the materials and the styles that took on the representation of the various stations in life."[25] In other words, a person's rank or status was indicated by the cut of his or her clothes.

The loom was an innovation, together with every aspect of pharaonic society, appearing suddenly and fully developed in the Nile Delta around 3100 BC.

Ilax   After immigrating from Atlantis, Ilax became "the princess of fire" in rituals of the Law of One cult. She was the mistress of shamanistic ecstasies, wherein her altered states of consciousness were meant to establish communication with the spirit world. Her renowned transformations contributed to the mystery cults later instituted by Isis, Ra, and Hermes, but after achieving substantial influence and prestige, Ilax mistakenly sided with the wrong faction in a native rebellion and lost all her political power. She subsequently devoted herself to the performance of menial tasks in active service to the Law of One cult.

Iltar   With just ten followers, this member of the household of Atlan and follower of the Law of One cult left Atlantis to settle on the shores of Yucatán. Several temples were built there, but they were destroyed during the almost worldwide geologic upheavals that destroyed his forsaken Atlantean homeland. He survived these natural turmoils to rebuild many new sacred structures, which profoundly influenced the development of Mesoamerican architecture. Cayce predicted that "the temple of Iltar will then rise again."[26]

Cayce also said in this reading that "Those in Yucatán, those in the adjoining lands as begun by Iltar, gradually lost in their activities; and came to be that people termed, in other portions of America, the mound builders."[27]

Ishod   An Atlantean metalsmith and forger of weapons, including chariots. He also worked in more decorative silver and gold.

In Plato's description of Atlantis, he characterizes its chief industry as metallurgy and its craftsmen as busy in the production of military bronzes, as well as the manufacture of luxury items in more precious metals, with which they even bedecked the walls of their public and sacred buildings.

Ishuma   During the second series of major geologic upheavals that afflicted Atlantis, Ishuma was a low-ranking, albeit ambitious priestess in the Temple of Light, and she belonged to the Law of One cult. Advancement through the religious hierarchy was obstructed by her superiors, particularly the elders, who unsuccessfully sought her dismissal. They were scandalized by Ishuma's giving birth to "seventeen sons by seven different men."[28]

Not even powerful cult leaders were able to force her removal from the prestigious Temple of Light, some indication, perhaps, of the moral freedom that prevailed in Atlantean society, at least during its middle period. Similarly, the Law of One elders identify themselves here as less open-minded.

Istulo   An Atlantean immigrant in Egypt, where she was a "healing assistant" (nurse) specializing in the care of children. Nevertheless, Istulo somehow fell afoul of her superiors—so much so that she was forced to leave Egypt. She resettled in Abyssinia and there tried to continue her practice among the native young people, but she was so intoxicated by the local culture that her scientific medical practices gradually degenerated into "the rhythm of incantations"[29] and primitive superstitions. Like Kurz in Joseph Conrad's novel *Heart of Darkness,* instead of converting the savage to civilization, Istulo was herself made savage.

Her reading is additionally interesting, because it shows that Atlantean impact reached even as far as East Africa. A remnant of this influence appears to have survived as late as the fifth century BC, when Nubia (modern Sudan, incorporating much of present East Africa) was ruled by an Atlanersa, meaning "prince or royal descendant (*ersa*) of Atlan."

M

Mayr   She was an Atlantean priestess who resettled in Egypt, where she became an emissary to lands as far away as the Indian and Pacific Oceans.

Meg   "Before the second of the upheavals," this priestess "interpreted the messages that were received through the crystals and the fires that were to the eternal fires of nature (natural energies)."[30] In Meg's time, there were "new developments in air, in water travel . . . these were the beginning of the developments at that period for the escape."[31] Although the first examples of this evacuation technology were becoming available, "when the destructions came, the entity chose rather to stay with the groups than to flee to other lands."[32]

In ancient British myth, Meg was a giantess able to throw huge boulders over great distances. Her memory still survives in the Royal Navy, where battleship guns are referred to as Mons Megs, from Long Meg. It is not inconceivable that Cayce's Meg and the Atlantean cataclysm were transmuted over time into the British Meg, which seems to describe an erupting volcano ejecting its lava bomb.

Mu-Elden   A woman survivor from the destruction of Atlantis who immigrated to the Nile Valley, where she assisted in the Temple of Sacrifice and the Temple Beautiful. Her name indicates Lemurian origins.

Mufuti   Enigmatically described by Cayce as "an Atlantean and a Lemurian in purpose."[33]

Muglo   This female spiritual advisor in Atlantis with a decidedly Lemurian name indicates Pacific impact on the Atlantic civilization.

O

Ogriae   A princess at a time when Atlantis was reaching the zenith of its greatness, she "kept away from those of the opposite sex, for the love was given in one of low estate and could not bring self to the conditions necessary for the consummation of the desires in each other's inner self."[34] Doubtless, those "conditions" would have entailed Ogriae's renunciation of her high place in the royal family.

Her name belongs to a theme often describing aspects of the Atlantis phenomenon surviving among some of the cultures influenced by the lost civilization. Appropriately, names comprising or deriving from Og are associated in ancient Irish and biblical contexts with some world-class deluge, such as the former's Tir-nan-Og, a kingdom beneath the sea, and the Hebrew Scriptures' Og, who, in Genesis, was a giant hitching a ride on Noah's Ark. After a terrible flood destroyed their homeland, Ogllo (alternate spelling, Ocllo), together with her husband, Manco Capac, arrived in South America, on the shores of Lake Titicaca, Bolivia, to found Andean civilization, according to the Inca's story of creation.

In Greek myth, Ogyges was the son of Poseidon (the sea god) and the first king of Greece, who reigned during a great flood. Homer wrote of Ogygia, a mid-Atlantic island where Calypso was the high priestess of a magic cult that turned men into servile beasts, not unlike the genetically engineered "Things" Cayce said made up the unfortunate laboring classes of Atlantis. He described a genetically engineered subclass deliberately modified by the Atlanteans to serve as human beasts of manual labor.

In Cayce's life readings, Og is one of the three principle islands belonging to Atlantis at the time of its final destruction.

P

Pfstxie   She was the priestess of a sun-worshiping cult in what is now the Ohio Valley, where hundreds of ancient earth mounds may still be found. Cayce said these mounds "were called the replica or representative of the Yucatán experiences, as well as the Atlantean. . . . All of these are as one consciousness in the entity's activity."[35]

Archaeologists agree with Cayce that the prehistoric Mound Builders probably worshipped in a cult of the sun god, judging from important solar alignments, particularly orientations to the solstices, originally built into many of the structures. Diffusionist scholars point to abundant evidence that connects the Mississippian period of pyramidal mound building throughout the Midwest and much of the South to close parallels in Yucatán.

An earlier phase of mound building, known as the Adena, spread from the Atlantic seaboard to Wisconsin after the final destruction of Atlantis, about 3,000 years ago. Although most of North America's prehistoric mounds were not tombs, all of them were undoubtedly sacred. Surviving Native American tradition depicts some of the earthworks as "schools" for students of shamanism. Most mounds appear to have been raised in communal efforts under the direction of these holy men and women (like Pfstxie), as concentrations of telluric or Earth energies. Hence, the creation of sacred sites where tribal members sought spiritual power.

Cayce suggests that these structures were Atlantean in the sense that the mounds ritually duplicated Mount Atlas, the holy mountain from which the city, Atlantis, the daughter of Atlas, derived her name. Plato informs us that Atlas was not a god but a semidivine being, a Titan, the son of a god—Poseidon—by a mortal woman—Kleito.

Pfstxie was a native priestess who perpetuated the Ohio Valley's sun-worshiping cult brought to North America before her time and memorialized in the Midwestern earthworks.

R

Rariru She was instrumental in blending newly arrived Atlanteans into prehistoric Peruvian society. She instituted "the worship of the sun and the solar forces,"[36] and took charge of every detail of the new "ritualistic forces," even those "pertaining to court hangings."[37] Rariru "was the first High Priestess to the Sun in the land, making the first human sacrifice in that period."[38]

Rariru adopted the name some time in the early stages of her priestly career, or she may have been simply born into the sun cult, given the solar significance of her name. Ra, of course, was the supreme Egyptian sun god, but he never demanded human sacrifices. On the other side of the world, on Easter Island, Ra was used in many mythic contexts with the deified sun. In Rariru's Peru, the Inti-Rai-mi was the Incas' most important ceremony (still performed today) on behalf of their sun god, who likewise received no human sacrifices.

Rhea In describing this high priestess of the Law of One, Cayce provides some indication of the high levels of spiritual enlightenment reached by the Atlanteans, especially with regard to progress they made in elevating the group mind. Rhea and her colleagues achieved "the concentration of thought for the use of the universal forces, through the guidance or direction of the saints (as would be termed today)."[39]

"There are few terms in the present that accurately describe their state of consciousness, save that through the concentration of the group mind of the Children of the Law of One, they entered into a higher, fourth-dimensional consciousness—or were absent from the body. This was a state of mind or soul wherein behavior equaled identity and thought equaled action. It was a level achieved in a "light" or "astral" body, separate from but connected to the physical body. Thus they were able to have that experience of crystallizing through the Light the speech from what might well be termed the saint realm, to impart understanding and knowledge to the group gathered."[40] Rhea became proficient as "the interpreter to the groups of the messages attained or gained from the periodical meetings with those from the universal realm, for instruction, for direction, for understanding in those periods of activity."[41]

It appears that progress in psychic development among the Atlanteans went beyond almost anything known since. In this respect, the difference between their time and ours is crucial, because modern Western society generally dismisses paranormal phenomena as useless superstition, invalid or nonscientific. In Atlantis, however, psychic research was universally acknowledged as not only authentic science, but the highest scientific endeavor. Consequently, modern Western humans can be thought of as spiritually vacuous and provincial materialists, while the Atlanteans touched the higher forces of Creation.

The ancient Greeks revered Rhea as the Great Mother Goddess, the Mother of the Gods, and the daughter of Gaia and Uranus (Mother Earth and Father Sky). It is this parentage that reflects Cayce's Rhea, whose psychic work was connecting the mundane Earth with the spiritual heaven. Her husband was Cronos, associated with the Atlantic Ocean. His fellow Titan Atlas assumed leadership of the war against the gods after Cronos resigned his foremost position. All this places Rhea in the Atlantic realm at a time defined by Plato as the war between Athens and Atlantis—the same conflict reflected in Greek myth.

Who, then, was the Rhea described by Cayce? Did she derive her name from a goddess worshipped first in Atlantis, then whose cult spread to Greece? Or perhaps the high priestess achieved such renown that she was remembered and eventually deified by the Greeks as one of their most important goddesses.

S

Saail He was a defrocked priest, punished because he used splendid temples belonging to the Law of One church as rendezvous sites for "sin." Turning to the Sons of Belial, Saail participated in active rebellion against his former faith.

What makes his reading of particular interest is Cayce's mention of "the mysteries of the black arts"[42] practiced by Belial cultists. We thus learn that the followers of the Law of One were opposed not simply by another spiritual doctrine, but by a sophisticated satanic movement with its own set of mysteries.

Sailuen   Traumatized by the overwhelming geologic cataclysm she experienced in the destruction of Atlantis, Sailuen's spirit would be troubled by inexplicable, inborn fears of earthquakes and panic—the intuitively felt recollections of her Atlantean sojourn—throughout successive incarnations.

Before the advent of these troubles, she tried to "prevent the activities of the peoples towards self-engorgement, or the taking on of self in the manner of worshiping self's abilities, rather than applying self as a channel or the motive through which universal forces might act."[43]

Here, Cayce acted as a psychiatrist, explaining for his client the root of her deep-seated but unreasonable fear of seismic and social upheavals. In view of his statement that numerous Atlantean souls are reincarnating into our time, we can wonder how many people today are suffering from the same inexplicable (to them) anxieties.

His description of Atlanteans just prior to their destruction as wallowing in the "engorgement" of vulgar materialism could just as well apply to modern Americans more interested in "worshiping self's abilities"[44] than becoming "the channel or the motive through which universal forces might act."[45] This last and wonderfully succinct characterization of the self's true function is at the core of all genuine spiritual attempts and is the central goal of meditation striven for by practioners of Tibetan Buddhism.

Segferd   He lived in Atlantis during its technological heyday as the modern equivalent of an electrical engineer. In this reading, Cayce gives us some insight into the applied science and kind of research known to the Atlanteans. Like us, they were able to transmit sounds, electricity, and "color" (movie projection, television?), but were similarly interested in the transmission of thoughts.

He described the Atlanteans as "well advanced in those things that are still being sought today—the very means and manners of turning the forces of nature into that channel as a servant for the mind of man."[46]

Segund   "Before the breaking up of the Atlantean land," he was "very close to those in authority" as "the keeper of the portals, as well as the messages that were received from the visitation of those from the outer spheres." Who or exactly what these visitors might have been is not made clear.[47]

Immediately prior to the worst outbreaks of seismic violence, Segund used his position as a "messenger . . . or the means through which transmissions of activities were set up,"[48] to organize evacuations to nearby Og (one of the Atlantean islands, it too would be later destroyed), Yucatán, the Pyrenees, Greece, and Egypt, and as far away as India, Southeast Asia, and Mongolia. The vast extent of these mass migrations is some measure of the Atlantean population, which must have been enormous.

She-Aba   Born in Egypt of Atlantean parents, she designed "the various characters of robes, the dress of the peoples of the various positions in the court, as well as in the fields of service," in the Temples of Sacrifice and Beauty.[49]

Shu-Su-Mu-Lu-r   Born of mixed Atlanto-Egyptian parentage, she appears to have been a propagandist "for the presenting of ways and manners in which the race might be changed."[50]

With their homeland utterly destroyed, many (most?) Atlanteans resettled in the Nile Valley, where they sought to create a new society by interbreeding with the natives. Shu-Su-Mu-Lu-r was one of the first members of this hybrid race. She must have been a positive example, because she was chosen to represent it and promote the ongoing process of miscegenation. Judging from the results (i.e., pharaonic civilization), the blended outcome was successful, perhaps in some measure because the indigenous Nilotic stock was probably related (at least distantly) to the Atlanteans, with whom Egypt had been in contact for centuries prior to their mass migrations.

Shu-Su-Mu-Lu-r's name reflects the purpose assigned her, Shu being the Egyptian Atlas.

Shu-Tu   After becoming a priestess in the Law of One, she was forced to leave Atlantis during the terrible geologic upheavals, which eventually sank her homeland beneath the sea.

Arriving in Yucatán, she learned that survivors from another, somewhat similar but earlier catastrophe settled in what is now southern California and New Mexico. These were refugees from the Pacific Ocean civilization of Mu, long familiar to the Atlanteans. Although temperamentally poles apart, the two peoples engaged in amiable spiritual dialogue, and visitors from Atlantis (mostly diplomats, scientists, and theologians) were not unknown in the Pacific.

The Lemurians were not as outgoing or aggressive and less frequently seen outside their spheres of influence, a notable exception being the queen of Mu's journey to Egypt for the Great Pyramid's consecration. These spheres expanded to include Asia and the Americas after the destruction.

Shu-Tu embarked on a long journey to find these lost Lemurians. Her quest was successful and she learned a great deal about the spiritual ideas that originated in Mu. These were then beginning to impact religious thought in India and Southeast Asia, where they would survive to varying degrees in Buddhism, particularly in Tibet, and Japanese Shintoism. She was fascinated by these new (to her) concepts, which, however different from what she knew from the Law of One, were still complementary to her Atlantean beliefs and even, in some instances, expanded upon them. Shu-Tu began "correlating the tenets" of the two belief systems.

It is this synthesis of Atlantean and Lemurian, together with local spirituality, which survives in the largely secret lodge traditions of the Hopi, Navajo, and other tribal peoples of the American Southwest.

Sonl   A living example of the familiar axiom that "absolute power corrupts absolutely," he "ruled with an unlimited power" over the sacred Atlantean city of Peos, much "to his soul's undoing."[51]

His tyranny nonetheless provides us with a glimpse of the authoritarian political system that governed Atlantis. In the hands of enlightened leaders, their great personal power went to good effect, raising civilization to heights of material and spiritual greatness never seen before or since. But when it surrendered to the abuses of Sonl, authority declined into self-destruction. That is the supreme lesson of Atlantis for our time and civilization.

Su-Er-To   A princess high in Atlantean aristocracy, she was also a gifted priestess in the Law of One. Su-Er-To fled for her life from the cataclysm that obliterated Atlantis, suddenly reduced to a mere refugee dependent upon the hospitality of foreigners. Emotionally disoriented, she had great difficulty adjusting to a new life in the Nile Valley, where her former greatness now counted for little.

Yet she had not lost "the ability to aid by the very high vibrations of the body itself,"[52] and Su-Er-To eventually regained her former self-confidence through healing others with the laying-on of her hands, a natural power that continued through her numerous incarnations into Edgar Cayce's twentieth-century client.[53]

Sululon   An aggressive leader of the Sons of Belial, his beliefs did not prevent him from indulging in a torrid affair with a female follower of the despised Law of One. They were lovers at a time when strife between the two cults was approaching its peak, and Sululon was forced to flee Atlantis under the accusation of traitor.

He landed on the shores of Yucatán, the first Atlantean to arrive there, and was welcomed as a god. Together with a few friends who accompanied him, they organized the willing populace into work crews for the creation of the first stone temples and palaces in America.

Sululon and his fellow Atlanteans established law and order; temporarily put an end to human sacrifice; and instituted agriculture, irrigation, astronomy, literature, the arts, metallurgy, medical care, and all the advantages of the distant home left behind forever.

Restless by nature, he decided to leave after a few years of civilizing the natives, who wept to see him and a few of his original companions go. (Some remained behind as chief administrators married to local women.) He tried to comfort them by saying that he would return some day. If not, then surely one of his descendants would come back to reclaim the kingdom he was leaving in their hands.

Sululon journeyed south into Bolivia and Peru, where he repeated the same series of culture-founding events. Again, he grew unsettled after a few years and left his sorrowful new people with a promise to return. This time, he traveled north, far beyond Yucatán, into what is now the state of Virginia. There his civilizing mission occurred for the last time. Eventually, his wanderlust got the better of him, and he vanished into American myth as the Feathered Serpent.

Su-Son   One of the most peculiar individual cases in the life readings, Su-Son was regularly mistaken for the most powerful prince in Atlantis. The two men were physically identical, although utterly unrelated, a situation that inevitably led to numerous misunderstandings with serious political ramifications—"until the union of their purpose and activity made for the preventing of turmoils arising from the experience of Su-Son."[54]

T

Tek-Ia-Eln   He was in Egypt "when there were the coalitions made with the Atlanteans, as well as the natives, and those of other lands."[55] Tek-Ia-Eln matched work assignments and careers to those men temperamentally suited to them: "the stonecutters, the farmers, the herdsmen, the miners. All of these were trained for the service to the peoples as a unit, not as individuals."[56] This last statement is a credible, hence revealing look at a part of ancient Egyptian society as it was being forged by combinations of cultures.

Tujar   A kind of servant or combination nursemaid-teacher who lived and worked in the household of an Inca prince at a time when Atlantean influences were transforming Peru. Tujar applied herself "to the edifying of the young"[57] by excelling in basket-weaving, painting, bookmaking, and rug designing, while dutifully attending to the weak and disabled.

In her twentieth-century incarnation, her talents lived on as a painter of pastoral scenes. "But ever to the entity there must be either the mountain or the sea in the viewing of same," recalling Tujar's soul-memories of ancient days.[58]

Z

Zurumu   An Atlantean priestess with a Lemurian name in Yucatán's Temple of the Sun.

LAST CHANCE OR
JUDGMENT IN 2012?

The people of Atlantis were alleged to have created a long-lived, culturally rich, and economically powerful and virtuous society. Over time, however, in Plato's words, they

> . . . became too diluted too often, and with too much of the mortal mixture, human nature got the upper hand. Then, they being unable to bear their fortune, became unseemly, and to him who had an eye to see they began to appear base, and had lost the fairest of their precious gifts. But to those who had no eye to see true happiness, they still appeared glorious and blessed at the time when they were filled with unrighteous avarice and power.[1]

To some investigators, such as the renowned French Freemason scholar Serge Hutin, these words refer to the Atlanteans' racial purity ("the fairest of their precious gifts"),[2] which became less important to them than the pursuit of material gain. As he writes, "Plato tells of the growing decadence that afflicted the Atlantean people. He attributes it to increased cross-breeding. In a sense, the great Greek philosopher was clearly a racist: he regarded the increase in cross-breeding as a calamity."[3]

To other researches, such as Desmond Lee, a British translator of the Dialogues, Plato meant to say that the Atlanteans, being originally descended from Poseidon, diluted their godly inheritance by intermarrying with ordinary mortals. Yet this interpretation lacks conviction, because the Atlanteans never interbred with other deities following Kleito's encounter with Poseidon.[4]

In any case, Cayce's life readings take up where Plato left off to explain that not all Atlanteans succumbed to materialism and miscegenation. There were, he said, two rival factions in Atlantis warring for control of their people's destiny: the Children of the Law of One, and the Sons of Belial. The Law of One does not appear to have been merely some monotheistic cult, but instead seems to refer to the One Law, or the predominance of natural law, with emphasis on healing and psycho-spiritual values. The Sons of Belial, however, were interested in using natural resources only for their own material gain. The origin of contention between the two groups was, as Plato explained, rooted in racial problems. Cayce agreed: "And there crept those pollutions, or polluting themselves with those mixtures that brought contempt, hatred, bloodshed and desires of self without respect to others freedom, others' wishes—and there began then, in the later portion of this period, dissentings and divisions among the peoples of the lands."[5]

Cayce told another client that he once lived "in Atlantean land during those periods when there was the divisions between those of the Law of One and the Sons of Belial, or the offspring of what was the pure race and those who had projected themselves into creatures that became 'the sons of men', as the terminology would be, rather than the creatures of God."[6] Three days later, he described a different client as having dwelled "in Atlantean land when there were the greater questioning between the Sons of the Law of One and the Sons of Belial, or between those that were purified by keeping the pure strain."[7]

One of Cayce's last life readings about Atlantis included

. . . a priest of the Law of One pitted self against many of those things that were presented by a people that were being drawn gradually into self-indulgence. This was during the time when there was the breaking up of the Atlantean land. When there was then waging of the eternal Laws of One with those that worshiped Belial—and those that worshiped the satisfying of physical desire—those that worshiped ease and pleasure in the material world.[8]

This spiritual-materialist struggle preceded the natural catastrophe, as Cayce described for a client who lived "in Atlantean land when there were those activities that caused the first upheavals and the use of those influences that brought destruction to the land—among those of the Law of One, but was persuaded by and with leaders of the land to apply spiritual laws for material gain—thus brought or aided in bringing what eventually became the destruction of the material lands."[9]

Plato reported that the island of Atlantis was swallowed up by the ocean after "a day and night" of exceptionally violent seismic activity, followed by an extraordinary degree of magmatic debris that pervaded the seas beyond the Straits of Gibraltar for literally centuries thereafter. Its final destruction, however, may not be entirely understood in purely geologic terms. With fascinating consistency, from Plato to Cayce and beyond to the folkish traditions of Wisconsin's Ho Chunk Indians and the Basque in Spain, the cataclysm is linked to the spiritual decline of the Atlanteans.

Formerly known as the Winnebago, the Ho Chunk preserve generational accounts of an ancestral people who sinned against their original goodness by fighting among themselves until they were punished by God with a terrible flood. Basque racial memory of the Green Isle, Atlaintika, lost in a cataclysmic storm brought about by the immorality of its inhabitants, is a self-evident version of Plato's Atlantis. The precise relationship between social decay and physical annihilation is defined in none of these accounts, although they do provide a model for what might have occurred.

Cayce said that "the terrible crystals," which concentrated limitless energy from the hidden wellsprings of nature itself, were taken over by the materialistic Sons of Belial to dig into Earth for the extraction of wealth in the form of precious minerals. They penetrated too deeply, however, and set off subterranean forces that resulted in catastrophic seismic upheavals. Remarkably, several Native American tribes, such as the Menominee of the Upper Great Lakes region, recount in their oral traditions how a world flood was precipitated by greedy foreigners, the white-skinned Marine Men who dug into Earth Mother for underground riches, especially copper.

The Tuaoi stone, the great crystal at the center of Atlantis, affected, according to Cayce, "the application of spiritual power in the physical world."[10] It was to this end that the Tuaoi was abused. If this fantastic version of the destruction of Atlantis was limited to the musings of psychics, we might feel inclined to dismiss it as so much unfounded imagination. Yet despite the apparently natural disaster that obliterated the oceanic civilization, Plato also argued that the Atlanteans brought about their own demise. Their sins against the very foundation of not only society but also life itself so offended the natural order of the universe that the keepers of that divine order, the gods, condemned them to oblivion.

Cayce, who never read the Dialogues, seconded the *Kritias* redaction of a corrupt people punished with the annihilation of their fabulous island. The theme of an Atlantean judgment stated in Plato was repeated in faraway cultures he never dreamed existed, from the Hopi of the American Southwest to African tribes of the Ivory Coast. This world memory, indelibly printed in the folkish consciousness of dozens of peoples often separated by thousands of miles and as many years, substantiates the verity of lost Atlantis. On another level, its resemblance to the present condition of world civilization is more than uncanny.

Perhaps the ultimate significance and power of Atlantis to impact our time will be revealed when modern humans realizes that we have allowed our own society to slip almost as far. Cayce wondered if comparisons between the modern world and Atlantis are being drawn by an influx of Atlantean souls into our time: "Be it true that there is the fact of reincarnation, and that souls once occupied such an environ (Atlantis) are entering the Earth's sphere and inhabiting individuals in the present, is it any wonder that—if they made such alteration in the affairs of Earth in their day, as to bring destruction upon themselves—if they are entering now, they might make many changes in the affairs of peoples and individuals in the present?"[11]

Apparent collapse of long-established religious and political institution and the rapid deterioration of the so-called global economy, with its attendant corporate corruption and larceny of an unprecedented magnitude, suggest to some that the spirit of Atlantis is reemerging in our time, as Cayce said it would. Perhaps the Children of the Law of One have returned as the idealists who today work for the protection of our natural environment, while the despoilers of our planet's rain forests or the industrial exploiters are the reincarnated souls of the Sons of Belial.

According to Hugh Lynn Cayce, his father believed that

> . . . many individual souls (or entities) who had one or more incarnations in Atlantis are reincarnating in the Earth in this century (the 20th Century), particularly in America. Along with technological abilities, they bring tendencies for being extremists. Often they exhibit individual and group karma associated with selfishness and exploitation where others are concerned. Many of them lived during one of the periods of destruction or geological change in Atlantean history.[12]

As Edgar Cayce himself said, "Even today, either through the direct influence of being reincarnated in the Earth, or through mental effect on individuals' thoughts, they may influence individuals, groups and nations in the present."[13] The Atlanteans failed the crisis they themselves brought about and therefore were utterly destroyed. Now, as the world again approaches a question of "to be or not to be," their spirits are returning to work out once more the eternal dilemma of survival.

Certainly, the most compelling parallel afforded by Cayce's life readings is the destruction of Atlantis itself. Insatiable for unlimited material prosperity, all the values that made the Atlanteans great and powerful were discarded, even despised. They broadened their uncontrolled exploitation of the natural environment until Earth, pushed too far for too long, turned on them with overwhelming fury, annihilating them and all their works. "In a single day and night," their wealth, technology, and self-indulgent power were reduced to ashes floating on the sea.

The deities associated with Atlantis—Poseidon, Atlas, Thaut, Kukulcan, Viracocha, and the rest—metaphorically represented the forces of history and nature to complement poetically Cayce's life readings. Thanks in large measure to him and Plato, it seems more than significant that the Atlanteans' fate has come down to us at this critical moment for our planet.

They made their indelible imprint on America's pre-Columbian civilizations, which rose to their own heights of cultural greatness as pyramid builders and astronomers. Fearing the loss of control over an expanding population, however, they increasingly resorted to physical coercion of the bloodiest kind. When a regime has sunk so low on the scale of civilization as to require mass murder for the prosecution of state policy, it has abrogated any right to exist and dooms itself to extinction.

The Aztecs were neither the first nor last such example in America. Ancient as well as modern history is tragically replete with governments in which power developed as an end in itself and security became inseparable from terror. The cosmic balance between ethical behavior and its physical consequences was centered at the focal point of the Mayas' cosmological understanding of humanity's relationship to life and was expressed in their calendar. It later evolved into the Cuauhtlixicalli, the so-called Aztec Calendar Stone. This was the ominous Vessel of Time that accurately ticked off the final moments before the great city over which it stood was razed to the ground. Now, the same Mesoamerican calendrics point to the morning of December 21, 2012.

The Maya would have explained that the events of that date will be an outcome of humankind's harmonious interdependence with nature or fall upon us as a condemnation for too many generations of self-indulgence. In other words, civilization either will be rewarded with continued existence, perhaps even the advent of a new golden age, or our species will be judged "when Bolon Yokte descends" with all the demons of the underworld.

To be sure, there are positive energies at work in the world, striving to correct the destructive imbalance created by past centuries of unlimited, unnatural gratification. Compassion for all sentient beings, love of all things natural, and spontaneous generosity have not yet been eradicated from human nature by unmitigated self-indulgence, intolerance, and tyranny. Yet whether our higher instincts weigh in the scales sufficiently to tip them in favor of all humankind might be disclosed on the winter solstice of 2012.

Even if no apparent change is noticed on that day, its minimum significance is still astounding. From a prehistoric vantage point of at least 22 centuries ago, the Maya selected that date for the end of their calendar to coincide with the termination of a 26,000-year-period—the Precession of the Equinoxes. The same rising sun ascends into the middle of our Milky Way Galaxy, thereby forming an alignment between the galactic center, Earth, and our star, which will reverse its own magnetic poles after reaching the conclusion of a current 11-year sunspot cycle.

These astronomical occurrences bespeak a temporal termination, an end to time. That they were predicted with targeted accuracy by the Maya and their Atlanto-Olmec predecessors many thousands of years ago alone represents an unbelievable achievement. Yet Earth changes anticipated for 2012 cannot be brought about solely by that year's geo-solar-galactic alignment, because it is only an illusion arising from our terrestrial perspective and is not caused by the actual position of our planet in relation to the Milky Way. It is, in short, a visual phenomenon. Moreover, the distances separating Earth and the sun from our galaxy are far too great for gravitational forces to act upon one another in any way. If any geophysical change does occur on the winter solstice of 2012, it will be brought about instead by the precessional wobble that alters our planet's angular relationship with the sun, the cause of ice ages and the next glaciation, perhaps beginning in 2012.

How likely is that to happen? Before his death at 90 years of age in 2002, the renowed Australian geologist S. Warren Carey observed, "Our present interglacial has probably nearly run its course. While the world worries about a nuclear winter, we may suddenly find the seas lowering by one hundred meters or more, as the next glacial stage advances over Europe, Asia, and North America."[14] According to John Imbrie, the paleoceanographer at Brown University, who received numerous scientific awards for verifying Milanković's theory of Earth rotation as the cause of glaciation: "[D]uring the past two million years, no interglacial lasted more than twelve thousand years. Most lasted only ten thousand. Statistically speaking then, the present interglacial is already on its last legs, tottering along at the advanced age of ten thousand years."[15] Columbia University professor James D. Hays, quoted here in chapter 6, believes that "previous interglacial mild intervals comparable in warmth to the present one lasted only about ten thousand years. If it is truly similar to earlier ones—and if man's activities do not alter natural trends—it should be nearly over."[16]

Long before 2012's galactic alignment predicted by the Mayan calendar was generally known, scientists were already concerned about the unknown repercussions of just such an event. As long ago as 1970, Craig B. Hatfield and Mark J. Camp broached the subject of "mass extinctions correlated with periodic galactic events" in the *Geological Society of America Bulletin*.[17] Fourteen years later, astronomers Richard D. Schwartz and Philip B. James described "periodic mass-extinctions and the Sun's oscillation about the galactic plane" for readers of *Nature* magazine.[18] More to the point of 2012, a "possible relation between periodic glaciation and the flexure of the galaxy" was suggested by astronomer George E. Williams in 1975.[19]

Though an impending ice age is inevitable, its beginning in 2012 seems uncertain, however possible. More likely is the arrival of a solar hurricane, because such an event could coincide with that year's heighted sunspot activity, which is responsible for coronal masses of plasma hurled at our planet. Their collision with Earth's magnetosphere might short modern civilization's electronically run infrastructure. Resulting social dislocation may push the Western world toward extinction, thereby fulfilling the darkest hints of the Maya prophecy and its dreaded end date.

A cataclysm of that global magnitude, if not too severe, might be, in fact, the catalyst for positive change that some researchers interpret for 2012. Drastic reduction of world population could restore the lost balance between ourselves and our environment, removing in one stroke the fundamental cause of civilization's self-destructive traits. While downsizing us from 6,763,557,000 individuals to a few million survivors seems the worst holocaust of all time, nature regards such die-offs as nothing more than necessary readsjustments.[20] Gene studies show, for example, that radical climate change 150,000 years ago virtually exterminated humankind. "At one point," reports *National Geographic,* "our species may have been down to as few as two thousand individuals."[21] Yet it was this near-extinction resulting in our genetic hardihood that made us everything we are today, enabling us to survive and evolve over time. Perhaps another cataclysmic restructuring for the greater good of our species is in the offing.

For all the illumination their genius casts on the subject, the Atlantis code is not to be found among the words of Plato or Edgar Cayce, but in the Mayan calendar itself. The science that went into this ancient conception of time was a legacy that the pre-Columbian peoples of Middle America inherited from their Atlantean founding fathers, remembered as Kukulcan, Quetzalcoatl, or Itzamna—the Feathered Serpent. It was among the gifts he brought from his lost kingdom across the Sunrise Sea. It was obviously of such supreme importance to the Mayas—and to all those Mesoamericans who preceded and followed them—that they preserved his sacred almanac intact over thousands of generations, until its final message has come down to us.

The Atlantis code *is* the Mayan calendar. One may be broken by understanding the other. In it, the Maya promised a dark end for our age, but they at least extended us a single hope in our ability to reestablish civilization's cosmic balance before time runs out. Whether or not their prognostications for the near future were correct will be revealed to the world only when the sun rises on the first day of winter, 2012.

GLOSSARY

Atlas The first king of Atlantis, from whom the city, island, and surrounding Atlantic Ocean derived their names.

Azaes One of Plato's Atlantean kings who gave his name to a Maya people, the Itzás, in coastal Yucatán, where Chichén Itzá, with its depiction of Atlas-like figures, was built.

Aztlán A "White Island" in the Atlantic Ocean, homeland of Mexihcah ancestors, who brought with them the first sacred calendar to Middle America.

Bolon Yokte The Maya god of the underworld, who will close out the Fifth Sun.

Bronze Age The pre-classical milennia from 3100 BC to 1200 BC characterized by a transition from copper to superior bronze metallurgy.

Chalchihuitlicue The Mexihcah Lady of the Turquoise Skirt, a mythic figure personifying the final destruuction of Atlantis and the cataclysmic deluge that terminated 4-Atl, the Fourth Sun or Age.

Children of the Law of One According to Edgar Cayce, a monotheistic cult that failed to achieve control of Atlantis before the island was destroyed.

Cuauhtlixicalli   The Eagle Bowl or Vessel of Time, the original Mexihcah name for the Aztec Calendar Stone.

Fimbulvetr   In Norse sagas, the Great Winter, three consecutive years of unbroken winter conditions preceeding the end of the world.

Hun yecil   Described in the Mayas' *Popol Vuh*, or Book of Counsel, as the Drowning of the Trees, a deluge that ravaged the world just before Kukulcan arrived on the shores of Yucatán.

I Ching   The ancient Chinese Book of Changes, a system of symbols believed to discern, as a means of divination, order or patterns from the apparent chaos of random occurrences.

Kleito   Described in Plato's *Kritias* as the Atlantean woman who bore Poseidon five pairs of male twins, progenitors of the royal houses of Atlantis.

Kukulcan   The Maya Feathered Serpent, the bearded founding father of Mesoamerican civilization.

Macuilli-Tonatiuh   Clenched Fist, the destructive aspect of the sun depicted at the center of the Aztec Calendar Stone, who will preside over the close of our age in 2012.

Mictlán   The Mexihcah realm of the dead.

Magdalenians   Upper Paleolithic Europeans contemporary with Plato's Atlanteans.

Nahui-Ollin   The Mexihcah' 4-Ollin, Movement, our present Age or Sun.

Ragnarok   The Ending of the Gods in Norse cosmology, a recurring cycle of global destruction.

remote viewing   Acquiring information about distant or unseen targets through extrasensory perception.

Saquasohuh Katchina   The Hopi Blue Star, said to appear as a messenger of worldwide chaos and calamity.

Semsu-Hr and the Mesentiu   Respectively, the Followers of Horus and the Harpooners, described by ancient Egyptians as the progenitors of dynastic civilization who arrived at the Nile Delta after their homeland, Sehket Aaru, was overwhelmed by the sea.

Sons of Belial   A materialistic or satanic cult that Edgar Cayce stated was in charge of Atlantis at the time of its destruction.

taurobolium   Bull sacrifice as practiced by the kings of Atlantis in the Temple of Poseidon.

Tenochtitlán   The Aztec capital, a city originally built by the Mexihcah.

Tezcatlipocha   Smoking Mirror, the virtuous Feathered Serpent's evil twin, synonymous with the darkness and annihilation that time cyclically visits upon the world.

Tortuguero   Place of the Turtles, near the Mexican border with Guatemala, where the earliest and so far only known written Maya reference to the end of their calendar has been found.

Tuaoi   Described by Edgar Cayce as "the terrible, mighty crystal" that the Atlanteans abused and which led to their own self-destruction.

Yonaguni   A small island at the end of a Japanese chain known as the Ryukyus, where a sunken "citadel" associated with Lemuria was discovered in 1985.

yugas   Hindu epochs or eras within a cycle of four ages.

NOTES

INTRODUCTION.
END TIMES OR GOLDEN AGE?

1. Robert T. Bakker, *The Dinosaur Heresies* (New York: William Morrow and Company, 1986).

2. Krzys Wasilewski, "Computer Software Says Armageddon Will Arrive in 2012," *The Student Operated Press,* http://thesop.org/index.php?article=11011, 1 May 2008.

3. Ibid.

4. Zechariah Sitchin, "Olmec Civilization Older Than Believed," in *Ancient American* 9, no. 6 (April 2001).

5. Alfonso Caso, *The Civilizations of Ancient Mexico* (New York: Prescott Publishers, 1960).

6. *Oera Linda Bok*, trans. Howard Schnell (London: Truebner and Company, 1876).

CHAPTER 1. WHAT WAS ATLANTIS?

1. Ramses Seleem, *The Illustrated Egyptian Book of the Dead, A New Translation with Commentary* (New York: Sterling, 2001).

2. *The Edfu Texts*, trans. Robert Kohlmann (Dallas: University of Texas Press, 1968).

3. Philipp August Boeckh, *Commentary on Plato,* trans. Robert Pearson (London: London University Press, 1928).

4. Plato, *The Timaeus and the Kritias,* trans. Desmond Lee (London: Penguin Books, 1977).

5. Ibid.

6. Kenneth Caroli, private e-mail correspondence with the author, February 20, 2009.

7. Plato, *The Timaeus and the Kritias.*

8. Kenneth Caroli, private e-mail correspondence with the author, February 20, 2009.

9. Desmond Lee, translator of Plato's *The Timaeus and the Kritias* (London: Penguin Books, 1977).

10. Kenneth Caroli, private e-mail correspondence with the author, February 20, 2009.

CHAPTER 2. THE OTHER SIDE OF THE MIRROR

1. Plato, *The Timaeus and the Kritias.*

2. Ian Kerner, *She Comes First* (San Francisco: Collins Living, Harper Collins, 2004).

3. Joseph Wells, http://greekatlantis.warpco.com/Sexcentric.html.

CHAPTER 3. SACRED NUMERALS

1. Plato, *The Timaeus and the Kritias.*

2. Carl Olson, *The Theology and Philosophy of Eliade: A Search for the Centre* (New York: St Martin's, 1992).

CHAPTER 4. THE ATLANTO-MAYAN CALENDAR

1. Daniel G. Brinton, *The Books of Chilan Balam* (Philadelphia: Stern, 1882).

2. Teobert Maler, in Louis Carpenter, *Art and Archaeology Magazine* 22, no. 18 (March 1981).

3. Brinton, *The Books of Chilan Balam.*

4. Ibid.

5. *Popol Vuh: The Sacred Book of the Maya,* trans. Allen J. Christenson (Norman: University of Oklahoma, 2003).

6. Bernal Diaz Del Castillo, *The True History of the Conquest of New Spain,* trans. Alfred P. Maudslay (London: Hakluyt Society, 1910).

7. Marc Davis, et. al., "Extinction of Species by Periodic Comet Showers," *Nature* 308 (1984).

8. Kenneth Caroli, private e-mail correspondence with the author, February 20, 2009.

9. Plato, *The Timaeus and the Kritias.*

10. Max Heindel, *The Message of the Stars* (New York: Cosimo Classics, 2006).

11. Jorge Luis Borges, *Atlas of the Mountain* (New York: Pranger Publishers, 1980).

12. C. A. Burland, *The Gods of Mexico* (London: Eyre and Spottiswoode, 1970).

13. Graeme R. Kearsley, *Mayan Genesis, Migrations and Iconography in Mesoamerica* (London: Yelsraek Publishing, 2001).

14. *Popol Vuh: The Sacred Book of the Maya.*

15. C. A. Burland, and Werner Foreman, *Feathered Serpent and Smoking Mirror* (New York: G. P. Putnam and Sons, 1975).

16. Michael D. Coe, *Mexico* (New York: Praeger Press, 1966).

17. *Popol Vuh: The Sacred Book of the Maya.*

18. Victor von Hagen, *The Ancient Sun Kingdoms of the Americas* (Cleveland: World Publishing Company, 1957).

19. Lars Franzen, and Thomas B. Larsson, in *Natural Catastrophes During Bronze Age Civilizations: Archaeological, Geological, Astronomical and Cultural Perspectives,* ed. Trevor Palmer and Mark E. Bailey (Oxford, England: Archaeo Press, 1998).

20. Zelia Nuttall, *The Fundamental Principles of Old and New World Civilizations,* vol. 2 (Cambridge, Mass.: Harvard University Press, 1900).

21. Bernal Diaz Del Castillo, *The True History of the Conquest of New Spain.*

CHAPTER 5. A REBELLION OF THE EARTH

1. John Van Auken, "December 21, 2012—Mayan Year of Destiny," www .edgarcayce.org/2012.asp.

2. David Stewart translation: UT Mesoamerica Center Discussion Board http:// groups.google.com/group/utmesoamerica/browse_thread/thread/2ad64b039cb6 0983/0396cfd4957fd61e?pli=1.

3. Nikolai Grube, Simon Martin, Martin Zender, The Proceedings of the Maya Hieroglyphic Workshop, March 9–10, 2002, University of Texas at Austin: "Palenque and its Neighbors."

4. John Major Jenkins, "Comments on the 2012 text on Tortuguero Monument 6 and Bolon Yokte K'u", May 2006, http://Alignment2012.com.

CHAPTER 6. THE GREAT WINTER

1. Gregory F. Fegel, http://english.pravda.ru/science/earth/106922-earth_ice_ age-0, 11.01.2009.

2. Oleg Sorokhtin, http://english.pravda.ru/science/earth/106922-earth_ice_age-0, 11.01.2009.

3. Khabibullo, Abdusamatov, http://english.pravda.ru/science/earth/106922-earth_ ice_age-0, 11.01.2009.

4. Gregory F. Fegel, http://english.pravda.ru/science/earth/106922-earth_ice_ age-0, 11.01.2009.

5. Peter Harris, and John Faraday, "An Urgent Signal for the Coming Ice Age," Western Institute for Study of the Environment Colloquium, Western Institute for Study of the Environment, Lebanon, Oreg., www.westinstev.org/2008/04/28, 2008.

6. Edmund Rouse, *A Dictionary of Scientists* (New York: Oxford University Press, 2003).

7. James Croll, *Climate and Time in Their Geological Relations* (London: Trafalgar Press, 1875).

8. Wikipedia, http://en.wikipedia.org/wiki/Milutin_Milanković.

9. Wallace Broecker, www.absoluteastronomy.com/topics/Wallace_S._Broecker.

10. Harris and Faraday, "An Urgent Signal for the Coming Ice Age."

11. John Imbrie, James Hays, and Nicholas Shackleton, "Variations in the Earth's Orbit: Pacemaker of the Ice Ages," *Science* 238, no. 12 (June 1976).

12. Gregory F. Fegel, http://englishpravda.ru/science/earth/106922-earth_ice_age-0, 11.01.2009).

13. Daniel Carnahan, "Are We Entering a New Ice Age?" *Time* 91, no. 18 (June 24, 1974).

14. Ibid.

15. Nigel Calder, *International Wildlife* 12, no. 15 (July 1975).

16. Ken Caldera, and F. Kasting, "Susceptibility of the early Earth to irreversible glaciation by carbon dioxide clouds," *Nature* 359 (September 17, 1992).

17. Gifford H. Miller, and Anne de Vernal, "Will Greenhouse Warming Lead to Northern Hemisphere Ice-Sheet Growth?" *Nature* 355 (January 16, 1992).

18. Caldera and Kasting, "Susceptibility of the early Earth to irreversible glaciation by carbon dioxide clouds.

19. Terry Devit, www.jsonline.com/news/obituaries/29471324.html.

20. Ibid.

21. John Kutzbach, www.jsonline.com/news/obituaries/29471324.html.

22. Robert Felix, *Not By Fire, But By Ice* (Bellevue, Wash.: Sugarhouse Publishing, 1997).

23. Abdusamatov, http://english.pravda.ru/science/earth/106922-earth_ice_age-0, 11.01.2009)

24. Felix, *Not By Fire, But By Ice.*

25. www.indiadaily.com/editorial/1753.asp.

26. Ibid.

27. David Loper, www.gly.fsu.edu/fac/loper/main.php.

28. James Hays, "Variations in the Earth's Orbit: Pacemaker of the Ice Ages," *Science* 238, no. 12 (June 1976).

29. I. K. Crain, "Possible Direct Causal Relation between Geomagnetic Reversals and Biological Extinctions," *Geology Society of America Bulletin* 82 (1971).

30. C. G. A. Harrison, and J. M. Prospero, "Reversal of the Earth's Magnetic Field and Climate Changes," *Nature* 250 (August 16, 1974).

31. Thomas Crowley, www.gcrio.org/CONSEQUENCES/winter96/crowley.html.

32. David M. Raup, www.scientificblogging.com/howard_bloom/mother_nature_ and_the_evolutionary_mandate.

33. Geneviéve M. Woillard, "Grand Pile Peat Bog: A Continuous Pollen Record for the Last 140,000 Years," in *Quarternary Research* 9 (1978): 1–21.

34. W. F. Ruddiman, and A. McIntyre, http://gsabulletin.gsapubs.org/content/vol93/ issue12/.

35. Felix, *Not By Fire, But By Ice.*

36. Ibid.

37. Woillard, "Grand Pile Peat Bog: A Continuous Pollen Record for the Last 140,000 Years."

CHAPTER 7. THE SUPER SOLAR STORM

1. National Academy of Sciences, www.pnas.org/content/105/20.toc.

2. Michael Brooks, "Space Storm Alert: 90 Seconds from Catastrophe," *New Scientist* 23 (March 2009), www.newscientist.com/article/mg20127001.300-space-storm-alert-90-seconds-from-catastrophe.html?full=true.

3. Stuart Clark, *The Sun Kings: The Unexpected Tragedy of Richard Carrington and the Tale of How Modern Astronomy Began* (London: Princeton Publishers, 2007).

4. Ibid.

5. Bruce Tsurutani, http://socioecohistory.wordpress.com/2009/05/09/nasa-warns-of-super-solar-storm-2012/.

6. Tony Blair, Science@NASA, http://science.nasa.gov/headlines/y2009/21jan_ severespaceweather.htm?list5029.

7. Ibid.

8. John Kappenmann, "Severe Space Weather Events—Understanding Societal and Economic Impacts Workshop Report," http://books.nap.edu/catalog. php?record_id=12507.

9. Ibid.

10. Paul Kintner, www.newscientist.com/article/mg20127001.300-space-storm-alert-90-seconds-from-catastrophe.html?full=true.

11. Tsurutani, http://socioecohistory.wordpress.com/2009/05/09/nasa-warns-of-super-solar-storm-2012/.

12. Uniform Crime Reports of the Federal Bureau of Investigation, 2008, www.fbi
.gov/ucr/08aprelim/index.html.

13. Kappenmann, "Severe Space Weather Events—Understanding Societal and
Economic Impacts Workshop Report."

14. Brooks, "Space Storm Alert: 90 Seconds from Catastrophe."

15. Mike Hapgood, www.newscientist.com/article/mg20127001.300-space-storm-
alert-90-seconds-from-catastrophe.html?full=true.

16. James Green, www.newscientist.com/article/mg20127001.300-space-storm-alert-
90-seconds-from-catastrophe.html?full=true.

17. Daniel Baker, www.newscientist.com/article/mg20127001.300-space-storm-alert-
90-seconds-from-catastrophe.html?full=true.

18. Kappenmann, "Severe Space Weather Events—Understanding Societal and
Economic Impacts Workshop Report."

19. Robert Roy Britt, "The Great Storm: Solar Tempest of 1858 Revealed," www
.space.com/scienceastronomy/mystery_monday_031027.html.

20. Hapgood, www.newscientist.com/article/mg20127001.300-space-storm-alert-90-
seconds-from-catastrophe.html?full=true.

21. Daniel Baker, www.newscientist.com/article/mg20127001.300-space-storm-alert-
90-seconds-from-catastrophe.html?full=true.

22. Ibid.

23. "After 19 years, Ulysses solar probe to go dark," http://news.yahoo.com/s/
ap/20090626/ap_on_sc/us_sci_sun_probe. Click on the article title on this
page.

24. *Scientific American*, www.sciam.com/article.cfm?id=timeline-the-1859-solar-
superstorm, 29 July 2008.

25. Hapgood, www.newscientist.com/article/mg20127001.300-space-storm-alert-90-
seconds-from-catastrophe.html?full=true.

26. *Scientific American,* www.sciam.com/article.cfm?id=timeline-the-1859-solar-
superstorm, 29 July 2008.

27. Tsurutani, http://socioecohistory.wordpress.com/2009/05/09/nasa-warns-of-
super-solar-storm-2012/.

28. "Sunspot credited with rail tie-up," *New York Times*, May 16, 1921, page 2.

CHAPTER 8. THE COMING OF THE BLUE STAR

1. Kenneth Caroli, private e-mail correspondence with the author, February 20,
2009.

2. Ibid.

3. *The Bhagavad Gita*, trans. Laurie L. Patton (New York: Penguin Classics, 2008).

4. Chief Dan Evehema, www.geocities.com/Athens/Oracle/9007/HopiDeath .html.

5. Allen C. Ross, www.ipl.org/div/natam/bin/browse.pl/A279.

6. Ibid.

7. Frank Waters, *The Book of the Hopi* (New York: Viking Press, 1963).

8. Snorri Sturluson, *The Prose Edda,* trans. Jesse L. Byock (New York: Penguin Classics, 2006).

9. Ibid.

10. Kevin Crossley-Holland, *The Norse Myths* (New York: Pantheon Books, 1980).

11. Ibid.

12. Padraic Colum, *Nordic Gods and Heroes* (New York: Dover Publications, 1996).

13. Dennis J. and Terence McKenna, *The Invisible Landscape: Mind, Hallucinogens, and the I Ching* (New York: Seabury Press, 1975).

14. Ibid.

CHAPTER 10. DOOM NUMBER

1. Leonardo Tarán, *Academica: Plato, Philip of Opus, and the Pseudo-Platonic Epinomis* (Philadelphia: American Philosophical Society, 1975).

2. Maria Valla, *The Power of Numbers* (Camarillo, Calif.: DeVorss and Co., 1971).

3. Erica Vidnjevitch, "Lunatics or Solartics?," *Psychology Today* 7, no. 4 (December 1979).

4. Dennis Duda, "Whale Song of the Sun," *Natural History* 53, no. 11 (August 1982).

5. Frank Godwin, "Fish Behavior Surprises Marine Biologists," *Chicago Today* 13, no. 10 (December 30, 2006).

6. Burland, *The Gods of Mexico*.

7. Edward Turner, "Scientists warn time is short for environment," *Columbine Gazette* 2, no. 4 (January 5, 2002).

CHAPTER 11. HOW COULD THEY HAVE POSSIBLY KNOWN?

1. Erich Von Daniken, *Chariots of the Gods* (New York: Berkley Books, 1999).

CHAPTER 12. PLATO OR CAYCE?

1. Herbert M. Vaughan, *The Medici Popes* (New York: G. P. Putnam and Sons, 1908).

2. Edgar Cayce, *Atlantis, The Edgar Cayce Readings,* vol. 22 (Virginia Beach, Va.: Association for Research and Enlightenment,1987), 1601–1602.

3. Ibid.

4. Hugh Lynn Cayce, *Cayce on Atlantis* (Virginia Beach, Va.: Association for Research and Enlightenment, 1980).

5. Ibid.

6. Edgar Cayce, *Atlantis, The Edgar Cayce Readings,* vol. 22, 1391–1 F.28, 1935.

7. Ibid., 1874–1 F.39, 5/6/39.

8. Alfred North Whitehead, *Process and Reality* (New York: Free Press, 1979).

9. Plato, *The Timaeus and the Kritias.*

10. Scholasticus, http://en.wikipedia.org/wiki/Society_of_Biblical_Literature.

11. Ibid.

12. J. Barnes, *The Cambridge Companion to Aristotle* (Cambridge, England: Cambridge University Press, 1995).

13. Aelian, *On the Characteristics of Animals,* vol. 3, books 12–17 (Cambridge, Mass.: Loeb Classical Library, 1958).

14. Auguste Helaine, *Astronomy Across Cultures: The History of Non-Western Astronomy* (Netherlands: Kluwer Academic Publishers, 2000).

15. Thomas L. Pangle, *The Laws of Plato* (New York: Basic Books, 1980).

CHAPTER 13. LOST MOTHERLAND, DROWNED FATHERLAND

1. Edgar Cayce, *Atlantis, The Edgar Cayce Readings,* vol. 22, 274–1 M.34, 2/13/33.

2. Ibid., 877–26 M.46, 5/23/38.

3. Ibid., 442–1 M.57, 11/15/33.

4. Ibid., 2713–5 F.43, 9/23/29.

5. Ibid., 57–201 M.45, 9/4/38.

6. Ibid., 2464–2 F.24, 11/13/41.

7. Ibid.

8. Ibid., 618–3 F.61, 3/6/35.

9. Ibid., 2262, F.22, 10/11,40.

10. Ibid., 787–23 M.44, 1/12/37.

11. Ibid,. 2750–1 F.44, 3/12/30.

CHAPTER 14. EDGAR CAYCE'S DREAM OF LEMURIA

1. Edgar Cayce, *Atlantis, The Edgar Cayce Readings,* vol. 22, 877–26 M.46 5/23/38.
2. Ibid., 364–13, 11/17/32.
3. Ibid., 2801–5 F.43, 5/11/25.
4. Vada F. Carlson, *The Great Migration* (Virginia Beach, Va.: Association for Research and Enlightmenment, 1970).
5. Edgar Cayce, *Atlantis, The Edgar Cayce Readings,* vol. 22, 4349–1 M.14, 10/13/24.
6. Carlson, *The Great Migration.*

CHAPTER 15. HE SAW ATLANTIS

1. Benjamin R. Foster, trans. & edit., *The Epic of Gilgamesh* (New York: W. W. Norton, 1997).
2. Edgar Cayce, *Atlantis, The Edgar Cayce Readings,* vol. 22, 1743–1 M.28, 11/11/38.
3. Ibid., 364–3, 2/16/32.
4. Earth Changes, www.unexplained-mysteries.com/forum/lofiversion/index.php/t50714.html, 1958.
5. Edgar Cayce, *Atlantis, The Edgar Cayce Readings,* vol. 22, 5748–6, 7/1/32.
6. Ibid., 2688–1 M.2, 1/16/42.
7. Ibid., 797–1
8. Ibid., 440–5 M.23, 12/20/33.
9. Ibid.
10. Ibid., 2462–2 M.35, 6/19/41.
11. Ibid., 440–5 M.23, 12/20/33.
12. Ibid., 2012–1 M.26, 9/25/39.
13. Ibid.
14. Ibid., 1073–4 F.51, 2/17/36.
15. Ibid., 1210–1 M.54, 6/29/36.
16. Ibid., 1486–1 M.55, 11/26/37.
17. Ibid.
18. Ibid.
19. Ibid., 691–1 F.20, 8/17/34.
20. Ibid., 2688–1 M.2, 1/16/42.

CHAPTER 16. THE TERRIBLE, MIGHTY CRYSTAL

1. Edgar Cayce, *Atlantis, The Edgar Cayce Readings,* vol. 22, 263–F.23, 3/6/35.

2. Ibid., 528–14 F.29, 12/30/34.

3. Ibid., 440–5 M.23, 12/20/33.

4. Ibid., 2072–10 F.32, 7/22/42.

5. Ibid., 440–5 M.23, 12/20/33.

6. Ibid., 3004–1 F.55, 5/15/43.

7. Ibid., 440–5 M.23, 12/20/33.

8. Ibid.

9. Ibid., 378–16 M.56, 10/29/33.

10. IBM stockholders' report, ftp://ftp.software.ibm.com/annualreport/2004/2004_ibm_10k.pdf, 1989.

11. Edgar Cayce, *Atlantis, The Edgar Cayce Readings,* vol. 22, 440–5 M.23, 12/20/33.

12. Ibid., 1298–1 F.43, 11/27/36.

13. "Physical Review Letters, Coherence, Narrowing, Directionality, and Relaxation Oscillations in the Light Emission from Ruby," cos.cumt.edu.cn/jpkc/dxwl/zl/zl1/Physical%20Review%20Classics/science/ 058.pdf (October 1, 1960).

14. Edgar Cayce, *Atlantis, The Edgar Cayce Readings,* vol. 22, 440–5 M.23, 12/20/33.

15. Plato, *The Timaeus and the Kritias.*

16. Edgar Cayce, *Atlantis, The Edgar Cayce Readings,* vol. 22, 440–5 M.23, 12/20/33.

CHAPTER 17. NORTH AMERICA'S ATLANTO-LEMURIAN LEGACY

1. Joseph H. Wherry, *The Totem Pole Indians* (New York: Funk and Wagnalls, 1964).

2. Edgar Cayce, *Atlantis, The Edgar Cayce Readings,* vol. 22, 1215–4 M.17, 6/4/37.

3. Ibid., 5750–1, 11/12/33.

4. Ibid,. 3004–1 F.55, 5/15/43.

5. Ibid., 5750–1, 11/12/33.

6. Ibid., 1286–1 F.30, 11/8/36.

7. Flavius Josephus, *The New Complete Works of Josephus,* trans. by William Whiston (New York: Kregel Academic and Professional, 1999).

8. Edgar Cayce, *Atlantis, The Edgar Cayce Readings,* vol. 22, 691–1 F.20, 8/17/34.

9. Ibid., 3528–1 M.36, 12/20/43.

10. Ibid., 1219–1 F.40, 7/13/36.

11. Ibid, 509–1 F.54 2/18/34).

12. Ibid., 851–2 F.44, 8/23/40.

13. Ibid., 691–1 F.20, 8/17/34.

14. Ibid., 812–1 F.48, 2/4/35.

15. Carlson, *The Great Migration*.

16. Edgar Cayce, *Atlantis, The Edgar Cayce Readings*, vol. 22, 440–5 M.23, 12/20/33.

17. Ibid., 1252–1 F.2, 4/26/36.

18. Ibid., 470–22 M.48, 7/5/38.

CHAPTER 18. MIDDLE AMERICAN CRUCIBLE

1. Edgar Cayce, *Atlantis, The Edgar Cayce Readings*, vol. 22, 5750–1, 11/12/33.

2. Carlson, *The Great Migration*.

3. Edgar Cayce, *Atlantis, The Edgar Cayce Readings*, vol. 22, 364–3 F.26, 3/30/34.

4. Ibid., 851–2 F.44, 8/23/40.

5. Ibid., 2073–2 F.39, 4/12/40.

6. Ibid., 3384–3 M.22, 12/5/43.

7. Ibid., 2397–1 F.39, 11/11/40.

8. Ibid., 5750–1, 11/12/33.

9. Ibid.

10. Richard N. Luxton, trans., *The (Chilam Balam) Book of Chumayel; The Counsel Book of the Yucatec Maya* (Walnut Creek, Calif.: Aegean Park Press, 1995).

CHAPTER 19. THE INCAS' ATLANTO-LEMURIAN HERITAGE

1. Edgar Cayce, *Atlantis, The Edgar Cayce Readings*, vol. 22, 470–2 M.35, 5/15/25.

2. Alexander P. Braghine, *The Shadow of Atlantis* (Kempton, Ill.: Adventures Unlimited Press, 1997).

3. Edgar Cayce, *Atlantis, The Edgar Cayce Readings*, vol. 22, 470–2 M.35, 5/15/25).

4. Ibid., 3345–1 F.47, 10/24/43.

5. Ibid., 5252–1 M.29, 6/14/44.

6. Ibid., 1159–1 F.80, 5/5/36.

7. Ibid., 845–1 F.36, 3/5/35.

8. James Churchward, *The Books of the Golden Age—The Sacred & Inspired Writings of Mu* (Albuquerque: Brotherhood of Life Publishing, 1997).

9. Edgar Cayce, *Atlantis, The Edgar Cayce Readings,* vol. 22, 2365–2 M.68, 8/9/29.

10. Ibid., 364–4, 2/16/32.

11. Ibid., 4805–1 F., 12/3/25.

12. Ibid., 2887–1 F.57, 5/25/31.

13. Ibid., 2688–1 M.2, 1/16/42.

14. Ibid., 772–2 F.42, 8/5/36.

CHAPTER 20. EDGAR CAYCE'S
ATLANTEANS AND LEMURIANS

1. Vincent Scramuzza, *The Emperor Claudius* (Cambridge, Mass.: Harvard University Press, 1940).

2. Edgar Cayce, *Atlantis, The Edgar Cayce Readings,* vol. 22, 813–1.

3. Ibid., 470–2 M.35, 5/15/25.

4. Ibid., 1219–1 F.40, 7/13/36.

5. Ibid., 2537–1.

6. Ibid., 615–1, 487–17, 961, 1007–3, 1035–1, 1217–1, 1574–1.

7. Ibid., 440–5 M.23, 12/20/33.

8. Ibid., 5750–1, 11/12/33.

9. Ibid,. 3004–1 F.55, 5/15/43.

10. Ignatius Donnelly, *Atlantis, the Antediluvian World* (New York: Harpers, 1882).

11. Walter B. Emery, *Archaic Egypt* (New York: Penguin, 1974).

12. Donnelly, *Atlantis, the Antediluvian World.*

13. Veronica Ions, *Egyptian Mythology* (London: Hamlyn, 1968).

14. Edgar Cayce, *Atlantis, The Edgar Cayce Readings,* vol. 22, 38–1.

15. Ibid., 5750–1.

16. Ibid., 1523-4.

17. Elena Maria Whishaw, *Atlantis in Spain* (Kempton, Ill.: Adventures Unlimited Press, 1994).

18. Edgar Cayce, *Atlantis, The Edgar Cayce Readings,* vol. 22, 5232–1.

19. Ibid., 303–1.

20. Ibid., 2545–1.

21. Ibid., 1219–1.

22. Ibid., 1743–1.

23. Ibid., 5750–1.

24. Ibid.

25. Ibid., 1690–1.

26. Ibid., 1523-4.

27. Ibid.

28. Ibid., 3004–1.

29. Ibid., 5252–1.

30. Ibid., 5232–1.

31. Ibid.

32. Ibid.

33. Ibid., 2725–1, 364–6.

34. Ibid., 2887–1.

35. Ibid., 2464–2.

36. Ibid., 2886–1.

37. Ibid.

38. Ibid.

39. Ibid., 2655–1.

40. Ibid., 1827–1.

41. Ibid.

42. 1610–2.

43. Ibid., 1681–1.

44. 3344–1.

45. 2988–2.

46. Ibid., 2690–1.

47. Ibid., 1695–1.

48. Ibid.

49. Ibid., 2856–1.

50. Ibid., 3004–1.

51. Ibid., 5252–1.

52. Ibid,. 2655–1.

53. Ibid.

54. Ibid., 1610–2.

55. Ibid., 3344–1.

56. Ibid.

57. Ibid., 2988–2.

58. Ibid.

CHAPTER 21. LAST CHANCE
OR JUDGMENT IN 2012?

1. Plato. *The Timaeus and the Kritias.*

2. Serge Hutin, *Alien Races and Fantastic Civilizations* (New York: Berkley Books, 1975.

3. Ibid.

4. Plato, *The Timaeus and the Kritias.*

5. Edgar Cayce, *Atlantis, The Edgar Cayce Readings,* vol. 22, 1416–1 M.34, 7/27/37.

6. Ibid., 2690–1.

7. Ibid., 1417–1 M.8, 7/30/37.

8. Ibid., 3345–1 F.47, 10/24/43.

9. Ibid., 1695–1.

10. Ibid., 1523–4.

11. Ibid., 1688–6 F.30, 2/14/41.

12. Hugh Lynn Cayce, *Cayce on Atlantis.*

13. Edgar Cayce, *Atlantis, The Edgar Cayce Readings,* vol. 22, 2856–1.

14. S. Warren Carey, www.todayinsci.com/C/Carey_Samuel/CareySamuel-Quotations.htm.

15. Imbrie and Shackleton, "Variations in the Earth's orbit: Pacemaker of the Ice Ages."

16. Hapgood, www.newscientist.com/article/mg20127001.300-space-storm-alert-90-seconds-from-catastrophe.html?full=true.

17. Craig B. Hatfield, and Mark J. Camp, "Mass Extinctions Correlated with Periodic Galactic Events," *Geological Society of America Bulletin* 18 (March 1970).

18. Richard D. Schwartz, and Philip B. James, "Periodic Mass Extinctions and the Sun's Oscillation about the Galactic Plane," *Nature* 308 (April 19, 1984).

19. George E. Williams, "Possible Relation between Periodic Glaciation and the Flexure of the Galaxy," *Earth and Planet Science Letter* 26 (1975).

20. U.S. Census Bureau, www.census.gov/ipc/www/popclockworld.html, 30 May 2009.

21. Amitabh Avasthi, "After Near Extinction, Humans Split into Isolated Groups," *National Geographic News,* http://news.nationalgeographic.com/news/2008/04/080424-humans-extinct.html, 24 April 2008.

BIBLIOGRAPHY

Aldred, Cyril. *The Egyptians*. New York: Praeger Press, 1962.

Alexander, William. *North American Mythology*. New York: Harcourt Brace, 1935.

Anklin, M. "Climate Instability during the last Interglacial Period recorded in the GRIP Ice Core." *Nature* 364 (July 1993): 203–207.

Arribas, A. *The Iberians*. New York: Praeger Press, 1958.

Baines, John, and Jaromir Malek. *Atlas of Ancient Egypt*. New York: Oxford University Press, 1980.

Banincourt, Michael. *Five Letters of Cortez to the Emperor*. New York: W. W. Norton and Company, 1962.

Baran, Michael. *Atlantis Reconsidered*. New York: Exposition Press, 1981.

Boylan, Patrick. *Thoth, the Hermes of Egypt*. New York: Oxford University Press, 1922.

Braghine, Col. A. *The Shadow of Atlantis*. Kempton, Ill.: Adventures Unlimited Press, 1997.

Brestead, James. *A History of Egypt*. New York: Scribner's and Sons, 1909.

Briggs, Cabot. *The Stone Age Races of Northwest Africa*. London: Oxford Press, 1973.

Brinton, Daniel G. *The Books of Chilan Balam*. Philadelphia: Stern, 1882.

Broecker, Wallace S., D. L. Thurber, J. Goddard, Te-lung Ku, R. K. Matthews, and K. L. Mesolella. "Milankovitch Hypothesis Supported by Precise Dating of Coral Reefs and Deep-Sea Sediments." *Science* 159 (January 19, 1968): 297–300.

Brown, George. "Illiterate Man Becomes A Doctor When Hypnotized, Strange Power Shown by Edgar Cayce Puzzles Physicians." *New York Times* 22, no. 13, March 3 1910.

Bryant, Alice. *The Message of the Crystal Skull*. Woodbury, Minn.: Llewellyns, 1989.

Budge, E. A. Wallis. *Ancient Egyptian Amulets and Talismans*. New York: University Books, 1968.

Burland, C. A. *The Gods of Mexico.* London: Eyre and Spottiswoode, 1970.

Burland, C. A., and Werner Foreman. *Feathered Serpent and Smoking Mirror.* New York: G. P. Putnam and Sons, 1975.

Bushnell, G. H. S. *Peru.* New York: Praeger Press, 1967.

Carey, S. Warren. *The Expanding Earth, Developments in Geotectonics.* New York: Elsevier/North Holland, 1976.

Carlson, Vada F. *The Great Migration.* Virginia Beach, Va.: Association for Research and Enlightment, 1970.

Caso, Alfonso. *The Civilizations of Ancient Mexico.* New York: Prescott Publishers, 1960.

Catlin, George. *Illustrations of the Manners, Customs, and Conditions of the North American Indians.* New York: Dover Publications, 1970.

Cayce, Edgar. *Atlantis, The Edgar Cayce Readings,* vol. 22. Virginia Beach, Va.: Association for Research and Enlightenment, 1987.

Cayce, Hugh Lynn. *Cayce on Atlantis.* Virginia Beach, Va.: Association for Research and Enlightenment, 1980.

Cerve, W. S. *Lemuria, the Lost Continent of the Pacific.* San Jose, Calif.: AMORC Printing and Publishing, 1942.

Childress, David Hatcher. *Lost Cities and Ancient Mysteries of South America.* Kempton, Ill.: Adventures Unlimited Press, 1986.

———. *Lost Cities of Ancient Lemuria & the Pacific.* Kempton, Ill.: Adventures Unlimited Press, 1988.

———. *Lost Cities of China, Central Asia and India.* Kempton, Ill.: Adventures Unlimited Press, 1985.

———. *Lost Cities of North and Central America.* Kempton, Ill.: Adventures Unlimited Press, 1992.

Churchward, James. *The Children of Mu.* Albuquerque: BE Books, 1988.

———. *Cosmic Forces of Mu,* vol. 1. Albuquerque: BE Books, 1998.

———. *Cosmic Forces of Mu,* vol. 2. Albuquerque: BE Books, 1998.

Clark, R. T. Rundle. *Myth and Symbol in Ancient Egypt.* London: Thames and Hudson, 1959.

Coe, Michael D. *Mexico.* New York: Praeger Press, 1966.

Colum, Padraic. *Nordic Gods and Heroes.* New York: Dover Publications, 1996.

"Computer Models predict Magnetic pole reversal in Earth and Sun can bring end to human civilization in 2012." www.indiadaily.com. Search title on homepage.

Cooper, C. W. *Crystal Magic.* London: Faber and Faber, 1986.

Corliss, William R. *Ancient Structures.* Glen Arm, Md.: The Sourcebook Project, 2001.

Crossley-Holland, Kevin. *The Norse Myths.* New York: Pantheon Books, 1980.

Crow, Robert. *Crystal Handbook.* Vt.: Hathaway Press, 1984.

Daniel, Glyn. *The Illustrated Encyclopedia of Archaeology.* New York: Thomas Y. Crowell, 1970.

Dansgaard, W., and J. Duplessey. "The Eemian interglacial and its termination." *Boreas* 10 (1981).

Davies, Nigel. *The Ancient Kingdoms of Mexico.* London: Penguin Books, 1982.

De Ayala, Felipe Guaman Poma. *Nueva corónica y buen gobierno* [New Chronicle and Good Government]. Translated by David L. Frye. New York: Hackett Publishing Company, 2006.

De Camp, L. Sprague. *Lost Continents, The Atlantis Theme in History, Science and Literature.* New York: The Gnome Press, 1954.

De Onis, Harriet, trans. *The Incas of Pedro de Cieza de Leon.* Norman: University of Oklahoma Press, 1959.

Doake, Christopher S. M. "Climate Change and Geomagnetic Field Reversals: A Statistical Correlation. *Earth and Planet, Science Letters* 38 (1978).

Donnelly, Ignatius. *Atlantis, the Antediluvian World.* New York: Harpers, 1882.

Dorland, Frank. *Holy Ice.* Lakeville, Minn.: Galde Press, Inc., 1995.

Duran, Fray Diego. *Book of the Gods and the Rites of the Ancient Calendar.* Translated by Fernando Horcasitas and Doris Heyden. Norman: University of Oklahoma Press, 1971.

Earth/Matrix. www.earthmatrix.com/aztec/spatial/introduc.htm williams .

Ebon, Martin. *Atlantis, The New Evidence.* New York: New American Library, 1977.

Ellis Davidson, H. R. *Gods and Myths of Northern Europe.* New York: Penguin Books, 1982.

Ellis, Ralph. *Thoth, Architect of the Universe.* Kempton, Ill.: Adventures Unlimited Press, 2001.

Emery, Walter B. *Archaic Egypt, Culture and Civilization in Egypt Five Thousand Years Ago.* London: Penguin Books, 1961.

Engl, Lieselotte, and Theo Lieselotte. *Twilight of Ancient Peru.* New York: MacGraw Hill, 1969.

Erman, Adolf. *Life in Ancient Egypt.* New York: Dover Publications, Inc., 1966.

Felix, Robert W. *Not By Fire, But By Ice.* Bellevue, Wash.: Sugarhouse Publishing, 1997.

Gaddis, Vincent H. *Native American Myths & Mysteries.* New York: McDonald, 1972.

Gallenkamp, Charles. *Maya.* London: Frederick Muller, 1960.

Garvin, Richard. *The Crystal Skull.* New York: Doubleday, 1971.

Geological Society of America, http://gsa.confex.com/gsa/inqu/finalprogram/ abstract_53841.htm.

Giovannini, A. "Peut-on démythifier l'Atlantide?" *Museum Helveticum* 42 (1985): 151–56.

Graves, Robert. *The Greek Myths,* vols. 1 and 2. Harmondsworth, Middlesex, England: Penguin Books, 1984.

Grimstad, William R., "Climate Instability during the last Interglacial Period recorded in the GRIP ice-core." *Nature* 364 (July 15, 1993).

Hennes, D. *The American Aborigines: Their Origins and Antiquity.* New York: Cooper Square, 1963.

Hodge. F. W. *The Handbook of the American Indians North of Mexico,* thirty volumes. Washington, D.C.: Bulletins of the Bureau of American Ethnology, 1907.

Hunter, Bruce C. *A Guide to Ancient Mexican Ruins.* Norman: University of Oklahoma Press, 1978.

Imbrie, John, James Hays, and Nicholas Shackleton. "Variations in the Earth's Orbit: Pacemaker of the Ice Ages." *Science* 238, no. 12 (June 1976).

Imel, Martha Ann, and Dorothy Myers. *Goddesses in World Mythology, A Biographical Dictionary.* New York: Oxford University Press, 1993.

Ions, Veronica. *Egyptian Mythology.* London: Hamlyn, 1968.

Jakeman, M. Wells. *The Origin & History of the Mayas.* Los Angeles: Research Publishing Co., 1957.

Jenkins, John Major. "The How and Why of the Mayan End Date in 2012 A.D." *The Mountain Astrologer* (December 1994).

Jimenez, Randall C., and Richard B. Graeber. *The Aztec Calendar Handbook.* Santa Clara, Calif.: Historical Science Publishing, 2001.

Joseph, Frank, *Atlantis and Other Lost Worlds.* London: Arcturus Publishing, 2008.

———. *The Destruction of Atlantis.* Rochester, Vt.: Inner Traditions, 2002.

———. *Discovering the Mysteries of Ancient America.* Franklin Lakes, N.J.: New Page Books, 2005.

———. *Edgar Cayce's Atlantis and Lemuria.* Virginia Beach, Va.: Association for Research and Enlightenment, 2001.

———. *The Lost Civilization of Lemuria.* Rochester, Vt.: Bear and Co., 2006.

———. *The Lost Pyramids of Rock Lake,* revised edition. Lakeville, Minn.: Galde Press, Inc., 2003.

———. *Opening the Ark of the Covenant.* Franklin Lakes, N.J.: New Page Books, 2007.

Josephus, Flavius, *The New Complete Works of Josephus.* Translated by William Whiston. New York: Kregel Academic and Professional, 1999.

Katsonopoulou, Dora. "Helike and Her Territory in Historical Times." *Pallas* 58 (2002): 175 182.

Kenny, Andrew. www.ourcivilisation.com/aginatur/iceage.htm.

Knappert, Jan. *Indian Mythology, An Encyclopedia of Myth and Legend.* London: Diamond Books, 1995.

Kramer, Noah. *A Sumerian Lexicon.* New York: New York University Press, 1975.

———. *The Sumerians.* Chicago: University of Chicago Press, 1969.

Kronkheit, C. A. *A Dictionary of Ancient Egyptian Terms.* Chicago: University of Chicago Press, 1929.

Krupp, Edwin C. *Echoes of the Ancient Skies: The Astronomy of Lost Civilizations.* New York: Harper and Row, 1983.

Lanning, Edward P. *Peru Before the Incas.* Englewood Cliffs, N.J.: Prentice-Hall, Inc., 1967.

Leicht, Hermann. *Pre-Inca Art and Culture.* New York: Orion Press, 1960.

Le Plongeon, Augustus. *Sacred Mysteries Among the Mayas and the Quiches.* New York: Cosimo Classics, 2007.

Lomas, Victor. *The Magdalenians.* Toronto: MacPherson Press, 1971.

MacCana, Prosinas. *Celtic Mythology.* London: Hamlyn, 1970.

Malkowsky, Edward. *Egypt Before the Pharaohs.* Rochester, Vt.: Bear and Company, 2006.

Malkus, W. V. R. "Precession of the Earth as the Cause of Geomagnetism." *Science* 160 (April 19, 1968).

Maloney, Evan Coyne. http://brain-terminal.com/posts/2008/10/01/fear-the-coming-ice-age.

Marriott, Alice, and Carol K. Rachlin. *American Indian Mythology.* New York: New American Library, 1968.

Massa, Aldo. *The World of the Etruscans.* Geneva, Switzerland: Editions Minerva, 1973.

Matthew, William Diller. "Plato's Atlantis in Paleogeography." *Procedures of the National Academy of Sciences* 6 (1920): 17f.

McKenna, Dennis J., and Terrence McKenna. *The Invisible Landscape, The Mind, Hallucinogens, and the I Ching.* New York: Seabury Press, 1975.

McMoneagle, Joseph. *Memoirs of a Psychic Spy: The Remarkable Life of U.S. Government Remote Viewer 001.* Charlottesville, Va.: Hampton Roads Publishing, 2006.

Men, Hunbatz. *Secrets of Mayan Science/Religion.* Rochester, Vt.: Bear and Company, 1990.

Mercatante, Anthony S. *Who's Who in Egyptian Mythology.* New York: Clarkson N. Potter, Inc., 1978.

Mercer. A. B. Samuel. *Horus, the Royal God of Egypt.* Cambridge, England: Society of Oriental Research, 1960.

Metraux, Alfred. *The History of the Incas.* New York: Pantheon Books, 1969.

Milewski, J. V., and V. L. Harford, eds. *The Crystal Sourcebook.* Sedona, Ariz.: First Editions, 1987.

Miller, Mary, and Karl Taube. *The Gods and Symbols of Ancient Mexico and the Maya.* London: Thames and Hudson, 1993.

Morehouse, David. *Psychic Warrior: The True Story of America's Foremost Psychic Spy and the Cover-Up of the CIA's Top-Secret Stargate Program.* New York: St. Martin's, 1998.

Morley, Sylvanus. *The Ancient Maya.* Palo Alto, Calif.: Stanford University Press, 1946.

Moseley, Michael E. *The Incas and their Ancestors.* London: Thames and Hudson, 1994.

Namkhai Norbu. *Drung, Deu and Boen, Narrations, Symbolic Languages and the Boen Tradition in Ancient Tibet.* Translated by Adriano Clemente and Andrew Lukianowicz. New York: Library of Tibetan Works and Archives, 1988.

Nicholson, I. *Mexican and Central American Mythology.* London: Hamlyn, 1967.

Nuttall, Zelia. *The Fundamental Principles of Old and New World Civilizations,* vol. 2. (Cambridge, Mass.: Harvard University, 1900.

O'Brien, Henry. *The Round Towers of Atlantis.* Kempton, Ill.: Adventures Unlimited Press, 2002.

Olivier, Guilhem. *Mockeries and Metamorphoses of an Aztec God Tezcatlipoca, "Lord of the Smoking Mirror."* Boulder: University Press of Colorado, 2003.

Olson, Carl. *The Theology and Philosophy of Eliade: A Search for the Centre.* New York: St Martin's, 1992.

Osborne, Harold. *South American Mythology.* London: Hamlyn, 1970.

Pallottino, M. *The Etruscans.* New York: Harper and Row, 1978.

Peithmar, Irwin M. *Echoes of the Red Man.* New York: Expectation Press, 1955.

Petrie, W. M. Flinders. *A History of Egypt,* vol. 3, *The IX and XX Dynasties.* London: Methuen, 1896.

Plato. *The Timaeus and the Kritias.* Translated by Desmond Lee. London: Penguin Books, 1977.

Popol Vuh: The Sacred Book of the Maya. Translated by Allen J. Christenson. Norman: University of Oklahoma, 2003.

Porch, Douglas. *The Conquest of the Sahara.* New York: Alfred Knopf, 1984.

Powell, T. G. E. *The Celts.* New York: Praeger Press, 1959.

Pravda. http://english.pravda.ru/science/earth/106922-earth_ice_age-0, 11.01.2009.

Prescott, William H. *The Conquest of Peru.* New York: New American Library, 1961.
———. *The Conquest of Mexico.* New York: Julian Messner, 1950.

Radin, Paul. *The Winnebago Tribe,* 37th Annual Report of the Bureau of American Ethnology, Smithsonian Institution, Washington, D.C., 1923. Lincoln: University of Nebraska Press, 1970.

Ramoino, Michael R. "Possible Relationships between Changes in Global Ice Volume, Geomagnetic Excursions, and the Eccentricity of the Earth's Orbit." *Geology* 7 (December 1979).

Sahagún. *Florentine Codex, General History of the Things of New Spain.* Translated by A. J. O. Anderson and C.E. Dibble. Santa Fe: School of American Research, Inc., 1963.

Santesson, Hans. *Understanding Mu.* New York: Paperback Library, 1970.

Savoy, Gene. *On the Trail of the Feathered Serpent.* New York: Bobbs-Merrill, 1974.

Scofield, Bruce. *Day Signs.* N.p.: One Reed Publications, 1996.

Seleem, Ramses. *The Illustrated Egyptian Book of the Dead, A New Translation with Commentary.* New York: Sterling Publishing, 2001.

Sharkey, John. *Celtic Mysteries, the Ancient Religion.* London: Thames and Hudson, 1970.

Sitchin, Zechariah. "Olmec Civilization Older Than Believed." *Ancient American* 9, no. 6 (April 2001).

Smith, Richard J. *Fathoming the Cosmos and Ordering the World: The Yijing (I Ching or Classic of Changes) and Its Evolution in China.* Charlottesville: University of Virginia Press, 2008.

Space Weather. www.solarstorms.org/SS1921.html.

Spence, Lewis. *The Problem of Lemuria.* London: Rider, 1930.

Steinhoff, George, and Kenneth Seele. *When Egypt Ruled the East.* Chicago: University of Chicago Press, 1957.

Sturluson, Snorri. *The Prose Edda.* Translated by Jesse L. Byock. New York: Penguin Classics, 2006.

Swanson, Claude. *The Synchronized Universe.* Tucson, Ariz.: Poseidia Press, 2003.

Sykes, Edgerton. *Lemuria Reconsidered.* London: Markham House Press, 1968.

———. *Who's Who in Non-Classical Mythology.* New York: Oxford University Press, 1993.

The Aztec "Sun Stone." Washington, D.C.: Smithsonian Institution, National Museum of Natural History, Department of Anthropology, Public Information Office, 1987.

The Bhagavad Gita. Translated by Laurie L. Patton. New York: Penguin Classics, 2008.

The Edfu Texts. Translated by Robert Kohlmann. Dallas: University of Texas Press, 1968.

The Oera Linda Bok. Translated by Howard Schnell. London: Truebner and Company, 1876.

Thunderhorse, Iron. "The Calendar Stone: Myths and Facts." *Ancient American* 7, no. 44 (March/April 2002).

Thompson, Gunnar. *American Discovery, the Real Story.* Seattle: Misty Isles Press, 1995.

Tozzer, Alfred M. *A Maya Grammar.* New York: Dover, 1978.

Tyler, H. A. *Pueblo Gods and Myths.* Norman: University of Oklahoma Press, 1964.

University of Vermont. www.uvm.edu/whale/GlaciersAgeEnd.html.

University of Wisconsin, Madison. www.news.wisc.edu/15316.

Vaillant, George C. *Aztecs of Mexico.* New York: Doubleday, 1962.

Van Over, R. *Sun Songs, Creation Myths from Around the World.* New York: New American Library, 1980.

Von Hagen, Victor. *The Ancient Sun Kingdoms of the Americas.* Cleveland: World Publishing Company, 1957.

Wasilewski, Krzys. "Computer Software Says Armageddon Will Arrive in 2012." *The Student Operated Press.* http://thesop.org/index.php?article=11011, 1 May 2008.

Wasson, R. Gordon. *Persephone's Quest: Entheogens and the Origins of Religion.* New Haven: Yale University Press, 1986.

Waters, Frank. *The Book of the Hopi.* New York: Viking Press, 1963.

Whishaw, Elena Maria. *Atlantis in Spain.* Kempton, Ill.: Adventures Unlimited Press, 1994.

Wikipedia. http://en.wikipedia.org/wiki/Solar_storm_of_1859.

Wikipedia. http://en.wikipedia.org/wiki/Yuga.

Wilkins, Harold T. *Mysteries of Ancient South America.* Kempton, Ill.: Adventures Unlimited Press 2000.

Williams, Mark R. *In Search of Lemuria.* San Mateo, Calif.: Golden Era Books, 2001.

Xu, H. Mike. *Origin of the Olmec Civilization.* Norman: University of Oklahoma Press, 1996.

Zimmerman, J. E. *Dictionary of Classical Mythology.* New York: Bantam Books, 1971.

INDEX

Page numbers in *italics* refer to figures.
Page numbers preceded by CP indicate color plate pages.